MEET AT DAWN, UNARMED

Front Cover: 'One Night in Flanders' by Bruce Bairnsfather from an article in the December 1929 issue of *The American Magazine.* © *Barbara Bruce Bairnsfather*

'Then one of our sergeants climbed over the trench ... the Germans sent up a star shell which lit up the place lovely ... and then for the first time we saw friend and foe.'

From a letter by Charlie Pratt of the Warwickshire Regiment, written on December 27th 1914.

Andrew Hamilton retired in 1989 from teaching History at schools in Hereford and Worcester. He turned a restored working watermill into a popular tourist attraction in Warwickshire which he managed until 2004. He is involved with the management of the Walton Estate and is committed to its preservation for future generations. Inspired by research in Flanders and British museums and archives for *Meet at Dawn, Unarmed*, he hopes that this will not be his last publication on the Great War.

Alan Reed retired from full-time teaching in Cheshire in 1996 to concentrate on guiding school and adult groups on the Western Front. His interest in the Great War was inspired by his father who worked for the Commonwealth War Graves Commission in Northern France. A fluent French speaker, his vast knowledge of France and Belgium, combined with a detailed appreciation of the region's history and culture, have been invaluable in research for *Meet at Dawn, Unarmed*.

Published by Dene House Publishing
Dene House, Walton, Warwick, CV35 9HX
www.meetatdawnunarmed.co.uk

Designed by Ruth Smith, Damson Creative Ltd.
www.damsoncreative.co.uk

Printed and bound in the United Kingdom by Henry Ling Ltd.
www.henryling.co.uk

ISBN 978-0-9561820-0-5

MEET AT DAWN, UNARMED

UNARMED

Captain Robert Hamilton's account
of Trench Warfare
and the Christmas Truce in 1914

Commentary and historical reconstructions by
Andrew Hamilton
and
Alan Reed

Maps by
George Sayell

Contents

Maps

Sketches

Photographs

All photographs are the property of Andrew Hamilton and the Hamilton family unless stated otherwise.

We should like to thank all those who have kindly granted us permission to reproduce their material- acknowledgement is to be found in the captions.

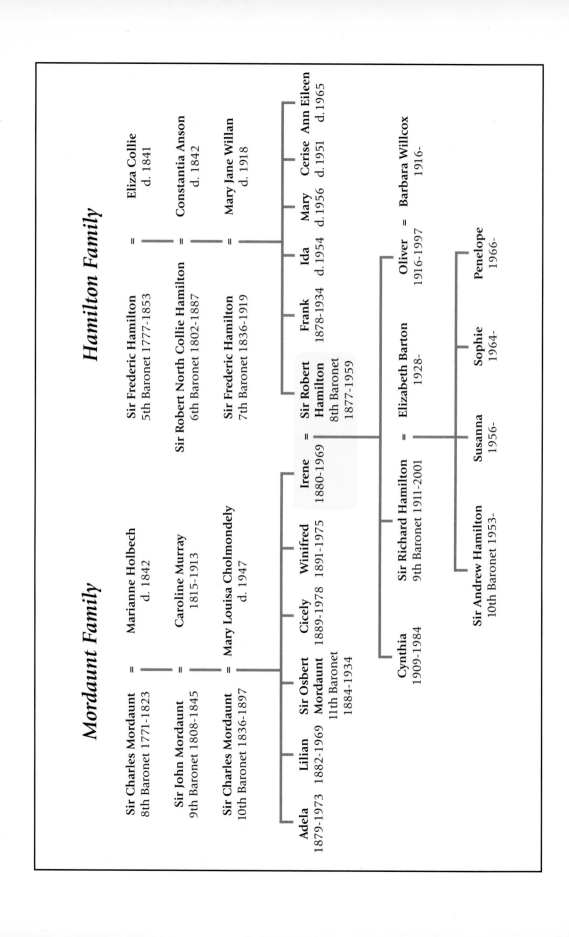

Mordaunt Family

Hamilton Family

Captain Robert Caradoc Hamilton
1877 - 1959

Meet at Dawn, Unarmed
is dedicated to all the soldiers
mentioned in the text who died
in the Great War

🌺 *Each name is marked by a poppy*

1

'One more piece of extraordinary luck'

Armed with trench and O.S. maps, we had pinpointed the precise location. There were neat rows of young potato plants growing in soil scorched by a hot sun. It was here in 'No Man's Land' that my grandfather Captain Robert Hamilton had fraternised with his German counterpart on Christmas Day 1914. Soldiers from both sets of trenches then followed their lead, met and exchanged gifts and seasonal greetings. Robert was in no doubt as to the significance of what had occurred. In the warmth of his dug out later that evening, he recorded in his diary that it had been 'A DAY UNIQUE IN THE WORLD'S HISTORY' and claimed that it was he who had set in motion a wave of similar fraternisations along No Man's Land.

Whether or not that was the case, it was a proud moment to be standing on ground in Flanders where, ninety four years earlier, my grandfather had played a key role in an episode that will never fail to fire the imagination of this and future generations.

In 1980, I was browsing through a shelf packed with leather-bound diaries that he had painstakingly kept in the period from 1913 to 1950. Much of the content of each year's diary was unexceptional and rather dull, but my eye was drawn to a slim, hardback volume which stood out awkwardly from the rest. It was inscribed on the front cover- 'Diary kept by Captain R.C. Hamilton from August 5th 1914 to January 12th 1915'. Unlike the other volumes, it had not been hand written but specially typed.

At the time, I was a History teacher and could scarcely believe my good fortune in stumbling on original material which would be ideal for use in lessons on the Great War. Each page was a rich seam of evidence about life on the Western Front during the first six months of the War. Robert chronicled in detail the campaign and exploits of the 1st Battalion of the Royal Warwickshire Regiment. There were comprehensive descriptions of trench warfare- the dangers and discomforts, the incessant rain, the mud and cold, the camaraderie and loyalty amongst officers and men and the overriding spectre of wounding and death. Marching, singing, trench digging...it was all there jumping out of the pages at me. There was even criticism of the Generals, comfortably ensconced behind the lines at their Headquarters in St. Omer. Then, as I neared the end of the forty page diary, I came across the undoubted highlight- Robert's description of the Christmas Truce.

The incorporation of the diary into my students' studies of the Great War helped to bring the events to life for them as well as for myself. Teachers always remember the lessons and material that inspired their charges and the diary generated some outstanding work. The most memorable came from an unlikely source; the son of the owners of a local Chinese restaurant designed and drew a spectacular version, in cartoon form, of the events of Christmas Day 1914. It is a great source of regret that I failed to keep a copy of his work.

Soon after the diary's discovery in 1980, I took it to the Royal Fusiliers Museum in Warwick which houses information and artefacts about the Royal Warwickshire Regiment. I proudly offered use of this valuable material about the Regiment's campaign in the first months of the Great War but it was one of those unfortunate days when the main curator was absent and his deputy for the day proved to be a model of indifference. After a few minutes of research, he returned to inform me that Robert Hamilton had not been a serving officer with the Regiment. I pointed out that the forty pages in my hand suggested otherwise! The offer of the opportunity to make a copy was declined, so I left a little bemused and deflated.

"They've evidently seen me."

One of Bruce Bairnsfather's famous cartoons, first published by The Bystander *on April 21st 1915*
Barbara Bruce Bairnsfather

For twenty years, the diary's future lay in abeyance until my daughter Alice went on a school visit to the First World War battlefields and cemeteries in northern France and Belgium. After an inspirational talk by the tour guide Alan Reed, I approached him with the diary. He took a quick look at it and in measured tones declared that "this could well prove to be an incredible piece." He took it home with him and phoned me a few days later. He was in no doubt that it was one of the best contemporary descriptions he had read of the first six months of the British military campaign in the early part of the War. The account of the Christmas Truce was of major importance and he was excited that my grandfather should have been a friend of two soldiers in the Royal Warwickshire Regiment who went on to achieve great fame- Bruce Bairnsfather, for his morale boosting contemporary cartoons of the trials and tribulations of the British Tommy in the trenches, and Bernard Montgomery, the future Field Marshal and architect of victory over Germany in the 2nd World War.

For several years, Alan was too busy with other projects to concentrate on the diary until Christmas time in 2007, when he orchestrated the publication of articles that appeared in *The Daily Telegraph* and local Warwickshire newspapers. Alan, Alice and I enjoyed our two minutes of fame on Boxing Day's BBC news programmes.

Once the presenter and cameraman had departed, Alan and I vowed to publish the diary. It only dawned on us later that its publication would mark the 90th anniversary of the end of the Great War, so work started in earnest to achieve our publication date of Armistice Day, November 11th 2008. Sadly, we failed by five months!

It was fortuitous that I should have had the opportunity to collaborate on the diary's publication with such an enthusiastic and deeply knowledgeable student of the Great War. On a four day tour following the 1914 campaign of the 1/ Royal Warwicks, I found that there is little that Alan Reed does not know about the theatre of war in France and Belgium. Driving through the Flemish countryside, he was never short of a fascinating tit bit of information- he would point to a cemetery where a nurse, killed through shelling, was buried or another cemetery where two soldiers were buried after 'execution at dawn' for desertion or cowardice. Within seconds of walking through the 'No Man's Land' potato field, he had picked up a large handful of metal objects.

He handed me two unprepossessing pieces of rusty metal- "There you are- a shell fragment and this one is German barbed wire. It's much thicker than that used by the British Army and proves we are in the area of the German trenches."

Bernard Law Montgomery in the uniform of the Royal Warwickshire Regiment wearing his medals' ribbon which includes his Distinguished Service Order- at the time of the photograph he was a Lieutenant-Colonel
Imperial War Museum HU 45593

It was with relief that I found that his knowledge was fallible. On arrival at St. Omer, he announced that there are rare examples nowadays of cafés being called 'estaminets'. There are many references in Robert's diary of officers' visits to them when off duty behind the lines- I looked across the square and there, staring us in the face, was an *estaminet*, the first of many we encountered for the rest of the tour!

Ironically for Alan, work on the diary has meant his life has, in a way, gone full circle. His father worked for the Commonwealth War Graves Commission and early in his career was employed as Head Gardener at the cemetery where several hundred soldiers who fell at the Battle of Méteren on October 13th 1914 were buried. For many of those who served with Robert Hamilton, it was their final resting place.

Alan's profound interest in the Great War had its roots in the endless rows of white gravestones inscribed with the names of thousands of unsung heroes who lost their lives for their King and Country. Half a century later, he returned to his roots when researching for *Meet at Dawn, Unarmed*. His enthusiasm and dogged determination to hunt down photographs, maps, locations and information for the diary commentary have been invaluable and without his efforts and inspiration, this book would never have seen the light of day!

Modern day estaminet in St.Omer

George Sayell, who spent many painstaking hours producing the excellent maps in the book, has connections of a different sort to the Great War. No less than 21 Sayells served in France and Belgium, of whom 7 were killed and were buried or commemorated there. An 8th died on his return to England a few months after being discharged. George commissioned a plaque in St. George's Church, Ypres, in memory of three of his family who fell in the Ypres Salient:

- **Corporal Edward Thomas Sayell of the Machine Gun Corps** (Dozinghem Cemetery)

- **Private Milford Sayell of the Royal Fusiliers** (Menin Gate)

and

- **Private Samuel Sayell- a Royal Fusilier and George Sayell's great great uncle** (Lijssenthoek Cemetery)

British Military Cemetery at Méteren

Every family was affected in some way by the War. Wendy Godfrey, the mother of Ruth Smith, the designer of this book, has provided an account of her family's experiences of the bombardment of the family's house in Scarborough on December 17th 1914 (see the commentary for that day on p.105).

The focal point of the book is chapter 10- Robert Hamilton's diary recorded from August 5th 1914 to January 12th 1915. His wife Renie wrote a diary concurrently, extracts of which I have interspersed with her husband's. Her contributions offer a valuable insight into the anxiety and

Robert Hamilton, promoted to Captain in September 1914, in his Royal Warwickshire Regiment uniform. The regiment's badge of an Antelope is on his lapel

Irene (Renie) Hamilton

fear suffered by all wives who were left at home to look after their families. Rumours were rife and letters from the Front were censored. Increasingly, their fears were confirmed by the return of hundreds of wounded soldiers and the news of considerable losses. She, like Robert, soon realised that the War would not be 'Over by Christmas'.

I have used content from his diaries and other material to create a 'factional' narrative of the main events of his life prior to the outbreak of War: chapters 2 to 6 chart Robert's journey from the cricket and rugby fields of his Scottish public school and his early army career and marriage, to the hell of the trench warfare which he was to describe so graphically. Chapters 7 to 9 concentrate on the chain of command in the British Army, the British Expeditionary Force and the campaign of the Royal Warwicks in 1914; they help to place in context Robert's role in the War effort.

The ingredients of his background were not untypical of an officer in the Great War: Army, Empire and Land. His father, Sir Frederic, had been an Army officer and his grandfather Sir Robert, a distinguished member of the British Raj in India, had played an influential role during the Indian Mutiny of 1857 for which he received a formal Vote of Thanks from both Houses of Parliament. Robert was educated at a public school in Scotland which prepared its pupils for careers defending and administering Britain's imperial interests. He married into a wealthy landowning family- his wife, governess-educated Irene, was the daughter of Sir Charles Mordaunt Bart., owner of a large estate in Warwickshire and an M.P. for South Warwickshire.

The final diary entry to record Robert's time in Flanders on January 12th 1915 is followed in chapter 11, by a reconstruction of the Royal Warwicks' unofficial Christmas armistice in No Man's Land with soldiers of the 134th Saxon Regiment. It has been possible to pin-point accurately where the truce took place due to the wealth of contemporary evidence available and to paint a detailed picture of the Christmas Truce from the written and oral descriptions of soldiers who served in the Royal Warwicks and the German 134th Saxon Regiment. Of all the regiments involved in the Yuletide fraternisation, the Royal Warwicks produced more detailed descriptions than most. In addition to Hamilton's, there are accounts by Lieutenant Frank Black, an officer's servant Private William Tapp, regulars Mattey and Charlie Pratt, Captain Bruce Bairnsfather who became an instant celebrity because of his written contributions and cartoons in the The Bystander magazine and Private Harry Morgan. Sergeant J. Philpotts recorded his memories of the War for the B.B.C. in 1963 and Corporal Samuel Judd kept a diary in 1914. We have been able to use a German source, the diary of Leutnant Kurt Zehmisch and a trench map he drew, which have provided vital clues as to the precise location of the Truce and what took place there.

After January 1915, in chapter 13, my grandfather's diary extracts detail his bitter disillusionment with his changed role in the Army, his health and spirit affected by his experiences at the Front and by the War Office's lack of support for him in his position of Commandant of the Military Detention Barracks in Hereford. He found dealing with large numbers of Conscientious Objectors to the War, a challenging and depressing experience after the exciting and enervating experiences at the Front. Fiercely loyal to his fellow soldiers and a staunch defender of the reasoning behind the War effort, coping with Conscientious Objectors and their supporters tested his patience and philosophy of life to the full.

The final chapter is an assessment of Robert's career as a soldier- much loved and respected by his men but why did he not ultimately achieve a higher rank than Major?

I hope that *Meet at Dawn, Unarmed* will offer something for a range of readers, whether they be a Great War aficionado, a student of the Royal Warwickshire Regiment, a Bruce Bairnsfather devotee, a Christmas Truce enthusiast or a casual reader dipping into the history of the Great War.

When I started work on the diary it was mildly irritating that the hand written version had yet to surface. It was exciting, therefore, when my mother unearthed an old trunk of papers which included two other versions of the diary- the original, written at the time in pencil and standard issue purple crayon and another more detailed copy of it, in beautiful hand writing which would act as the working copy for the third and final typed version. It is disappointing that the numerous letters Robert and Renie wrote to each other have not survived. He wrote at least seventy letters and postcards in the five months he was at the Front.

I was concerned that Robert's final typed-up version might have suffered from a 'surfeit of the truth' but on close examination it was clear that little had been amended, apart from the omission of occasional criticisms of the Generals based at Headquarters.

In his diary entry for August 25th 1916 he wrote- 'My diary of the War is finished' and two days later he took it to printers in Hereford 'who wanted to charge me £5 to print it, so my Q.M.S. and Orderly Sgt. will do it between them.' He must have believed from the evening of Christmas Day 1914, that his story was worth recording for posterity and his plan may have been to publish his reminiscences at a later date. His failure to do so will remain a mystery but the popularity of works by celebrated writers like Siegfried Sassoon, Wilfred Owen, Robert Graves and Bruce Bairnsfather may have discouraged him.

🔵 **Lieutenant Wilfred Owen M.C.** was killed on November 4th 1918- news of his death only reached his parents in Oswestry on November 11th, Armistice Day. He joined the Artists' Rifles in 1915 and the Manchester Regiment in 1916. He was buried at Ors Communal Cemetery in France.

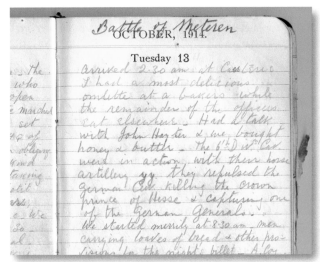

Robert Hamilton's 'original diary' written in the trenches and behind the lines

A handwritten and more detailed version of the original diary

pointed at him, Typically german. Gregory alone. Typically British. He got his ciga some magnificent yarns about the strength which amused us all very much when he told wanted me to meet their officer, and after shouting across, I said I would meet him a

Xmas Day:-   I went out and found a Saxon Saxon corps, who was fully armed. I pointe and pouch. He smiled and said seeing I was now". we shook hands, and said what we cou arranged a local armistice for 48 hours, a trenches. This was the signal for the resp come out. As far as I can make out this e extended itself on either side for some c The soldiers on both sides met in their h changed greetings and gifts. We buried ma did the same to ours. The chef of the Tre Saxons in front of us, and he seemed quite some of his former clients. They told us Russia with her nine million soldiers was Lieut Campbell of the Irish Fusiliers, wh and who had heard . but did not believe

The final version of the diary- typed in 1916 at Hereford

It has been an intriguing and humbling journey following my grandfather's route-marching footsteps through France and Belgium. His record of the events of the worst war in the history of mankind is a late but worthy addition to our pool of knowledge of the horrors of trench warfare and the futile waste of life it caused. On September 10th when 1/ Royal Warwicks engaged the Germans near the river Marne, Robert Hamilton's blunt assessment of the shelling was that 'This is the hell.' Death was never far from all soldiers' thoughts and on November 16th he wrote that he had enjoyed 'one more piece of extraordinary luck'. Many of his fellow officers and friends were not so lucky and never returned to their loved ones.

The pages of the diary emphasise how Robert Hamilton and his fellow soldiers in the Royal Warwickshire Regiment deserve the greatest admiration for struggling with their daily diet of inclement weather, cold, damp, noise, discomfort and danger with great stoicism and courage in the face of such extreme adversity. They did so with great humour; there are many occasions recorded in the diary when officers and men used it to raise their morale and cope with their predicament.

We have been most fortunate to have made contact with Mark Warby, editor of the *Old Bill Newsletter* and world expert on the works of Bruce Bairnsfather. It is appropriate that we have been able to include cartoons by Robert's friend Bairnsfather within the text of his diary. The humorous nature of the cartoons undoubtedly emanated from some of the raucous parties held by the Warwicks' officers at *estaminets* behind the lines.

The diary may not compare with the great literary works inspired by the War, but it is a valuable source of information about the conflict and I am delighted to have published, on my grandfather's behalf, nearly 100 years later, his personal and moving account of his experiences of the first six months of the Great War.

Andrew Hamilton, Walton, Warwickshire

2

'If you sometimes think of me'

Devon, August 5th 1914

Robert Hamilton woke with a start. There was another sharp bang on the door; he fumbled for his fob watch. It was the early call he had expected. Renie stirred, grumbled and turned over.

He hurried down the stairs and unbolted the sturdy front door.

"Telegram, Sir".

The bearer of bad tidings turned on his heel and pushed his bicycle noisily through the loose chippings.

Robert stepped barefoot over the driveway and walked onto his pride and joy- the tennis court he had lovingly created and tended since he and Renie had bought Collaven Manor near Tavistock in 1907 shortly after they were married.

He glanced at the telegram. 'Rejoin immediately. Arrive Shorncliffe 7 p.m.' The dawn chorus was reaching fever pitch. He pulled up a weed from the court surface and threw it on the cuttings heap.

After weeks of preparation at military barracks in Warwick and York, of endless route marches, rifle practice and bayonet training, the declaration of war against Germany meant that the time had at last arrived for him to perform his duties as a professional soldier in the British Expeditionary Force.

He returned to the bedroom and carefully put on his uniform. Renie slept on, undisturbed.

He hurried across the Tavistock to Sourton road, walked along the bridge over the railway line and climbed up on to Dartmoor. A buzzard circled and wheeled away on a current of wind. He strode over the peaty soil and breathed in familiar moorland scents.

He recalled the happy family outing the day before when he and Renie had taken their children, six year old Cynthia and three year old Dicky on horseback to Hunter's Pool high on the moor: he and Dicky on Gyp and Cynthia with Renie on Rhon. They tied the horses to granite boulders and climbed painstakingly down to the naturally created pool. Robert crouched over the water and caught their reflections in the still water. He felt he was still in his prime and physically ready for any challenges thrown at him by the German Army. "At least I don't look a day over thirty seven" he joked to Renie. Cynthia threw a pebble into the pool which disturbed the happy family picture. He told Dicky how to cup his hands and drink from the crystal clear water.

Robert woke from his reverie, looked up at the Sourton Tors and headed towards the tower of Sourton Church. A snipe zig-zagged up towards the rising sun. "I'll have you when I get back" he warned. He would miss his autumn shooting forays but he would make up for lost time after Christmas.

He hopped over the weather-worn fence at the perimeter of the graveyard and entered the small

The Church of St. Thomas à Becket, Sourton, Devon

7

The nave of Sourton Church

homely church of St. Thomas à Becket. He knelt in the front pew and prayed that the Lord would watch kindly over Renie, Cynthia and Dicky during his enforced absence.

He stood to attention in front of the altar, lowered his head and then walked back down the aisle. Renie would, he was sure, warn the Reverend Whitwell that he would be unable to carry out his Church Warden's duties for the foreseeable future.

He shut the graveyard's wicket gate behind him and briskly completed his three mile circular walk.

"For you, Lieutenant Hamilton". In the warmth of the dark kitchen, Robert accepted the cup of tea gratefully.

"The finest I'll have for several months, I'm sure."

"You'll be home soon?"

He put down the cup on the range. "Renie, this may not be as simple as the war in South Africa."

"Bob, the Hun must be sent packing and damned soon."

"Let's hope it's by Christmas."

Robert did not trace any hint of anxiety on his wife's face. She was the strongest and most determined woman he had ever met and was confident she would cope in his absence.

"Renie, I must catch the 9.45 train."

He took his tea upstairs and gently woke Cynthia and Dicky, knelt down and kissed them on each cheek.

"Good bye Toddles, I'll be back in time for Christmas Eve. Dicky, look after your big sister and mama won't you?"

"I want to be with you. I'm a big soldier now."

In 1900, Robert left for South Africa to fight the Boers with the Norfolk Regiment without a care in the world. But now, as he left their smiling faces, he was thankful that they were not old enough to understand the true meaning of 'war'.

Collaven Manor, Sourton, Devon
Jeff and Jacqui Mitchell, Collaven Manor Hotel, Devon

Renie brushed a hair from his uniform and straightened the Antelope badge of his new Regiment- the Royal Warwickshires.

"Will you miss the Holy Boys?" She appreciated that his move from the Norfolks was a disappointment to him.

"I'm sure I'll link up with some of the boys in France but there are some capital fellows in the Warwicks. Bruce Bairnsfather may rejoin us and I know Bernard Montgomery will keep me entertained- I'll be fine."

He placed his luggage on the gig and went down to the field behind the tennis court. He called to the horses: Rhon and Silver gambolled up to him. He chided Jock the collie for yapping under their feet and with a wistful sigh, looked up to the house and saw the smiling faces of his children at the window.

He climbed up alongside Renie who gave Gyp a flick with her whip; they both remained silent on the brief journey to Bridestowe station. He mused that on Saturday, he had crafted a fine 50 for Okehampton against Bude, and Renie's sow had produced a large litter of piglets. They both understood their world was about to change. She feared the coming weeks without Bob to help her with haymaking and tending the sheep and piglets. He could not dispel from his mind the possibility that she and the children might never see him again.

The little station was festooned with flags. He could feel the mood of excitement. Soldiers were milling around on the platform; young unattached soldiers, smoking ostentatiously, were engaged in excited bravado. Those with loved ones snatched a final embrace.

"Renie, I'll write to you every day. I promise."

"My dear Bob, take care of yourself- we will all pray for you."

Robert bought a copy of *The Times*. Frantic conversations were interrupted by the shrill blast of a guardsman's whistle; the train moved off past the clusters of bright mauve rhododendrons. He pulled down the window and continued waving until Renie was out of sight.

He settled into his seat and started to read his newspaper. 'This day will be momentous in the history of all time.' He would be in action in just ten days time if the Editor's speculation proved correct. 'The first decisive battles of the war are expected to take place between August 16th and 22nd.' Belgium's border, it was predicted, would be the probable scene of the first battle.

An officer of the Devonshire Regiment sitting opposite him, interrupted his read. "Which regiment?"

Robert explained that he had served with the Norfolks until he retired in 1909, went on the Special Reserve in 1912 and was called up into the Warwicks in early 1913. They speculated about the length of the War and agreed that despite reports of Germany's armaments programme, they could be home by Christmas.

The train laboured its way past Collaven on its way to Okehampton. He caught sight of Sourton church and graveyard. He returned to his paper which informed him that the Government was now in charge of the railways ensuring their use in the best interests of the State for the movement of troops, stores and food supplies.

It was reported that there had been a boom in recruiting. Robert was grateful that recruitment was in the hands of the inspirational Lord Kitchener. His eye was drawn to the notice that 'Your King and Country Need You.' He agreed with its central message that the British Empire was on the brink of the greatest war in the History of the World, and that if every patriotic man enrolled, England's Empire would emerge stronger and more united than ever.

His newspaper left Robert in no doubt that the next few weeks would be pivotal for his country, himself and his family. He would soon be in action against the German Army in defence of what he held so dear. Renie too would have to play her part- she would be expected to participate in training to tend the wounded and would follow Prime Minister Asquith's exhortations for the need for the 'strictest economy' on the Home Front.

He took his diary from his top pocket and removed the book mark. He wrote- 'A sad day for everybody, but it is a blessing to have a sensible and strong little wife- the chicks- they do not know. I kissed their smiling little faces but could not say a word.'

He lingered over the poem Renie had written for him on the bookmark when, after their engagement in 1904, he had to return to South Africa with the Norfolk Regiment:

My darling Bob I'm bored to death
I loathe this tiresome Ball
The dancing makes me out of breath
I hate them one and all.

There's no one here I've seen before
Or care to see again
My partners all have been a bore
The women are so plain.

I made this little poem up
When I was sitting out,
My partner brought me claret cup
What DID he talk about?

They trod upon my favourite corn
They tore my dress to rags
The second time that dress was torn
I never saw such snags.

The band is ripping far too good
For such a ball as this
Perhaps now you've understood
It's you I really miss.

My thoughts are with you all the same
In London at the play
It really seems to me a shame
You have to go away.

These things however have to be
So I will say good night
And if you sometimes think of me
Why then, 't will be alright.

Overwhelmed by melancholy, Robert gathered up his belongings and stepped on to the platform at Waterloo Station. He was struck by the capital's all pervasive war fever, a seething mass of flag waving well wishers and soldiers of the British Expeditionary Force busily on the move. A few skirmishes and it would not be long, he hoped, before the 'Hun' was sent packing from Belgium by Christmas time.

AH

3

'The knack of running through men'
Trinity College, Glenalmond, July 29th 1896

Robert Hamilton was surprised by the nostalgia he felt on his final full day at Trinity College, Glenalmond. For the last time, in brilliant sunshine, he walked across 'Big Cricket' ground and recalled two of his greatest exploits that summer- the 7 for 75 off 27 overs and his 49 not out. He scanned the heather-covered Perthshire hills behind the bowler's arm and accepted that he would miss the challenges of captaincy: plotting his opponents' downfall and coaxing match winning performances from his team mates.

He walked purposefully through Quad to the Library and returned some books he had borrowed for his final exams. He would have been the first to admit that the Library had been much less of an attraction for him than the College's sports fields but he was pleased to see Mr. Locke, the master in charge of the Library, whose French lessons he had enjoyed greatly. They exchanged the best of wishes for the future.

On his way out, he stopped at the racks of past copies of *The Glenalmond Chronicle* and pulled out the May edition for 1893,

'Big Cricket' ground at Glenalmond College, Perthshire, Scotland   Graeme Hart, Perthshire Picture Agency

which charted the beginnings of his sporting achievements, when only in his second year at 'Coll' he lost in the Fives final to William Kington, 15-5, 14-15, 13-15.

He glanced over the report of the cricket match against great rivals Fettes when his fledgling cricket career started disappointingly- he and his friend Hugh de Putron chalked up a 'duck' each. But for Kington's 81, 'Coll' would not have triumphed. It was an innings that merited the talismanic captain's commendation that 'he was the best bat we have seen here'. Robert's own end of season report suggested promise for the future- 'As a bat he has often proved himself in matches but is invariably caught from a half hit over the bowler's head, of which he ought to cure himself.' At least in a later edition he was congratulated for his 'brilliant tackling' at full back for the Rugby XV. His victory in the lawn tennis doubles tournament confirmed his burgeoning prowess as a sporting all-rounder.

Cricket teams at Glenalmond College
Glenalmond College

He lingered over the 1895 volumes which recorded his supremacy on the Fives courts and assessed him as the College's 'neatest and best gymnast.' With a wry smile he perused the description of his work on the horizontal bar- 'Hamilton's swinging and German circles were very well executed and the easy rhythmical motion with which he went through his complicated manoeuvres was admirable.' Quite a contrast he thought to his Rugby report- 'he picks up well and has the knack of running through men.'

He wondered how the autumn edition of *The Chronicle* after his departure from Glenalmond would assess his captaincy of the X1 in 1896. 'Skilful and imaginative' would be appropriate he thought, but reproached himself for such a lack of modesty. He felt he deserved a positive write-up for leading his team from the front with his 20 wickets and 268 runs that summer.

Wandering past the classrooms, he was distinctly unconcerned at the prospect of leaving behind his Latin, Greek and Scientific Studies. English Literature and Creative Writing had been his *forte*, or at least scurrilous verse that had entertained his peers.

Robert walked past New Wing, opened in 1893 by the Prime Minister W.E. Gladstone. All Glenalmond boys were reminded regularly that one of the College's founders was 'the greatest and foremost political figure in the great reign of Queen Victoria'.

It was his final Commemoration Day. Sharply dressed in his cadet force uniform, he joined the queue of prefects outside Chapel. They strode up the aisle and took their seats beneath the pulpit. His Christian faith had been fostered and encouraged in this fine building during his five years at the school. Sermons by the Warden, The Rev. Dr. John Huntley Skrine, had inculcated in him the role he and his fellow pupils would perform as 'Christian Gentlemen' in the management and defence of Britain's far flung Empire. Other speakers at 'Commem' had emphasised that schools like Glenalmond taught its pupils 'how to be a man' and 'how to govern themselves and others as the country's natural leaders'.

His father had sent his son to a public school in Scotland to prepare him for a career in the Indian Civil Service or the Army. Robert was placed in the Army Class academic stream for boys who were destined for the Army rather than University. He had been inspired by 'Coll's' training exercises and route marches in the wild Scottish countryside and had aspirations for greater excitement and physical challenges than those offered by a desk bound career.

He concluded early in his schooldays that his future lay with the British Army. He looked forward to playing a role in safeguarding Britain's pre-eminence in the world and defending his country and its interests against all aggressors. He accepted that much of the prize-giving ceremony in the

RAH.ROBERTSON. H.W.D.HILL. T.E.KEYDEN. T.E.A.DALYELL.
C.S.WILSON. A.D.SKRINE. R.C.HAMILTON. C.T.GRAHAM. D.K.TWEEDIE.
F.R.CROMBIE. H.GARDNER.
1896.

Trinity College, Glenalmond- 1st XI Cricket team in 1896- the crossed triangles on the blazers represent the Holy Trinity
Glenalmond College

Gymnasium would be spent applauding others who came up to receive their rewards for academic excellence.

After the proceedings in the Gymnasium, the 500 strong company of benefactors, guests, staff and pupils made their way to dining-hall for a luncheon presided over by the Warden who ended his speech with a toast to 'The Founders and Benefactors'. In reply, a member of the Governing Council, Canon Scott Holland, pronounced that 'the boys in Glenalmond will ever find that their boyhood is not repressed, but enlarged, is not fettered, but uncurtailed, because it is nourished and sustained by the faith and powers of Christ and his Church. It is because we believe in it to be always so, and that the great Powers now in force will ever work out the like issue, that we put all our hearts and souls into the toast of Floreat Glenalmond.' Robert was silently grateful that he would never have to listen to any more 'Commem' speeches.

In the afternoon on the slopes not far from the meandering river Almond, Robert performed his last military parade in Scotland. The Cadet Corps marched past and saluted Colonel Sir Robert Moncreiffe who commended the young aspiring soldiers for the accomplished style in which they performed various different marching movements. It wouldn't be long before Robert would be performing such exercises as a soldier in the Norfolk Militia.

Early next day, in the corridor between the boys' cubicles, Robert finished packing his trunk and carefully tucked the photo of his cricket team safely into the centre. Two young boys who were noisily kicking a ball, were ordered to carry his trunk to Front Arch where it was loaded on to a cart and transported to nearby Methven station.

Scores of boys were milling around waiting to be taken to the station. Robert shook hands with Hugh de Putron and wished him well. Many others made their final farewells and vowed and hoped that they would meet again in the new millennium.

William Miles Kington *was at Glenalmond from 1890-1894. He was a Captain in the Royal Welch Fusiliers, received a D.S.O. (Distintinguished Service Order) and was killed in action in France on October 20th 1914 aged 38. He is commemorated on the Menin Gate Memorial at Ypres. William Kington was the grandfather of Miles Kington, jazz musician,* Punch *humorist and popular feature writer for* The Independent *for many years, who died in 2008 at the age of 66. Miles also attended Glenalmond and on November 12th 2006 opened the refurbished Armstrong Reading Room in the Glenalmond College library. Following the ceremony, he laid a wreath on behalf of the O.G. Club and gave the address at the Remembrance Day service in chapel in which he referred to the death of his grandfather.*

• *157 former pupils of the College lost their lives in the Great War, about the number of students on the school roll in 1914 and 23% of the total of 685 who fought in the War. 97 were killed in action and 60 died of wounds or illness.*

• *William John Locke was appointed to the Glenalmond staff in 1891 to teach Mathematics. He did not find this conducive so changed to teach Modern Languages instead. He was at Glenalmond for six years. After he left, he became a well known novelist and had several best selling novels in the United States. One of his short stories, 'Ladies in Lavender' was made into a film starring Judi Dench and Maggie Smith in 2004. He wrote a piece in support of the King of the Belgians in 'King Albert's Book', produced in December 1914 by* The Daily Telegraph *for their Belgian Fund. Other contributors included the Prime Minister Herbert Asquith, Rudyard Kipling, Winston Churchill, Sir Edward Elgar and Claude Monet. Robert recalls in his diary that he met Locke in 1919.*

• *Trinity College Glenalmond, now known as Glenalmond College, was founded in 1847 by a number of Scottish dignitaries but the prime movers were Sir John Gladstone and his son William Gladstone, Prime Minister in the periods 1868-74, 1880- 85 and 1892-95. It is a Scottish Episcopalian foundation and the Church was heavily involved in its foundation. Daily services are still held in Chapel except on Saturdays although pupils from any faith may attend the school.*

• *Hugh de Putron served in the Manchester Regiment and achieved the rank of Brevet Lieutenant-Colonel.*

AH

4

'Till the Ganges did not flow'

Indore, India, March 1907

The Norfolk Regiment had been posted to Bombay (Mumbai) in India early in 1907. In March, Lieutenant Robert Hamilton took his leave and travelled to the Hill Station of Mussourie (Mussoorie) in the State of Uttanchal in the foothills of the Himalayas. He was preparing to spend a day walking in the hills and on leaving the Officers' Mess after a hearty English breakfast, he received a telegram from the Maharajah of Indore, ordering him to 'come and stay with me now'. This was an invitation that Robert suspected he could not refuse and so delayed his plans for the day and arranged an extension to his leave. He took the first available train to Bombay.

Robert recalled the two Votes of Thanks to his grandfather that greeted visitors in the Hall of the family home at Avon Cliffe near Stratford-on-Avon. As a young boy he had asked about the reasons for them and appreciated that the summons to Indore by the current Maharajah, was in gratitude for what his grandfather had achieved during the Indian Mutiny fifty years before.

Ever since they had left their Scottish family seat at Silverton Hill in Lanarkshire, most of Robert's ancestors had traditionally joined the Army. His grandfather, Sir Frederic the 5th Baronet had bucked the trend when he joined the East India Company's Civil Service in the 1790s. His son Robert North Collie, born in 1802, followed in his footsteps and joined the East India Company but after the death of his wife Constantia in 1842, moved into the political service of the ruling British Raj and in 1844 was appointed British Resident of Indore in the Central Provinces. A large part of India was still under the rule of the British but there were still many independent states ruled by a Maharajah. Hamilton's role was to act as a representative for the British Government and keep a watching brief that the state of Indore was efficiently and fairly governed in Britain's best interests.

In 1844, the young Maharajah Holkar was an immature young boy, who was prey to palace intrigues. Hamilton took an avuncular but politically expedient interest in the young Maharajah and arranged for him to be educated by a respected Brahmin teacher. Holkar regarded him as a father figure and the young boy befriended the many members of the Hamilton family with whom Robert Hamilton had surrounded himself in India.

Robert North Collie Hamilton
Paul Hamilton

In 1853 Robert North Collie Hamilton became the 6th Baronet and was appointed Agent in the Central Provinces in 1854. Wary of leaving the seat of government in Calcutta, the Governor-General Lord Canning was keen that the new Agent should maintain a watchful eye over the Central Provinces.

Sir Robert's health deteriorated in 1857 and he retired to Bombay to convalesce. He was aware of growing discontent in the region and soon after his departure, local troops mutinied at Meerut. He was confident that Maharajah Holkar and his family and advisers would deal with any problems that arose. Concerned by the mood of restlessness in the Central Provinces, Canning appointed a deputy, Colonel Durand, to take charge. A military man, Durand was less politically adroit than Hamilton and his arrogant and provocative manner caused a breakdown in relations with the Maharajah's household. When locals rebelled in Indore and killed European troops, women and children, they were joined by Holkar's troops who bombarded the Residency, and forced Durand to flee for the sake of the women and children who had taken refuge there. Durand was convinced that Maharajah Holkar was to blame.

A race ensued between the appeaser Hamilton and the hawkish Durand to arrive in Indore first. Newly appointed as political adviser to Sir Hugh Rose, commander of the Central India Field Force, Sir Robert returned as quickly as was possible by 'bullock tonga' from Bombay.

Durand was keen to wreak revenge on Holkar whom he accused of treachery. Sir Robert, however, strongly took the view that Holkar was innocent of the charge and that his troops had rebelled without his knowledge. He understood the importance of treating the Maharajah well as his financial help was needed in maintaining the Central India Field Force. During the Mutiny, the Treasury had been raided but Sir Robert's even handedness paid off as Holkar, convinced that Hamilton had saved his life as he was sure Durand would have put him to death, lent a large amount of money to the cash strapped British Government. Sir Hugh Rose was now able to re-equip his army and successfully marched through the Central Provinces, releasing fortified towns and defeating insurgent forces; he was indebted to Sir Robert for his deep knowledge and understanding of the area and for providing him with much needed funds.

The reward for the Maharajah was to be appointed one of the senior reigning princes of India and Sir Robert North Collie Hamilton was accorded official Paliamentary Votes of Thanks in 1858.

On hearing that the grandson of the 'Burra Sahib' (important man) had been posted to India, the current Maharajah was keen to invite the 'Chota Sahib' (small man) to his Palace and repay some of his family's debt to the Hamilton family.

Robert's journey from Bombay on the state railway coincided with the height of the monsoon season. It was stiflingly hot and he was grateful for his recently acquired silk pyjamas which he wore as a practical necessity and without embarrassment. When the train arrived, he was taken aback by the scene that greeted him. The station was ablaze with illuminations of all kinds and hundreds of local Hindus were prostrate on the platform, their foreheads touching the ground. He proceeded to the exit door and it soon dawned on him that this extraordinary welcome was in his honour. He felt humbled and a little awkward as he stood there in his silk pyjamas!

The Maharajah in all his regal finery, approached and shook Robert's hand enthusiastically and introduced himself. The Prince asked Robert's permission that the prostrated men "may arise." He nodded diffidently and they joined an even larger number congregated outside the station.

The Maharajah arranged for a room to be provided for Robert to change in and as quickly as possible he rejoined the Prince. The two of them were driven off in an open landau with two servants on the box, two standing behind and several others running alongside and in front, to clear a way through the dense crowd. Not long after the crowds had been left behind, the Maharajah pointed to three palaces. He explained that one was his, another would be for Robert's use and the third was for his wives and concubines.

Inside 'his' palace, Robert was taken up a magnificent stairway flanked on either side by more of the bodyguard and was shown into a palatial room covered with priceless carpets and adorned with English furniture. One bed was placed in the centre of the enormous room and another on the verandah, which had a spectacular view of the Nerbudda river.

The Maharajah left Robert and intimated that he would like to see him later in the morning once he had breakfasted and had a rest. Robert made the half mile trip to the Maharajah's palace by elephant.

Standing together on a verandah, Robert was not surprised to learn that the Maharajah had been educated at Eton and Oxford. He was struck by how well travelled he was; the prince told him of the many languages he could speak- the young lieutenant surmised that academically, he was somewhat inferior to his host.

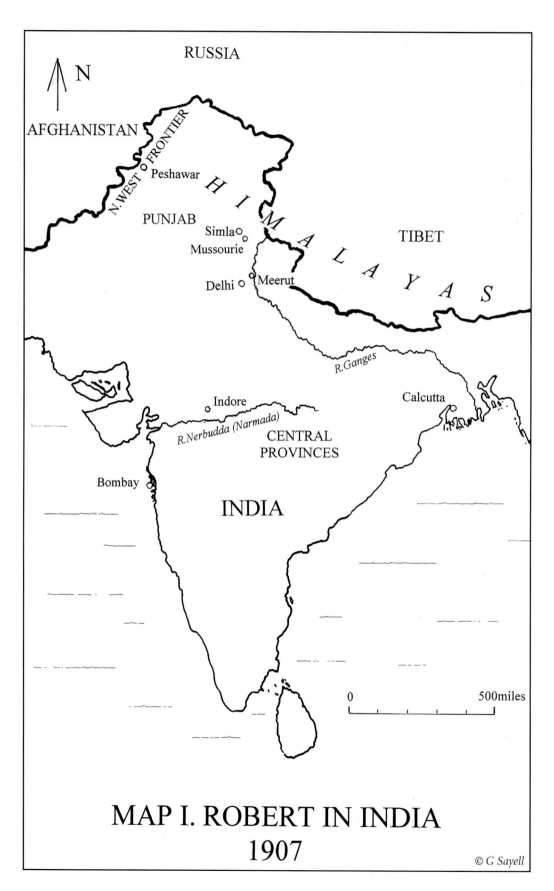

RUSSIA

AFGHANISTAN

N.WEST FRONTIER

Peshawar

PUNJAB

Simla

Mussourie

Delhi

Meerut

TIBET

H I M A L A Y A S

R.Ganges

Indore

Calcutta

R.Nerbudda (Narmada)

CENTRAL
PROVINCES

Bombay

INDIA

0   500miles

MAP I. ROBERT IN INDIA
1907

© G Sayell

The Maharajah handed Robert a large telescope and told him to focus it on a large clearance in the jungle. There he could see large numbers of wild boar being fed. Some gingerly descended a ramp to gambol and wash themselves in the river below.

The walls of the verandah were covered with maps of the British Empire of the kind Robert was familiar with from his schooldays at Glenalmond. There were maps of France, Italy and Germany and under each map rested a journal of each country.

Robert was told that ever since 1858 a Hamilton had been a tutor or adviser to each successive Maharajah and the reason for the visit became clear to him when the Maharajah offered him the post of Private Secretary. Robert was recited the deeds of 1858, and received a fulsome eulogy of his grandfather, the 'Burra Sahib.' The ageing potentate expressed his delight with the presence of the 'Chota Sahib' and to celebrate the event, he summoned a servant to bring champagne and glasses.

Robert thanked the Maharajah for his offer of a post in his household and considered it a great honour and privilege to have been asked. He expressed his sorrow at having to decline his kind offer; he was well advanced in his military career and he had pressing engagements to deal with at home in the very near future…

The Prince was disappointed that the Hamilton connection would end but led him to a private room where the household jewels were kept. He ceremoniously invited the young subaltern to choose whatever took his fancy as 'an inadequate but sincere payment for the debt incurred so long ago.'

Robert chose a breathtaking eight pointed diamond tiara which contained other smaller diamonds. The Maharajah made a short official speech, indicating that the tiara should be put in the keeping of Robert's mother until he should take a wife, after which it should be handed down from father to son "till the Ganges did not flow." Robert was overcome by the generosity of the gift and vowed that he would pass it on to his chosen wife.

Later that night, the young Lieutenant was invited as guest of honour to a gala of wrestling. He was transported to the ringside by the light of the moon on an enormous white elephant which was regarded as the greatest of honours. He found the wrestling a rather dull experience but proceedings at the end of each bout were enlivened when he was asked to throw handfuls of rupees amongst the crowd.

More to his liking was a Tiger Hunt which took place before daybreak the following day. The hunting party met in the courtyard of 'his' palace and from there, mounted on elephants with several attendants on board, set off with two local princes.

In the evening, he attended the 'blooding' ceremony when the bag of one tiger and two sambur (Indian elk) was accredited to Robert's gun, a claim he considered inappropriate to deny.

Next day's hectic programme included a drive in a carriage, accompanied by a mounted escort to a neighbouring palace on the Nerbudda river where a sumptuous repast was enjoyed, during which he was entertained by dancing girls whose athleticism did not escape his notice.

On the return journey, once again, all bent low to the ground as the carriage passed by and in the evening the old retainers who had asked to be allowed to 'do him honour' were admitted one by one to meet him. Self-conscious and accepting that protest was out of place, Robert sat on a canopied throne and was overwhelmed by the idea that the spirit of the 'Burra Sahib' still existed.

On his departure to Bombay, the Maharajah himself escorted his visitor to the station. The gardens of the Palaces were lit up by hundreds of coloured lanterns, and for Robert, the full moon was a perfect way to end the day.

His stay had been full of surprises, none more so than when the Maharajah made his fond farewells, he handed Robert an envelope. When he surreptitiously opened it later on his journey, he found that it contained 32,000 rupees which by his calculations was the equivalent of £3,000.

Robert could never have predicted the warmth of the welcome he received and the high esteem in which his family were held, in the very heart of India.

This account is adapted from a piece written 42 years after the event by Robert Hamilton in May 1949 when he was 72.

- Fortunately, the river Ganges does still flow but sadly, the eight-pointed diamond tiara does not seem to have been handed down from father to son nor grandson!

- I am indebted to Elizabeth Hamilton for detail about Sir Robert North Collie Hamilton Bt. and the Indian Mutiny.

AH

5

"Capital effort Herr Chef"
The Trocadero Restaurant, June 4th 1912

Lieutenant Hamilton and fellow officers of the Norfolk Regiment were enjoying cigars and port after the annual regimental dinner at the Trocadero Restaurant in Piccadilly, London.

The unanimous view was that this year's Dinner had been a first class event. The 1904 Perrier-Jouët champagne was a class act and the 1900 Château Gruaud-Larose was well received by the so-called experts for its luscious silkiness. Robert considered the long journey from Devon had been well worth it for the Médaillon de Boeuf Choron alone.

The Norfolk Regiment in 1903 in front of the Goojerat Barracks at Colchester- Robert Hamilton is seated on the ground in the front row on the far right

He was relaxed and comfortable in such company; several of those in attendance had served with him in South Africa. He calculated that he knew 28 of the 43 present.

He had been seated with Lieutenants Balders, Megaw, Ward and Captain 'Bootles' Cresswell. Proudly wearing their Queen's and King's medals for their successful efforts to quell the Boer uprising in the Transvaal, Orange Free State and Cape Colony, the conversation focused on tales of victorious skirmishes and ambushes. Memories of the intense heat and thick dust of high summer generated the excuse for another thirst quenching glass of 1904 Krug. The challenges posed by the terrain and climate were intensified by the shortage of water. In hushed tones, they berated their commanding officer, Colonel Borton, who was sitting out of earshot at the end of the table, for his repeated failure to ensure adequate supplies of drinking water for his men.

The Norfolk Regiment Fancy Dress Party, Bloemfontein in 1906.
Lieutenant Hamilton is seated second from left wearing a 'newspaper' suit. Lieutenant Cresswell is sitting on the ground,
Lieutenant Balders is standing far left and Captain Ward is second from right- all three died in the Great War

The officers had been stationed at Bloemfontein, capital of the Orange River Colony until 1906. Once the Boer insurgency had been quelled in 1902, life in Bloemfontein, the 'city of roses', was an undemanding and enjoyable social merry-go-round.

"Hammers, how's the old newspaper suit?"

Robert had caused a stir at the officers' fancy dress ball in 1906 when he dressed in a 'newspaper' suit. "I'm good news" he had proclaimed on arrival. He pointed out to Cresswell and Balders that their costumes that evening had been dreary and unimaginative in comparison.

The custom at previous regimental dinners had been for the Head Chef to receive the officers' plaudits after coffee had been taken.

"Capital effort, Herr Chef. The Ris de Veau Royal was quite splendid." The German Head Chef beamed with delight and accepted a large cigar for his efforts and a glass of his favourite five year old Berncastler Doctor.

They drank raucous toasts to the future good health of their respective monarchs and countries. The five South African veterans enjoyed a final glass of Dow's 1890 Port and unsteadily wove their way to their bedrooms on the third floor.

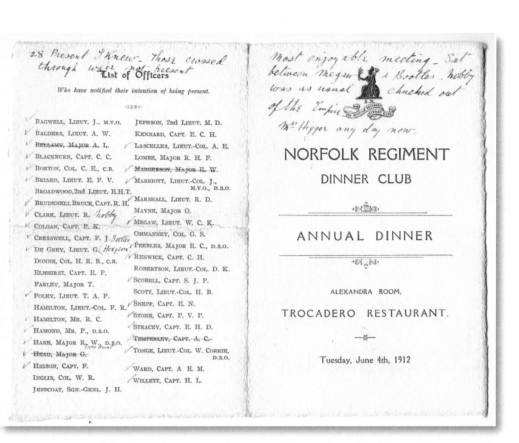

List of Officers

28 Present I knew - those crossed through were not present

Who have notified their intention of being present.

BAGWELL, LIEUT. J., M.V.O.	JEPHSON, 2nd LIEUT. M. D.
BALDERS, LIEUT. A. W.	KENNARD, CAPT. E. C. H.
BELLAMY, MAJOR A. I.	LASCELLES, LIEUT.-COL. A. E.
BLACKBURN, CAPT. C. C.	LOMBE, MAJOR R. H. F.
BORTON, COL. C. E., C.B.	MARGESSON, MAJOR R. W.
BRIARD, LIEUT. E. F. V.	MARRIOTT, LIEUT.-COL. J., M.V.O., D.S.O.
BROADWOOD, 2nd LIEUT. E.H.T.	
BRUDENELL BRUCE, CAPT. R. H.	MARSHALL, LIEUT. R. D.
CLARK, LIEUT. R. *hobby*	MAYNE, MAJOR O.
COLGAN, CAPT. P. K.	MEGAW, LIEUT. W. C. K.
CRESSWELL, CAPT. F. J. *Bootler*	OMMANNEY, COL. G. S.
DE GREY, LIEUT. G. *Hodgson*	PEEBLES, MAJOR E. C., D.S.O.
DONNE, COL. H. R. B., C.B.	RENWICK, CAPT. C. H.
ELMHIRST, CAPT. E. P.	ROBERTSON, LIEUT.-COL. D. K.
FARLEY, MAJOR T.	SCOBELL, CAPT. S. J. P.
FOLEY, LIEUT. T. A. F.	SCOTT, LIEUT.-COL. H. B.
HAMILTON, LIEUT.-COL. F. R.	SNEPP, CAPT. E. N.
HAMILTON, MR. R. C.	STONE, CAPT. P. V. P.
HAMOND, MR. P., D.S.O.	STRACEY, CAPT. E. H. D.
HARE, MAJOR R. W., D.S.O.	TEMPERLEY, CAPT. A. C.
HEAD, MAJOR G.	TONGE, LIEUT.-COL. W. CORRIE, D.S.O.
HIGSON, CAPT. F.	
INGLIS, COL. W. R.	WARD, CAPT. A. E. M.
JEFFCOAT, SGN.-GENL. J. H.	WILLETT, CAPT. H. I.

Most enjoyable meeting. Sat between Megaw & Bootles. hobby was as usual chucked out of the Empire.

Mr Higgor any day now.

NORFOLK REGIMENT
DINNER CLUB

ANNUAL DINNER

ALEXANDRA ROOM.

TROCADERO RESTAURANT.

Tuesday, June 4th, 1912

Menu card for the Norfolk Regiment's Dinner at the Trocadero, Piccadilly, London on June 4th 1912

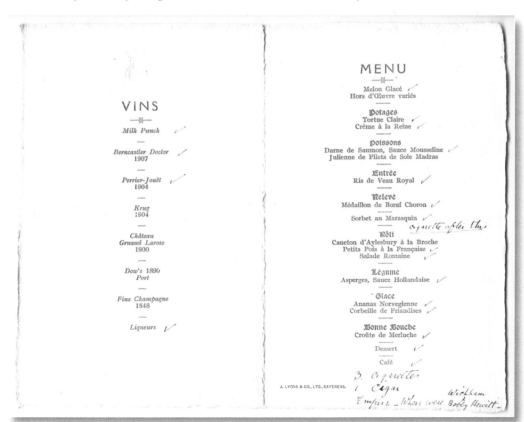

VINS

Milk Punch

Berncastler Doctor
1907

Perrier-Jouët
1904

Krug
1904

Château
Gruaud Larose
1900

Dow's 1896
Port

Fine Champagne
1848

Liqueurs

MENU

Melon Glacé
Hors d'Œuvre variés

Potages
Tortue Claire
Crème à la Reine

Poissons
Darne de Saumon, Sauce Mousseline
Julienne de Filets de Sole Madras

Entrée
Ris de Veau Royal

Relevé
Médaillon de Bœuf Choron

Sorbet au Marasquin   *cigarette after this*

Rôti
Caneton d'Aylesbury à la Broche
Petits Pois à la Française
Salade Romaine

Légume
Asperges, Sauce Hollandaise

Glace
Ananas Norvegienne
Corbeille de Friandises

Bonne Bouche
Croûte de Merluche

Dessert

Café

3. Cigarette
1. Cigar
Empire - When were Bobby Hewitt. Wickham

J. LYONS & CO., LTD., CATERERS.

BLOEMFONTEIN 1906.

1ST BATTN NORFOLK REGT

Capt. R.F.Day. L'& Q'. M'. W.J.Armstrong. Capt. J.C.Atkinson. L'. H.Lancaster. 'L'. T.R.Bowlby. 'L'. H.J.Dundas. 'L'. R.J.Filgate. 'L' WCK.Megaw. L'. R.C.Hamilton. L'. A.E.M.Ward. L'. E.A.Daunt. 'L'. A.W.Balders. Maj. A.L.Bellamy. Col. G.Massy. L'. F.J.Cresswell. Capt. C.V.Lanyon

2ND BATTN NORFOLK REGT.

Capt. C.G.Wickham d.s.o. 'L' E.W.Montgomerie. Capt. J.B.Orr. d.s.o. Capt. F.E.Walter. L' R.J.C.Otter. L' A.E.Bosher. L' W.J.O.B.Daunt. L' H.L.Willett. 'L' J.L.Whalley. 'L' C.E.L.Thompson. Capt. C.E.Luard d.s.o. L'& Q'. M'. P.Colgan. L' G.de Grey. Capt. F.C.Lodge. Col. F.Winfold. Capt. & Adj. B.S.Greswell.

The Norfolk Regiment on parade at Bloemfontein in 1906-
from F. Loraine Petrie's 'History of the Norfolk Regiment'

1ST BATTN NORFOLK REGT

Capt. R.F.Day. L'& Q'. M'. W.J.Armstrong. Capt. J.C.Atkinson. L'. H.Lancaster. 'L'. T.R.Bowlby. 'L'. H.J.Dundas. 'L'. R.J.Filgate. 'L' WCK.Megaw. L'. R.C.Hamilton. L'. A.E.M.Ward. L'. E.A.Daunt. 'L'. A.W.Balders. Maj. A.L.Bellamy. Col. G.Massy. L'. F.J.Cresswell. Capt. C.V.Lanyon

- Captain J. C. Atkinson: was Robert Hamilton's 'best man' in 1907.

Lieutenant Thomas Rupert Bowlby (later Captain) was killed in action at Missy-sur-Aisne on September 17th 1914. He was 33 and came from Hampstead, London. He is commemorated on the Memorial at La Ferté-sous-Jouarre.

- Lieutenant R.J. Filgate: Robert expressed surprise in his diary entry for December 30th 1914 to have met Filgate in Bailleul, France.

Lieutenant William Cecil Kennedy Megaw (later Captain) was killed in action on March 31st 1915 near Hill 60 aged 29. He was buried at Ramparts Cemetery, Ypres. He also met Robert in Bailleul. His family erected a plaque on the wall of St. George's Church, Ypres, in his memory.

Lieutenant Arthur Edward Martyr Ward (later Captain) was killed in action on August 12th 1915 at the Battle of Suvla Bay on the Gallipoli Peninsula aged 37. He is remembered on the Helles Memorial.

Lieutenant Captain Arthur William Balders (later Captain) was killed in action on November 27th 1915. His body was never found. His name is commemorated on the Zaria Memorial in Nigeria.

- Colonel G. Massy: Robert left his sword with him for safe keeping on August 24th 1914 when he arrived at Le Havre where Massy was Commandant- unfortunately he never saw his sword again.

Lieutenant F.J. Cresswell (later Captain) was killed in action on August 24th 1914 at the Battle of Mons aged 31. He was buried at the Auberchicourt British Cemetery. He was probably known to the Hamiltons as 'Bootles'.

The following attendees at the Dinner in 1912 were also killed during the war:

Lieutenant Ernest Felix Victor Briard (later Captain): was killed in action on August 25th 1914 at the Battle of Mons aged 25. He is buried at Élouges Cemetery.

Lieutenant Thomas Algernon Fitzgerald Foley: was killed in action on October 25th 1914 near Violaines aged 25. His name is to be found on the Le Touret Memorial.

- Robert met Lieutenant J. Bagwell and Captain R.H. Brudenell-Bruce in Bailleul on December 30th 1914.

AH

6

'Smile now, please, Mrs. Hamilton'

St. James's Church, Walton Hall, Warwickshire, Wednesday July 24th 1907

It was one of the highlights of the Warwickshire summer social calendar. The county's great and good had accepted invitations from the dowager Lady Mordaunt to the wedding of her second daughter Irene to Lieutenant Robert Caradoc Hamilton of Avon Cliffe, Tiddington near Stratford-on-Avon. The little Church of St. James, Walton Hall, built in 1740 and extended by Irene's grandfather Sir John Mordaunt in 1843, was bursting at the seams. Among the guests were Lord and Lady Leigh of Stoneleigh Abbey, the Marquess and Marchioness of Hertford, Lord and Lady Willoughby de Broke of Compton Verney, Sir Henry and Lady Fairfax-Lucy of Charlecote and Robert's parents, Sir Frederic and Lady Mary Hamilton.

Avon Cliffe, the Hamilton's family home at Tiddington, near Stratford-on-Avon. It was sold in 1921

When on extended leave from Bloemfontein in South Africa, Robert would ride over from the family home, Avon Cliffe to see Irene Mordaunt. They often rode out to various locations on the Mordaunt Estate; their favourite was the watermill on its northern edge where they would watch the massive wooden water wheel generating power to mill flour which was used for baking bread in the mill house's large bake oven. Sitting on the sluice gates, they watched carp and bream lazily basking in the mill pond and the miller, Henry Anderton, would bring the courting couple freshly baked rolls, butter and cheese.

Wellesbourne Watermill- 1890s postcard featuring the miller Henry Anderton, wife and mill hand

Another favourite trysting place was the Bath House, a hunting lodge set on a bank in the Bath Woods which overlooked the Hall and Church. Tethering their horses to the iron railings by the steps to the one octagonal room, they would go down to the grotto underneath it, which housed a bath filled by spring water from the hillside. Upstairs they enjoyed picnics and swapped gossip about local families.

"Renie, was this where your father's first wife and the Prince of Wales used to…"

"Robert" she interrupted testily "you must understand that what that woman did to my poor father is something I will never talk about, to anyone, EVER. That woman ruined the good name of my father and my family."

Robert understood that discretion in the matter was a sensible course of action. "The shell work in this room never ceases to amaze me" was the first thing that came into his head as he looked up at the intricate arrangements that encircled the room.

The Bath House, Walton, Warwickshire
Drawing by David Matthews

23

Walton Hall, Warwickshire

He, like many in Warwickshire and beyond, wanted to know more of the true inside story. Rumours had been rife about the 'Warwickshire Scandal' involving royalty and the family.

In December 1866, the thirty year old Sir Charles Mordaunt, 10th baronet, had brought his young eighteen year old bride, Harriett Moncreiffe, to his newly built neo-Gothic home in Warwickshire. Designed by Sir Gilbert Scott, no expense had been spared; it was, he believed, the perfect home for his new bride. For Harriett, life in sleepy Walton with her uninspiring husband was unexciting in the extreme and she soon became an attraction for the Prince of Wales and his hedonistic circle of friends.

Frank England
Stephen England

Increasingly, her husband must have suspected his wife and her furtive liaisons and when he returned early from a fishing trip in Norway, may not have been surprised to find Harriett showing off her driving skills of a carriage and two white ponies to an appreciative Prince. Enraged by the Royal's attention to his young wife, Sir Charles sent him post haste on his way to Moreton-in-Marsh train station.

Walton Village and the War Memorial which includes two soldiers who fought for the Royal Warwickshire Regiment. **Harry Hobday,** *son of George and Jane Hobday of Fosse Cottages, Walton, Wellesbourne, died on November 21st 1914 after the 1st Battle of Ypres and is named on the Ploegsteert Memorial*

Frank England, *son of Alfred and Martha England was killed aged 26 on the Somme, July 6th 1916 and was buried at the Caudry Old Communal Cemetery. Ironically he was born and brought up in one of the cottages in the background*

In an act of astonishing callousness, the jilted husband ordered his groom to lead the two ponies on to the lawn by the conservatory. There they were shot in front of Harriett's very eyes. Given his known love of horses, it was an extraordinary reaction that soon entered local folklore.

Not long afterwards, Harriett announced to Sir Charles that she was pregnant. Her husband was none too pleased to discover that, by her own admission, she was unsure of the father's identity.

A protracted divorce case ensued in which the Prince of Wales faced cross-examination in the witness box but was saved from further public embarrassment when his friend Lord Cole agreed to be cited as the only co-respondent.

The Moncreiffe family claimed and may well have encouraged their daughter to feign madness and thus spare herself and her family name from the humiliation of a divorce. Sir Charles was fortunate to benefit from a recent law change enabling him to obtain a divorce from Harriett, who sadly spent the rest of her life 'under restraint.'

Robert was taken aback by the vehemence of Renie's reaction. If she were to respond to reference to the humiliating and public goings-on with such vehemence and if he were to be allowed her hand in marriage, mention of the sorry affair would indeed never pass his lips again.

It was a beautiful cloudless day. As they waited for the bridal party in the nave of the church, Robert nervously confided in his best man, Captain John Atkinson of the Norfolk Regiment, that nothing he had experienced before had provoked such nervousness. Renie and her mother Mary Louisa, dressed in black as she had always done since her husband's death ten years earlier, hurriedly gathered up the bridesmaids- Renie's sisters, Adela, Cicely and Winifred and Robert's sisters, Mary and Cerise. Renie handed her bouquet of roses, lilies of the valley and azaleas to Cicely. They made their way down the aisle to the strains of Mendelssohn and when she arrived next to him, Robert was overcome by a warm flow of love for his wife-to-be. The sapphire and diamond pendant he had given her, sparkled on her ivory satin dress. The former vicar of the parish, the Reverend O'Brien, officiated and the current incumbent, the Reverend Alton gave an address declaring the duties of man and wife.

Wedding souvenir photographs of Robert and Irene Hamilton

The vows completed and rings exchanged, the happy couple exchanged smiles with family and friends as they made their way to the vestry, uplifted by Mendelssohn's Wedding March.

St. James's Church, Walton D'Eivile
Drawing by David Matthews

The marriage register duly signed, they stepped out into the sunshine to be showered in rose petals by excited local schoolchildren thankful for a day off school. They passed through a guard of honour of raised swords by Robert's fellow officers from Boer War days and entered the main Hall. The married couple stopped to look at some of the array of presents laid out on mahogany tables. Robert spotted a silver tea tray from his brother officers in the Norfolk Regiment and Renie's eye was drawn to a bright mauve prayer book signed beautifully by all the children of the village school. Robert picked up and turned in his fingers the gift from his 'best man'- a combined pencil, knife and cigar cutter.

Presented to
ROBERT CARADOC HAMILTON
on the occasion of his marriage
BY
HIS BROTHER OFFICERS
of the
1ST NORFOLK REGIMENT

Inscription on a silver tray, a wedding gift to Robert from officers of the Norfolk Regiment

"Capital, John, for the officer in relaxation mood".

"Let's hope you never need it in active combat."

Neither Robert nor Renie looked forward to small talk with guests many of whom they had not seen for years nor could put a name to. They found the meeting and greeting interminable. 25

Unenthusiastic posers for photographs, Renie was thankful the photographer was organised and confident enough to arrange the set up quickly and decisively- their guests would be desperate to eat.

"Smile please!" It all seemed such an effort.

Wedding photograph 1907.
Revd. O'Brien, Ida Hamilton, Robert Hamilton, Cerise Hamilton, Adela Mordaunt, Captain John Atkinson
Lady Mary Hamilton, Irene Hamilton, Lady Mary Louisa Mordaunt, unknown, Sir Frederic Hamilton,
Winifred Mordaunt, Cicely Mordaunt

Speeches, more small talk, but soon they would be on their way by Rolls-Royce to Rugby station and thence to Ballyhuish in Scotland for their honeymoon.

In the privacy of their own compartment, they collapsed gratefully into the comfortable seats. Robert took Renie's hand.

"Smile now, please, Mrs. Hamilton."

AH

Chain of Command and Composition of the British Expeditionary Force

When Lieutenant Robert Hamilton fought with the British Expeditionary Force in the summer of 1914, it was organised into four main sections under the command of Field Marshal Sir John French.

I Army Corps consisted of the 1st and 2nd Infantry Divisions and was commanded by Lieutenant-General Sir Douglas Haig.

II Army Corps was under the command of Lieutenant-General Sir Horace Smith-Dorrien and was made up of the 3rd and 5th Infantry Divisions.

III Army Corps was under the command of General Sir William Pulteney and consisted of the 4th and 6th Infantry Divisions which were sent out to France at the end of August and beginning of September.

The Cavalry Division was commanded by Major-General Edmund Allenby.

I and II Army Corps and the Cavalry Division fought at the Battle of Mons on August 23th 1914.

DIVISION:
Comprised of three Brigades and commanded by a Major-General. The 1st Battalion of the Royal Warwickshire Regiment was in the 10th Brigade of the 4th Division and was under the command of Major-General Thomas D'Oyly Snow C.B.

BRIGADE:
Consisted of four Battalions, commanded by a Brigadier-General and was about 4,500 strong. In August 1914, the four Battalions of the 10th Brigade commanded by Brigadier-General J.A.L.Haldane were the 1st Royal Warwickshires, the 1st Royal Irish Fusiliers, the 2nd Seaforth Highlanders and the 2nd Royal Dublin Fusiliers. On taking command of the 3rd Infantry Division in November 1914, he was replaced by Brigadier-General Charles Hull.

BATTALION:
Captain Robert Hamilton fought in one of two Battalions of the Royal Warwickshire Regiment in Belgium and France in 1914. Each was just over 1000 strong and commanded by a Lieutenant-Colonel. The 1/ Royal Warwicks had been commanded by Lieutenant-Colonel John Ford Elkington since February and the 2/ Royal Warwicks by **Lieutenant-Colonel Walter Latham Loring** who was killed in action at the age of 46 during the 1st Battle of Ypres on October 23rd and is remembered on the Menin Gate.

COMPANY:
The 1/ Royal Warwicks Battalion consisted of four Companies- A, B, C and D. Each was about 240 strong and commanded by a Captain. Robert Hamilton was in 'A' Company which was commanded by Captain C.A.C. Bentley until his death on October 23rd 1914 when Robert took over.

PLATOON:
A Company was made up of four Platoons about 50 strong, each under the command of a Lieutenant or 2nd Lieutenant. Hamilton was commanding a platoon when he was promoted to Captain on September 16th 1914.

SECTION:
A platoon was divided into four sections of about 12 each with a Corporal or Lance-Corporal in command.

Chain of Command for the 1/ Royal Warwicks:

- Lieutenant-Colonel

- Major

- Captain

- Lieutenant

- 2nd Lieutenant

Non-Commissioned Officers (N.C.Os):

- Sergeants

- Corporal

- Lance-Corporal

Those with no rank:

- Private

Alan Reed

"A Contemptible Little Army"

The British Expeditionary Force August 1914- January 1915

The British Expeditionary Force, made up of four Infantry Divisions (organised into two Corps) and one Cavalry Division, sailed to France in mid-August 1914 under the command of Sir John French. Britain had been drawn into War on August 4th when Germany invaded Belgium, whose neutrality had been guaranteed by the Treaty of London signed in 1839.

Within two weeks, the B.E.F. had entered Belgium to protect the left flank of the French Army and faced the might of von Kluck's 390,000 strong First Army.

Soldiers of the Royal Warwicks about to embark for France in August 1914   *David Vaux*

The British 'regular' was the best trained soldier in Europe and his expert use of the .303 Lee Enfield rifle held up the German advance at the Belgian mining town of Mons on August 23rd and 24th. When the French Fifth Army withdrew on their right, the B.E.F. retreated into France to Le Cateau where General Sir Horace Smith-Dorrien, against the wishes of Sir John French, organised a successful holding action on August 26th. The Allied Armies were forced to retreat, mainly due to the strength of the German Army and because the French High Command had been wrong-footed by the speed of the German thrust through Belgium. The B.E.F. crossed the river Marne on September 3rd.

Paris was in danger and taxis were used to rush troops to the Front. The B.E.F. took part in an allied counter-attack positioned in between the French Fifth Army commanded by d'Éspérey and the Sixth led by Galliéni, a manoeuvre which successfully made the Germans rethink their strategy. The British were able to recross the Marne and the Germans retreated to the heights north of the river Aisne. The 'Miracle of the Marne' ended German victory plans. Von Falkenhayn replaced von Moltke at the Head of the German Army and the French Commander, Joffre, became known as the saviour of France. The B.E.F., reinforced by III Corps, crossed the Aisne on September 13th. Thereafter, the Armies began to 'dig-in' with the Germans in strong positions on the Chemin des Dames but to the west, each side tried to outflank the other, a phase of the War known as the 'Race to the Sea'. In early October it was decided that the B.E.F. would be better used tactically by being transferred to Flanders. II Corps, commanded by Smith-Dorrien and the Indian Corps were sent south of Armentières. III Corps (including the 1/ Warwicks) led by Pulteney headed towards Lille. The Cavalry Corps (Allenby) attacked along the Messines Ridge and linked with IV Corps (Rawlinson) which had been ordered to Ypres after the Fall of Antwerp.

In order to stem the advance of the German Army on their front, the Belgians flooded the low lying countryside along the river Yser from the coast to Dixmude, north of Ypres.

The Germans were left with one chance of a breakthrough in the area around Ypres. By now Haig's I Corps had moved north of Ypres and the battle that followed, the 1st Battle of Ypres, lasted until mid-November. The German Armies made repeated assaults to achieve the expected breakthrough. So confident were they, that Kaiser Wilhelm II came to the Front to witness the victory of his troops.

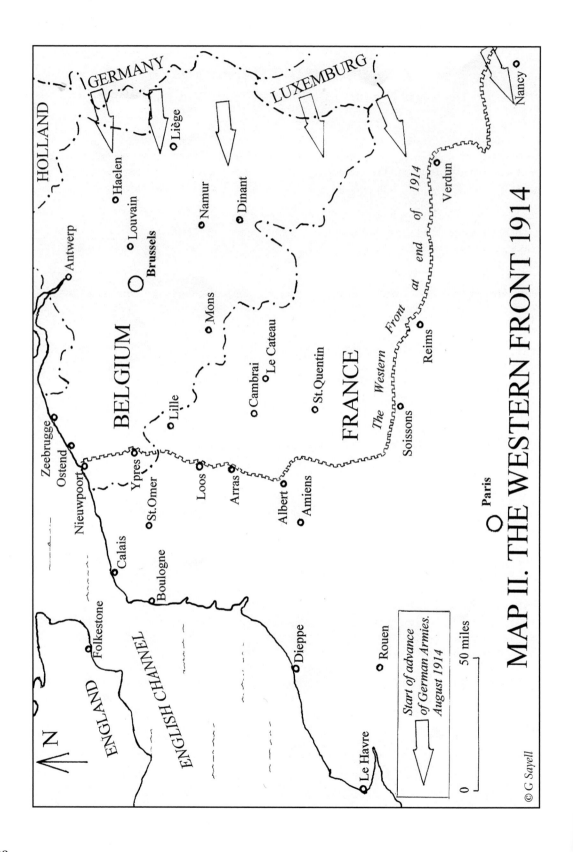

MAP II. THE WESTERN FRONT 1914

© G Sayell

Start of advance
of German Armies.
August 1914

0   50 miles

The Allies managed to hold out despite some days of crisis, notably on October 31st when the 2/ Worcesters saved the day at Gheluvelt east of Ypres. By the end of November, the front lines were static and a continuous system of trenches was to extend from the North Sea to the Swiss border along what would become the 450 mile 'Western Front'.

For the B.E.F. the first five months of the War would be costly in the loss of more than 3,600 officers and 86,200 men.

Territorials were sent out to increase the strength of the British Army and more than 1,100,000 men volunteered for action but had to be trained- a massive undertaking.

On December 26th 1914, two British Armies were created; the First, based south of Armentières, was commanded by Haig and Smith-Dorrien's Second, of which the Warwicks were part, was located south of Ypres.

The onset of winter offered the Allies some respite. The Germans were faced with the situation they had hoped to avoid- fighting on two fronts: the Western and now the Eastern Front against the Russians.

In early 1915, stalemate had been reached and thus the beginning of four dark years for the European powers.

AR

'Good Old Warwicks'

The 1st Royal Warwickshire Regiment, August 1914 - January 1915

During the reign of Charles II, the Sixth Regiment of Foot (sixth in order of seniority) was raised in 1673 for the service of the Dutch Monarchy. In 1782 it began its recruiting connection with Warwickshire and in 1832 the Regiment was given the Royal title by William IV. In 1881

when the Army was reorganised into county regiments, it became the Royal Warwickshire Regiment. Over the years, the Regiment served all over the world- in Ireland, Flanders, the Iberian Peninsula, the West Indies, North America, South Africa, India and the Sudan. In 1963 the Regiment became the Royal Warwickshire Fusiliers and after further restructuring on April 23rd 1968, they were amalgamated with other Fusiliers into the Royal Regiment of Fusiliers.

The Regiment's badge features an antelope whose origin is unclear. It may have featured on a flag captured at the Battle of Saragossa in Spain (1710) or it may have been borrowed from a badge of the Royal Family. The 1st Battalion has to this day kept a live antelope as a mascot, always known as 'Bobby'.

On June 19th 1914 Brigadier J.A.L. Haldane, commander of the 10th Brigade wrote in his diary that the Royal Warwicks were 'in good condition'. On July 29th, the Battalion was put in 'Precautionary Period' and the following day all officers and men were called from leave and on August 4th orders to

The Antelope Badge of the Royal Warwickshire Regiment
Alan Reed Collection

mobilize were received. The Rank and File, Reservists and Officers gathered at Shorncliffe Camp in Kent and the Battalion was then sent to York as a defensive measure in case the Germans invaded the north-east coast.

After a period of training, route marches and attack drills, led by Lieutenant-Colonel Elkington, the 1st Battalion arrived in Southampton on August 22nd, sailed on the *Caledonia* and arrived at Boulogne at 8.00 p.m. and temporarily encamped near Napoleon's column. Men and horses boarded the same train and were sent to Le Cateau on the 24th in time to cover the retirement of the 18th Brigade and its cavalry. Thereafter, the Warwicks joined the retreat and on the 26th fought over a ridge at Haucourt. Their first bayonet charge was, according to Captain Tomes (later in 1927 a Lieutenant-Colonel) 'an inspiring moment and a fine sight'. But they were met by shrapnel and sustained their first casualties- 47 in total.

By this time the situation was chaotic in the British Expeditionary Force. The Warwicks split into three groups, one of which was commanded by Major Poole for whom no orders were received to move back. Nonetheless, they escaped before being completely surrounded. Men were hungry and suffering from exhaustion and lack of sleep as some had covered more than 50 miles in 44 hours. On August 27th Elkington and his group arrived at St. Quentin looking for the railway station. The new Mayor, who had taken over from his predecessor who had fled, appealed to him and Lieutenant-Colonel Mainwaring (2nd Royal Dublin Fusiliers) not to fight the Germans to spare civilian lives. What followed became a matter of controversy. Mainwaring claimed he was made to sign a surrender document by Elkington who, for his part, stated at his trial that he had never seen 'the paper' that Mainwaring had allegedly handed to the Mayor. The two men were court-martialled on September 12th on charges of 'cowardice' and 'conspiring to surrender'. The charge of cowardice was dropped but they were found guilty of 'behaving in a scandalous manner unbecoming the character of an officer and a gentleman.' Both men were immediately 'cashiered' (barred from taking any public office). Elkington took full responsibility for what had happened and, showing his true character, joined the French Foreign Legion for whom he fought with distinction (see p.80). The British Army eventually reinstated him but not his colleague Mainwaring.

More than 400 men safely exited St. Quentin with a cavalry escort. Some of the Warwicks crossed the river Somme at Voyennes as Henry V and his army had done in 1415. On September 1st some Warwicks arrived too late to be of any assistance at Néry (south of Compiègne) where in a remarkable action, a battery of the Royal Horse Artillery held the German 4th Cavalry Division at bay. On September 5th Major Poole, who had rejoined via Rouen and Le Mans, took command of the 1st Battalion. Lieutenant Robert Hamilton had arrived with 88 Rank and File on September 4th as '1st reinforcement'. From then on full details of the Battalion's actions can be found in the commentary accompanying Robert Hamilton's diary entries.

At this stage, the retreat had ended and the French and British had been pushed back south of the river Marne. On September 6th, the Warwicks were on the counter-offensive as part of the Advance Guard, exploiting a gap in between two German armies and recrossed the Marne. They linked up with Zouaves, French colonial troops from North Africa.

On September 13th they helped to cover the 11th Brigade and crossed back over the river Aisne. Until early October warfare remained fairly static with much shelling and mounting casualties. Trenches were being dug and improvements to their design being carried out. By the end of September, the strength of the Battalion was 20 officers and 1045 other rank. In the Battalion War Diary, Major Poole showed concern for his men when he commented unfavourably about the soldiers' cap which he considered was 'unserviceable, easily lost, and does not shade back of head.' On their discipline, he remarked that it was 'noticeably worse than in South Africa probably due to socialistic ideas imbibed by reservists'!

Early in October the Warwicks enjoyed the luxury of an issue of 'night' blankets! On October 11th the Battalion was moved by train to the Pas-de-Calais where in 1816 their predecessors had been part of the British Army's occupation of France. The first major battle the Battalion fought was at Méteren on October 13th. According to Tomes, 'the mud of Flanders got into the mechanism of the rifles and often the bolts could only be made to work by hammering them open with stones.'

The Warwicks suffered 130 casualties. Major Christie was killed and wounds to Lieutenant Montgomery were severe enough for him to be returned to England. According to Sergeant Philpotts, Major Christie, 'a fine soldier' asked for volunteers to follow him to silence a machine-gun which the Germans had placed in Méteren's church tower. In the list of men deserving special mention, the Brigade War Diary commended Lieutenant B.L. Montgomery. Despite being severely wounded he 'led his men most gallantly and turned the Germans out of an entrenchment at the point of the bayonet. This officer set a striking example of gallantry under fire.' Also mentioned was Captain C.A.C. Bentley who, despite severe personal problems highlighted by Robert in his diary, 'early in the day had led his company to within 200 yards of the enemy's trenches and established himself there until reinforced by the general attack of the Brigade; all men near this officer were killed or wounded and he himself had two bullets through his clothes'. The Warwicks who died were buried near the scene of the action and after the War were reburied in the extension of the Méteren Civilian Cemetery.

Marching on across French Flanders, the Warwicks arrived in Armentières on October 17th. They pushed the Germans back despite heavy shelling. A gunner officer told Tomes 'what a magnificent sight it was to see the Battalion moving forward quite unperturbed by such shelling.'

The Front settled down to the east and south-east of Houplines where all men held an extended line. Sketch I on p.84 shows the area held by the Warwicks with Captain Robert

Hamilton's 'A' Company across the road from Houplines to L'Epinette. Most of the Warwicks had been campaigning without a break since late August and were suffering at the hands of the elements and enemy shelling and sniping. On November 11th, a German attack was repulsed and four days later the first snows of winter added to the problems and discomforts faced by the troops. Between November 18th and 21st, the Battalion enjoyed a short but well-earned rest at Pont de Nieppe.

The Battalion was sent for the first time on November 21st into Belgium to Point 63 as Reserve to the Brigade. For the rest of the year the Warwicks manned the front line at St. Yves and were relieved regularly by the Royal Dublin Fusiliers. About 200 casualties, many of them Warwicks, were buried at Prowse Point Cemetery just behind the British lines. Unusually for a Great War cemetery, it was unique on the Salient for being named after an individual- Major Charles Prowse (see below). Those whose bodies were never recovered or had no known grave, were commemorated on the Ploegsteert Memorial.

Tomes recorded that Christmas in 1914 produced for the Warwicks 'a curious truce which rather upset the higher command.' In the New Year on January 3rd, the Brigade War Diary noted the strength of the Battalion as 24 officers and 890 other ranks. Although the first five months of the War had tested the resolve of the 1/ Royal Warwicks, nothing could have prepared them for the carnage suffered on April 25th when they were sent to attack the Germans north of Ypres which they saw ablaze as they marched by.

The Menin Gate commemorates British soldiers who died in the Ypres Salient and have no known grave.

The Battalion would never be the same again as it lost nearly 500 men on that day- almost half the Battalion, many of whose names are engraved on panel 8 of the Menin Gate in Ypres (see opposite). For Tomes these men were 'good soldiers all and mostly irreplaceable'.

The central character in this book, Captain Robert Hamilton, had been dealt a good hand. Having survived the Battle of Méteren and trench warfare at Plugstreet Wood, by the time the 2nd Battle of Ypres took place, he had returned to England and his family, unscathed and with many tales to record.

Brigadier-General Charles Bertie Prowse: *a Major with the 1/ Somerset Light Infantry, in October 1914, he heroically made a stand north of Plugstreet Wood. Later as Brigadier-General Prowse, D.S.O., aged 47, he was killed on the first day of the Battle of the Somme July 1st 1916, whilst commanding the 11th Infantry Brigade and was buried in the Louvencourt Military Cemetery.*

'Prowse Point Cemetery was started by the 2nd Royal Dublin Fusiliers and the 1st Royal Warwicks and was used from November 1914 to April 1918. It contains 224 Commonwealth burials of the First World War.' (Commonwealth War Graves Commission)

AR

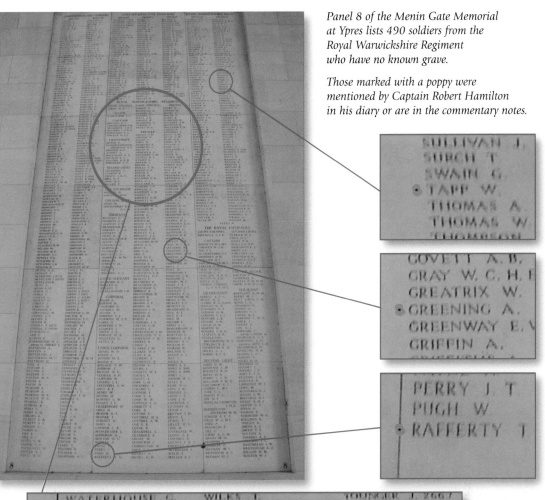

Panel 8 of the Menin Gate Memorial at Ypres lists 490 soldiers from the Royal Warwickshire Regiment who have no known grave.

Those marked with a poppy were mentioned by Captain Robert Hamilton in his diary or are in the commentary notes.

SULLIVAN J.
SURCH T
SWAIN G.
• TAPP W.
THOMAS A.
THOMAS W.
THOMPSON

GOVETT A. B.
GRAY W. C. H. E
GREATRIX W.
• GREENING A.
GREENWAY E. V
GRIFFIN A.

PERRY J. T
PUGH W.
• RAFFERTY J

WATERHOUSE G.   WILKS T.   YOUNGER J. 2667
WATSON T   WILLETT W.

ROYAL WARWICKSHIRE REGIMENT

LIEUT. COLONEL	LANCE CORPORAL	PRIVATE
• LORING W. L.	ROBBINS T.	DAVIES W.
	ROSSINDALE H.	DAWSON W.
MAJOR	SANDERS E.	DEELEY J.
• LANCASTER J. G.	SAWARD G.	DENNIS W.
	SCULL J. P.	DOBBS R.
CAPTAIN	SUMNER W.	DOBINSON W.
BRISCOE E. V.	URQUHART G.	DOUGHTY J. H.
CARLISLE-CROWE W. M.	VERNER D.	DRENNON R.
McCORMICK J. H. G.	WEEKS W. A.	DUCKERIN F. W.
METHUEN G. O'B. H.		EADON H.
SCHOOLING E. C.	PRIVATE	EDWARDS J.
• WALKER H. J. L.	ADAMS G. H.	ELLIS A. H.
	ADCOCK W.	ELLIS G. H.
LIEUTENANT	ALLEN A.	ELMS H. R.
DEANE D.	AMEY W.	EMMS W. T.
FETHERSTONHAUGH	ANDREWS A.	FALLON J.
FRAMPTON P. T.	ANDREWS G.	FANE E. J.
HUNTER N. F.	ANGUS D.	FAULKNER J.
JOWITT A.	ARMFIELD J.	FEIST J.
• MACLAGAN G. S.	ASSINDER C. W.	FINCH W.
• NICOLAI R. C.	ASTELL B. T.	FISHER W. E.
• TILLYER R. B. B.	ATKINS A.	FLETCHER E. A
WINDELER C. F.	AUSTIN J.	FLETCHER W.
	BACON J.	FODEN H. H.

10

The Diaries of Robert and Renie Hamilton
August 1914 to January 1915

This version of the diary was typed up by Robert Hamilton's staff at the Hereford Military Detention Barracks in 1916. Text in brackets was inserted by him after he had returned from France in January 1915. Commentary on the text is under the relevant diary entries. Punctuation, grammatical errors and spelling have not been altered in the diary entries.

Abbreviations: BWD- Battalion War Diary

1/ Royal Warwicks - 1st Battalion of the Royal Warwickshire Regiment

OD- Original Diary written in the trenches and behind the lines

Text coding for diary and notes: Robert Hamilton in this style type

Renie Hamilton in this style type

Montgomery in this style type

August 4th
A sad day expecting wire to summon Bob every hour. Things very serious. War declared, reservists and *terriers* called in to mobilise. The horrid wire came that evening at 9 telling him to join at once but not telling him where to go. He settled to go to Southampton.

August 5th
A telegram arrived at 5 a.m. with orders to re-join immediately. Started for *Shorncliffe* at 9 a.m. Renie behaved very well, and saw me off. The children gave me a smiling good-bye. Thank goodness they were not old enough to know what 'war' means.

A dreadful day. Bob got another wire at 5.30 telling him to go to Shorncliffe. Saw him off to the 9.45. Very sad for us both. *Nursing scheme* started which we will all join.

terriers: the Territorial Army was established in 1908 as a part-time force for home defence.

Shorncliffe: a military camp near Sandgate in Kent since the latter half of the18th century, was set up to counter the Napoleonic threat. After 1850, it was one of the military stations for troops travelling to and from India. At a nearby Military Cemetery, there are 471 First World War burials including over 300 Canadians soldiers. A Gurkha unit is currently based at Shorncliffe.

Nursing scheme: the Government set aside some money in the summer of 1914, to improve the delivery of healthcare by voluntary organisations in deprived areas.

August 6th

Numerous officers arriving from everywhere. *Colonel Elkington* very changed from the captain I knew who used to come over to Avon Cliffe for tennis and parties. Said I had too much kit. I said I had done three years' war, and was ready for the next. Lucky to have any kit at all. This was not a good start, and I began to wish that I had never left the *'Holy Boys.'* We sat down thirty three to mess. The barracks and condition of everything was filthy. Much discussion as to probable length of war. *I gave it to Christmas.*

Post card from Bob. Attended first *Red Cross* meeting at the Ramsdens. 34 people there, we all offered to lend beds, bedding etc. and the long room at Lew is to be turned into a hospital in the event of war here.

Colonel Elkington: John Ford Elkington became a Lieutenant-Colonel in 1910 and was appointed Commanding Officer of the 1/ Royal Warwicks on February 24th 1914. He was educated at Elizabeth College, Guernsey and the Royal Military Academy, Sandhurst. He followed his father into the Warwickshire Regiment, was promoted to Captain in 1886 and fought with distinction in the Boer War receiving 4 medals with clasps. As Robert served with the Norfolk Regiment in South Africa, it is unlikely that their paths crossed although the Elkington family visited the Hamiltons at their house Avon Cliffe in Tiddington near Stratford-on-Avon. Avon Cliffe was the Hamilton family home until 1921 when it was sold. As its name suggests, it was built on the banks of the river Avon.

'Holy Boys': the nickname for the Norfolk Regiment in which Robert Hamilton served from 1900 to 1909. Their motto is 'Firm', their march 'Rule Britannia' and their badge 'Britannia'.

I gave it to Christmas: the commonly held belief at the outset of the War that it would be over by Christmas. The traditional campaign, in which cavalry played an important role, tended to end with one major decisive battle settling the outcome. From early in the War, it soon became clear that the cavalry would not play a decisive role against well organised heavy artillery.

Red Cross: when war broke out in August 1914, the British Red Cross Society amalgamated with the Order of St. John to form a Joint War Committee to pool resources and work under the emblem of the Red Cross. Members of both groups were assigned to Voluntary Aid Detachments (VADs) and all members were trained in First Aid. Training was available in nursing, cookery, hygiene and sanitation. VADs worked on the Home Front in convalescent homes and medical supply depots and at the Front they worked in war zone hospitals and drove ambulances. The Red Cross was involved in recording the wounded and missing which entailed searches of villages where fighting had taken place. The VAD Emergency Hospital in Tavistock was at No.1 Bedford Villas. Red Cross Rooms in the town were a centre for the despatch of money and goods of all kinds that had been donated. Large numbers of boxes of sphagnum moss were sent off for use in surgical dressings. The women of Tavistock threw themselves into the War effort, about 300 raising £3,000 for the Red Cross. It was recorded in *The Tavistock Gazette* that Mrs. Hamilton had contributed £1.

August 7th

Loafing about. Nothing to do. Very much bored. Hoped that they would give me my company, and let me get down to it. Given command of the overseas base company. Said to be a soft job. In the middle of mess, orders were issued to pack up and move off to the station. Everything bar the *thirty five pounds* was left where it was. None of the doors of the quarters was even closed. We entrained at *Sandgate,* knowing absolutely nothing.

Four letters from Bob. He is to guard tunnel against German spies; last letter splendid news - he is to have a *safe but important post overseas.*

August 8th

Found ourselves at York, at 3.30 p.m. with only *half a battalion*. Nobody knew anything about the other half. Thought the Germans had landed on the East coast. We sat about on the common for an hour or two, and then somebody discovered we had been given the *Grandstand and enclosures*, and so we marched off there. *Bernard* and I walked down, and got our valises, which they refused to let us fetch. This was the first piece of regimental red tape rot, which Bernard and I quite made up our minds must cease. He was also an old campaigner. When we had obtained ours, the *C.O.* sent for a cart for the rest.

250,000 Germans repulsed by Belgians where losses were 7,000. Germans call for 24 hours armistice to bury their dead.

thirty five pounds: an artillery piece.

Sandgate: a village near Folkestone on the Kentish coast between Folkestone and Hythe and referred to as 'The Riviera of the Napoleonic Coast'. A redoubt or earth fortification had been built there as a defence against possible French invasion.

safe…post overseas: unfortunately for both Robert and Renie, his posting to Belgium and France was to prove anything but safe.

half a battalion: about 500 men.

Grandstand and enclosures: at York Racecourse which is south-west of the city.

Bernard: one of several references in the diary to Bernard 'Monty' Montgomery, later Field Marshal and Viscount Montgomery of Alamein. In October 1913, he was listed as a Lieutenant in 1/ Royal Warwicks' 'C' Company.

C.O.: Commanding Officer

250,000 Germans repulsed: reference to the siege of Liège which was protected by a ring of forts. The defending Belgians were attacked on August 5th and held out until 16th. The Germans were forced to bring in huge siege guns, including two 42 cm 'Big Bertha' howitzers. Their schedule was delayed by at least two days.

Sunday, August 9th

We had a practice attack on the common, the men losing hundreds of rounds in the rushes, to say nothing of their hats, which were blown in all directions. More loafing. Where were the *dixies* for the men? Who was our *Quartermaster*?

Very miserable day, pouring in torrents, blowing like mad. Church in the morning in the Mission room. Wonderfully appropriate psalms all about God protecting us in time of war. Just the right lessons too- 'If God is with us who can be against us?' Very cross all day but cheered by a letter from Bob who is getting on alright and has got his coat.

August 10th

Orders to march to the station, and billet the men, the billets consisting of the filthiest warehouses imaginable. Officers in third class railway carriages. A *cinder heap*. Everywhere else out of bounds. Even the restaurants. Bernard and I, however, had a good dinner, and arranged with the manager to feed all the officers while we were there. We told the C.O. we should have quite enough of roughing it, when we got out of England. He saw the point.

The first thing I see on waking up is Gyp and the foal kicking about on Bob's beautiful lawn. They ran through the gap so 'all's well that ends well'.

August 11th

Route march. Very hot. We had a bath and then a cheerful little dinner.

Letter from Bob from *Doncaster* saying they are roughing it very much, insufficient food and bad sleeping accommodation.

August 12th

Regiment for a route march. I spent the morning arranging the field sheets of my company, for Shorncliffe, and getting some of the men inoculated.

After supper we practise bandaging. Letter from Bob from Doncaster. Still roughing it very much. Papers say we are on the verge of a great battle between Germany, France and Belgium. Liège forts still hold out though town is occupied by Germans.

---

dixies: iron cooking utensils (of Hindustani derivation *'degchi'*) for making tea or stew.

Quartermaster: officer dealing with quarters, billets, transport, clothing etc.

cinder heap: probably a derogatory description of the state of the carriages.

Doncaster: Renie mistakenly thinks that Robert is writing from Doncaster Racecourse!

Officers in the B.E.F. would have been aware of a message conveyed to his soldiers by King George V on August 12th: 'You are leaving home to fight for the safety and honour of my Empire…I have implicit confidence in my soldiers…I shall follow your every movement with deepest interest and mark with eager satisfaction your daily progress…I pray God to bless you and guard you and bring you back victorious.' *(Imperial War Museum Q61356)*

August 13th

Walker and I left the cinder heap at 10 a.m. and got to *Shorncliffe at 6 p.m.* Found the whole place a veritable pig sty. No mess of any sort. All washing places and W.C.s in a filthy condition. Commandeered a clean pair of sheets. Got into my original quarters. Walked into Folkestone in uniform, and sat and listened to the band on the front.

August 14th

Reported *German advance.* Two battles. Germans reported defeated in both, and to have lost 2,000 men. Paid out 5/- per man of my company, and took on another 30 men. Two letters from Renie, one written last Sunday. Rumour has it that the regiment does not leave England until the German fleet are smashed up; I think the C.O. is responsible for this brilliant *bunkum.* Got into a suit of *John Haddon's* (he came out a couple of months later, and was wounded and taken prisoner almost as soon as he arrived) and he and I walked into Folkestone, had dinner and did the band.

Susan, Lily and I bicycle to Lew to attend Red Cross class. We learn how to make a bed. Small boy is practised on, undressed and washed. Not much war news today. Letter from Bob in the evening.

Walker: this is the only mention in the diary of Captain **Henry John Innes Walker** of the 1/Royal Warwicks who died at the 2nd Battle of Ypres on April 25th 1915. Just three months before his death he was recommended for a Distinguished Service Order by Brigadier-General Charles Hull who stated that 'he has been mentioned in despatches for previous good work; he has continued to be of great assistance to his battalion and is a valuable officer who fully deserves reward.' He is commemorated on the Menin Gate at Ypres.

Shorncliffe at 6 p.m: In the BWD, it was recorded that at '9.47, Lt. Hamilton and 69 men 1st Reinforcement left for Shorncliffe.' The rest of the Battalion moved to Strensall Camp north of York on 14th, then to Harrow Weald on 18th and finally to Southampton on August 22nd.

German advance: probable reference to the events at Liège and at Haelen. The Battle of Haelen was the first cavalry encounter of the War on August 12th north-east of Louvain where the Belgian cavalry temporarily halted the advanced German cavalry troops.

bunkum: nonsense or claptrap, of American derivation- the member for the County of Buncombe in North Carolina caused an obstruction to business in Congress by 'making a speech for Buncombe'.

John Haddon's: from John Ashby's 'Seek Glory, Now Keep Glory'- 'Haddon, Capt. J.B. date missing 18.12.14, interned Holland and repatriated 18.11.18.'

On January 20th 1919 Robert wrote- 'Heard some of John Haddon's awful experiences as a prisoner in the hands of the Hun. He can scarcely speak of his captivity so bitter is he.'

Susan: was the 'nurse' or 'nanny' for Cynthia and Richard.

August 15th
Paid out and gave the men a good talking to.

Letters from Bob who is tired of doing nothing.

Sunday August 16th
Went to the 11 o'clock service in a neighbouring village church. Stayed for the second service. John and I felt very depressed, so decided to go down to the beach, and laze on the sands. Two young ladies in bathing kit seemed rather sympathetic, and came and cheered us up.

No letter from Bob, but one from Mercy saying Uncle Harry is trying to get out in some capacity, but they won't have him. Don't wonder as he is in hospital having an operation. Children very good going to bed. Felt sad and lonely in the evening.

August 17th
Route march. A strong wind *caught my ears* on the cliffs, and has made me deaf. We did the band again.

Very hot day. Turned the stock into Nine Acre. No particular war news. Two letters from Bob. I painted calves' pen green. Took Cynthia and Dick for tea under the *viaduct*. We got up quite an excitement over 2 men in the viaduct who we took to be German spies about to blow up the bridge.

August 18th
Had a practice attack morning and afternoon. John Haddon and I did a stiff walk after tea.

The Driels motored Susan and I to the practical. Lecture first then bandaging collar bones ankles etc. Meeting at *Bridestowe* and Devonshire Patriotic Fund. I boldly propose that we stick to one fund instead of dividing between 2, Driel seconds it and it is carried 20 to 6, much to Mrs. France's annoyance. Mrs. O. says I've put my foot in it! 2 letters from Bob who thinks they are on the move to the London docks.

August 19th
I have reason to think that we are off pretty soon, so wired Renie to come down. Re-arranged my kit.

caught my ears: Robert suffered constantly from problems with his ears which were made worse by the cold and noise of gunfire and shelling. On January 27th 1915, two Doctor Colonels at the War Office decided that his ears were too bad for him to continue on active service.

viaduct: is less than half a mile from Collaven Manor, the Hamiltons' home outside Sourton village in Devon. When travelling south on the Sourton to Tavistock road, a footpath to the viaduct is on the left before the thatched Bearslake Inn at Lake. The viaduct commands superb views of Devon and Cornwall.

Driels: the Drielsmas were great friends of the Hamiltons, always known affectionately as the 'Driels'.

Bridestowe: a village two miles from Collaven. Robert played for Bridestowe Cricket Club and was Club President. His younger son Oliver followed in his father's footsteps.

Renie would have read in *The Tavistock Gazette* on August 19th, the Lord Lieutenant of Devon's exhortation that women should help in assisting the War effort- 'I earnestly ask the women of our county to bring all their influence to bear in obtaining recruits for His Majesty's Service.'

August 20th
My servant Pte. Taylor and I got ready one of the married officer's quarters, and I got Renie up to barracks for lunch. She quite enjoyed her ration meals. I had to dash off to inspect a tunnel guard five miles away, and so Renie had mess by herself, and a hot bath.

August 21st
We walked down to the beach. Renie had a bathe in a curious rented garment. Back for lunch. A Major, *two subs*, and a 100 men of the new army (Essex Regt. from Warley) arrived. Renie went to church after tea. Thunderstorm.

August 22nd
Went on the beach for another bathe, and then sat about. Orders to leave Southampton on Sunday. Dined in mess with John Haddon. Taylor woke us up early to say the transport was ready.

We went down to the beach for a bathe and then out and about. Bob had orders to leave Southampton Sunday. He and Haddon busy putting the transport together. We listened to the Sergeant's little speech to Bob's Company.

Sunday, August 23rd
Left Shorncliffe at 7.30 a.m. with poor Renie looking on, and the men singing 'The girl I left behind me.' Three other drafts with an officer in charge of each. Southampton at 1 o'clock. Loading all day. Fog came down, and we weighed anchor in the Southampton water till next morning.

I got up at 5.30 and I walked a little way with Bob. This second parting was worse than the first as one can't help feeling dreadfully anxious once he is over the sea. How I longed to go too. He went off outwardly cheerful, but I felt very miserable and went back to bed. I left at 10 for London and slept at 13 Margaret St. Beaten all round in my wish to attend Divine Service but having failed at 5 Churches, found a heated service going on at All Saints. Becoming quite fascinated by the *'tapis roulants'* in the underground. Lunched at Whiteleys where I bought a doll for Cynthia and a horse tricycle for Dick. Good journey home.

My servant: officers of the rank of Lieutenant and above had a batman or man-servant. They were Privates and during the course of his diary, Robert changed batman several times. Private Taylor was sacked for stealing his tobacco on October 1st. Wilkes suffered the same fate for being 'hopelessly drunk in St. Omer' on October 12th and was replaced by Baker who was

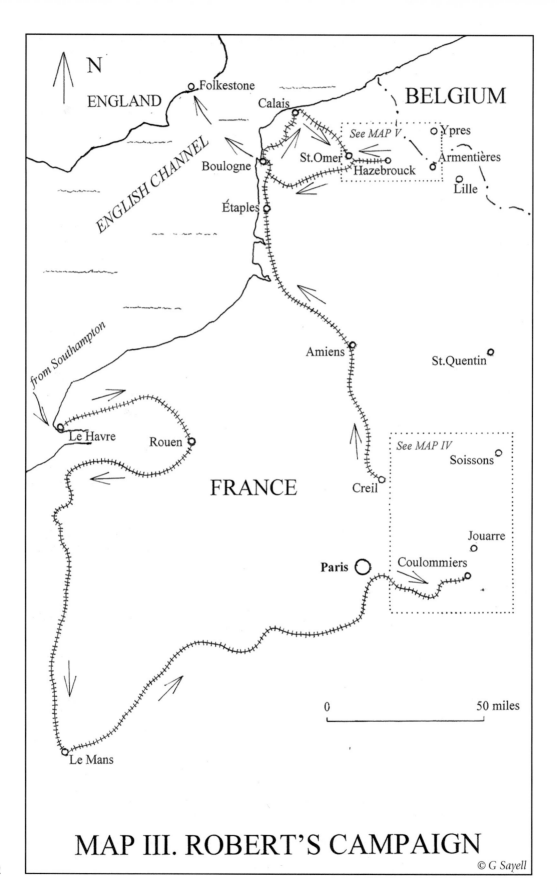

N

ENGLAND

Folkestone

BELGIUM

Calais

Ypres

ENGLISH CHANNEL

See MAP V

St.Omer

Armentières

Boulogne

Hazebrouck

Lille

Étaples

Amiens

St.Quentin

from Southampton

See MAP IV

Le Havre

Rouen

Soissons

FRANCE

Creil

Jouarre

Paris

Coulommiers

0   50 miles

Le Mans

MAP III. ROBERT'S CAMPAIGN

© G Sayell

killed on October 20th. Hall only lasted until November 8th when he was shot in the arm and Sperry was badly wounded on November 25th. Gregory was sacked for laziness on December 4th and was replaced by Casswell. Sperry and his wife both wrote most complimentary letters to Renie about her husband (see p.173-174).

two subs: subalterns are officers below the rank of Captain- i.e. Lieutenant and 2nd Lieutenant.

'tapis roulants': French for 'running carpets'- Renie was clearly much taken by the novelty of escalators in London's Underground.

August 24th
Arrived *Havre* mid-day. Unloading till 7 p.m. Stinking hot. Marched 7 miles to camp. Transport broke down. A good start. Nothing to eat. Got something at 11.30 p.m. and then orders arrived to march back to the station and entrain for the front. When we got to the station there was no train, so we hung about till 10.20 a.m. And then got off. A train load of wounded arrived. Colonel Massy (Norfolk regiment) was Commandant at Havre, so I left my *sword* with him. (I have never seen it again). It looks as if they want us pretty badly.

August 25th
Arrived at   10.30 a.m. Men in capital spirits after a grand sleep in the train. Carried on, and arrived at 11 p.m. Marched to *bivouacs* two miles away to the tune of the Farmer's Boy.

P.C. from Bob from Southampton. 'First off in the Roaumore.' Fall of *Nanuet*. Very unexpected. I went to the Nursing lecture and practised bandaging heads.

August 26th
The line is congested. Impossible to get on. Had a good wash in a builder's house, and an omelette done as only the French know how. The daughter of the house quite charmed the bearded pard *Campbell of the Irish*, and myself. She assured us there were plenty more like her where we were going. Think we will have another practice parade to-day. *Stood-to* all night. Very cold.

Havre: Le Havre a major port in Normandy, on the Seine estuary. The rest of the Battalion had sailed on the *Caledonia* from Southampton to Boulogne on August 22nd. On 23rd they boarded a train and arrived at Le Cateau the following day.

sword: similar to the one Montgomery was wearing in the photo on p.2.

Arrived at…: this may be a case of self censorship or more likely, Robert may have forgotten the correct names of the places.

bivouacs: where soldiers rested at night in the open, derived from the German word *beiwacht-* 'additional watch'.

Nanuet: she means Namur which lies between Liège and Mons in Belgium. It had been under siege since August 21st and fell two days later.

Campbell of the Irish: the 1/ Royal Irish Fusiliers was one of the 4 Battalions in the 10th Brigade. The others were the 2/ Royal Dublin Fusiliers, the 2/ Seaforth Highlanders and the 1/ Royal Warwicks. Campbell reappears famously in the diary entry for Christmas Day.

stood-to: 'stand to' is the time when soldiers have to be on alert. In the trenches, 'stand to' would have been at dawn. A sentry or officer would shout 'stand to' when under attack.

In the OD, Robert wrote 'The comfortable overseas base billet is rather a delusion.'

I am quite well.

I have been admitted into hospital
{ *sick* } *and am going on well.*
{ *wounded* } *and hope to be discharged soon.*

I am being sent down to the base.

I have received your { *letter dated_____*
telegram „ _____
parcel „ _____

Letter follows at first opportunity.

I have received no letter from you
{ *lately.*
{ *for a long time.*

Signature
only. }

Date_____

[Postage must be prepaid on any letter or post card addressed to the sender of this card.]

93509) Wt. W3497-293 1,125m. 6/16 J. J. K. & Co., Ltd.

August 27th: 'Posted a Field Post Card to Renie'
David Vaux

FRENCH MADE EASY
FOR OUR MEN WITH
THE EXPEDITIONARY FORCES.

ENGLISH	FRENCH	PRONOUNCED
I am English	Je suis Anglais	Sher swee songlay
I do not understand	Je ne comprends pas	Sher ner comprong-pah
Do you understand English?	Savez-vous l'Anglais	Savvay voo longlay?
Yes	Oui	Wee
No	Non	Nong
Will you give me if you please	Voulez-vous donnez-moi s'il vous plait	Voolay voo donnay m'wah seal voo play
(Things to eat)		
Bread	Pain	Pahng
Butter	Beurre	Burr
Cheese	Fromage	Fro marsh
Vegetables	Légumes	Laygoom
Meat	Viande	Veond
Fish	Poisson	P'wahsong
(Things to drink)		
Tea	Thé	Tay
Coffee	Café	Caffay
Water	L'eau	Low
Milk	Lait	Lay

August 28th: Robert wrote in his OD that the men still could not pronounce the French words correctly! National Army Museum

August 26th
Rather serious war news. British casualties over 2,000 near *Mons*.

August 27th
Posted a Field Post Card to Renie and arrived at *Rouen* at 8 p.m. A beautiful sight as we steamed in with the sun setting. Much excitement here, but can get no direct information as to the course of events. We marched through the town singing every kind of ditty. Had a tremendous reception. We found a camp pitched for us, and so after some bacon and biscuits, turned in.

Letter from Bob written in the 'Roaumore' and posted in Southampton. I walked down to Bridestowe to collect the post. Mrs. Holly called with an aged sister-in-law. She said to Dick "Are you going to be a little soldier?" to which he replied "I'm not going to be a little soldier, I'm going to be a big soldier!"

August 28th
Nice fine morning. The *Pathan* officer and I had a cheery cup of coffee and a roll, with the usual attendance, and then went to draw three days rations for the men. We all dined at the *Hotel Angleterre*, and drank health to the *King* and those we had left behind.

Mons: Mons marks the first encounter between British and German troops on August 23rd. Sir John French's troops were outnumbered by General von Kluck's First Army but the Germans suffered heavy losses to volleys of rifle fire. The professional British soldier could fire 15 rounds a minute with the .303 Lee Enfield rifle. After halting the German advance for a day, the B.E.F. started their retreat to Le Cateau in France.

Rouen: the largest city in Normandy lies 50 miles east of Le Havre on the river Seine. It was an important base for the B.E.F. and became a centre for several army hospitals. The cemetery at St. Sever, south of the city centre, has more than 3,000 burials and more than 8,000 in the extension plot.

Pathan: an Indian soldier in 1914 of Afghan origin.

Hotel Angleterre: it is described in the 'Guides Bleus: Normandie' of 1926 as 'un hôtel de premier ordre'!

King: George V.

In the OD - 'The men buy bits of paper with Eng. translated into Fr. for 5 cents but even then they cannot pronounce the words.'

August 29th

We had a route march. Very hot. Hear there is a chance of getting letters today. Five % of the men are to be allowed out to-night. Pathan and I bought khaki protectors for the back of the neck. With his mixture of French and Hindustani, he greatly amuses these French shop girls. Several services have been arranged for tomorrow, and a short route march without arms. At midnight the bugle sounded the Advance, and we were told to be ready to march off at 5.30 a.m. We all said this means 5.30 p.m.

Post card from Bob. 'All well.' Desperate fighting *round Cambrai*. Out of 2,000 only 30 British survive. *The Russians at Konigsberg. 5 German cruisers sunk.*

round Cambrai: She is referring to Le Cateau which is about 14 miles east /south-east of Cambrai.

The Russians at Konigsberg: Königsberg is a port on the Baltic Sea. It is noteworthy that Renie does not mention that south of Königsberg at the Battle of Tannenberg from August 26th to 30th, the Russian Second Army was severely defeated by the German Eighth Army commanded by General Hindenburg and Major-General Ludendorff. The Russian General Samsonov committed suicide on August 30th; an estimated 230,000 Russians were killed, wounded or captured.

5 German cruisers sunk: on August 28th, Sir David Beatty sent a force of cruisers and destroyers to raid German patrols and to lure enemy ships out of their base on the Baltic Sea. The Battle of the Heligoland Bight was the first important battle in the North Sea at the end of which a German destroyer and three of their light cruisers were sunk and about 1,000 German sailors lost. The British light cruiser *Arethusa* was damaged.

Sunday, August 30th

We struck camp and cleared up everything and then stood-by until 2 p.m.and eventually entrained at 4.20 a.m. The men have had no sleep, and have been in marching order for 20 hours. They don't seem to mind how long they keep the fighting troops just hanging about with no orders and nothing to do. The whistling of the infernal French engines which never go faster than ten miles an hour, is getting on my nerves.

Report that England is swarming with *Russians* on their way to the front. "Not bloody likely I'm afraid." How could they get there? Lots of extra trains running all today- some great movement of troops going on. Church in the morning. I took Cynthia and Dick to tea with the Tindalls. Cynthia behaved shockingly, Dick a perfect gent. Her manners are most distressing. They were loaded with good things and took home sweets, eggs and roses. Marvellous article in *The English Review* of 1910 predicting the Great War.

August 31st

Arrived at Le Mans at 9.30 a.m. Very hot. French girls bring bottle on bottle of French wine for the troops. *They cannot march on it,* and the practice must cease. Quartered in French cavalry barracks. *Sanitary arrangements are revolting.* We dined as guests of a civilian Frenchman, and his two daughters. They were trying to get down to the South of France, but only had enough petrol to take them 100 miles. We told them they had much better come along with us, the daughters were quite willing, but papa said he was too fat to fight. Met a cousin of the whiskey people of Crickhowell, and had a long chat.

More about the famous Russian report. We are convinced it is true. I said good bye to the Tindalls with much regret, but could not convince brother-in-law about the Russians. Bet him 5 to 1.

Russians: A rumour was sweeping the country that Russian troops had landed in Scotland to help their British ally; some had been seen in Edinburgh 'with snow on their boots'! The truth was that a few officers were on a mission to buy munitions.

The English Review: she may be referring to 'The Control of Foreign Affairs' by H.N. Brailsford in the 1909 edition of the learned *English Review* in which he quotes two imperialist statesmen- Sir Edward Grey, who regarded the build up of armaments by the major European powers as likely to 'submerge civilisation' and Lord Rosebery who warned that 'we are rattling into barbarism.' An article on the 'Flight of the Golf Ball' in the same edition would have been more appealing to Robert!

They cannot march on it: British soldiers would not have been used to drinking wine whereas French soldiers were given poor quality wine known as 'le pinard'.

Sanitary arrangements are revolting: a common reaction from British troops using French army accommodation or when taking over trenches previously occupied by the French.

September 1st
Reveille 6 a.m. Route march. Awful heat. Another ration lunch. My servant Taylor has got the other servants in hand again, and organised a small officers' mess. *De Putron*, an old Glenalmond boy turned up today. Met some more subs of the regiment in a café, who all seemed very cheerful, but say that the *regiment is so well scattered*, ditto the British Army after Mons, that it will take clever heads to concentrate before any big advance.

Russian report confirmed! Isn't it marvellous of Kitchener- they say they landed at Cardiff and went to Southampton. A train full of them actually passed Cowpers! Another meeting at Lew. Less instruction every time, no method, no nothing. Could do much better practising bandaging at home. Stayed to tea with them. No news of Bob. Bravo Kitchener of Khartoum!

September 2nd
Annoyed to find Mr. Taylor has been smoking my tobacco. Bought half a pound of capstan for 4 francs, my one pound tin is in my kit bag at the base (recovered the kit bag on January 16th, 1916 and found the tobacco as good as ever.) Paid the men 5 francs each, and so I suppose we will move. These dirty French troops spit all over the barracks. The more I see of them, the less I like them. Their blue coat is as thick as our great coat, how they can march in it beats me. Bugle sounds fall in, followed by the double. Entrained at 11.30 p.m.

P.C. and a letter (very much censored) from Bob written 29th August. He is on the move. I never felt so anxious till today. Boiling hot day and perfectly lovely. Glorious moon at night. Looked out clothes for *Belgian refugees*. Susan always refers to the Expeditionary Force as the Expedimentary Force.

De Putron: was a contemporary of Robert's at Trinity College, Glenalmond in Perthshire. They were in the same athletics team in 1892 and played together in the 1st XI cricket team in 1894.

De Putron was described in *The Glenalmond Chronicle* as 'a wild bat, with a resolve which too often proves in vain, to hit a boundary off his first ball.' Despite his dare-devil approach, De Putron survived the war (see p.13).

regiment is so well scattered: this was not unusual at the time and a great credit to the B.E.F. that disparate elements eventually found the main body of their battalion.

Lieutenant Montgomery kept a diary during the early weeks of the War- it was less detailed than Robert's and in style brief and very much to the point. It can be found in *The Antelope*, the magazine of the Royal Warwickshire Regiment for May 1938. He wrote in his diary: 'had a shave, bath, etc. The first since 24th August'.

Belgian refugees: in 1914 more than one million Belgians fled to France, Britain and the neutral Netherlands. About 110,000 Belgians arrived in Britain and by the end of the War 8,000 were assisted and cared for in Devon. A special committee to deal with the problem was set up in Tavistock.

September 3rd
These trains are the limit. The officials with their countless horns and whistles and flags cannot induce the trains to go faster than ten miles an hour. Had a bit of sleep last night, and today we are on a sort of Cook's tour round Paris. A party of French Red Cross ladies gave us tea with fresh milk in it, and later on champagne. Arrived at *Columbière* at 2 p.m. From here we are told we are going to march into action. Got off at 4 p.m. Fearfully hot. Through *Crécy*. On right through the night. Heavy sounds of guns. Men much excited.

First casualty list. Poor Bootles- the youngest is dead, *a good many of the Norfolk wounded*. A very jolly day. We motored to Trebarwith, it was blazing hot- we got there about 12 and had a heavenly bathe. We sent off a large bundle of clothes for wounded Belgians and refugees. Felt awfully anxious about Bob that night.

September 4th
Broke into our iron rations. Men fearfully done up. Their feet in a shocking way. *The Jocks* an awful nuisance, falling out in hundreds, drunk on anything they could lay their hands on. On we go. *Men throwing away everything* rather than carry them. Commandeered a horse. The heat was terrific and the roads vile. *The Scotch reinforcements are a disgrace to the army.* No heart. Drunk and disorderly. Arrived at 6 p.m. at Chévry, after 34 miles. *Four hundred of the regiment* arrive from Rouen, with Colonel Elkington, who was not in command. Later, other bodies arrived.

2nd casualty list. Jock Walford wounded. No news of Bob. Picked 9 lbs of blackberries. Devon Patriotic meeting at New Inn. Mr. Whitwell insisted on charging 5/- for use of the Parish Room, so they decided to hold the meeting elsewhere, needless to say Whitwells did not attend. There were 8 men and I the only woman. I made several valuable suggestions and proposed that we should call a ladies' meeting and undertook to interview Mrs. Whitwell and find out who would join.

Columbière: he is referring to Coulommiers, one of the railway stations near Crécy and 14 miles south-east of Meaux.

Crécy: not to be confused with the Crécy where a battle was fought during the Hundred Years War in 1346 when the English King, Edward III defeated Philippe VI of France. This is a reference to Crécy-la-Chapelle between Coulommiers and Meaux.

a good many of the Norfolk wounded: The 1/ Norfolk Regiment was present at the Battle of Mons on August 23rd. By the time they retreated, four of the regiment's officers had been killed, four

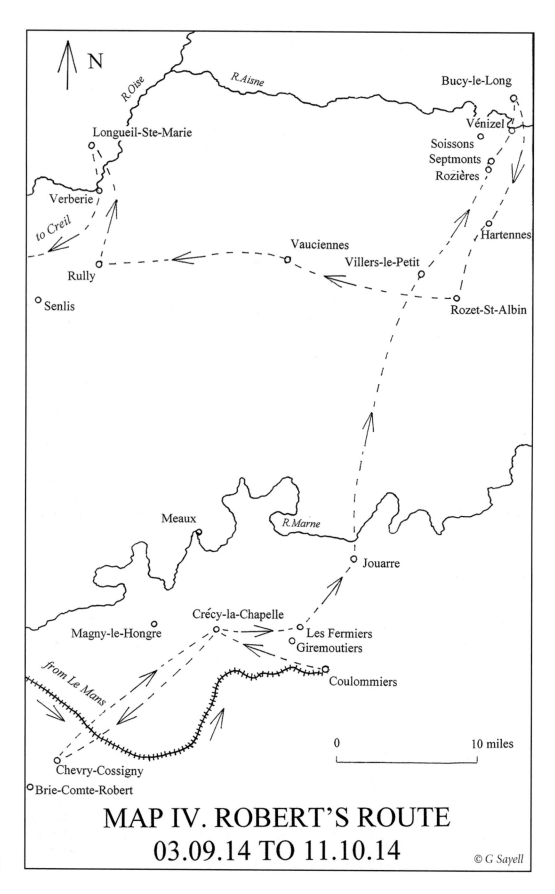

N

R.Oise

R.Aisne

Bucy-le-Long

Longueil-Ste-Marie

Vénizel

Soissons
Septmonts
Rozières

Verberie

to Creil

Hartennes

Vauciennes

Villers-le-Petit

Rully

Senlis

Rozet-St-Albin

Meaux

R.Marne

Jouarre

Crécy-la-Chapelle

Magny-le-Hongre

Les Fermiers
Giremoutiers

from Le Mans

Coulommiers

0   10 miles

Chevry-Cossigny

Brie-Comte-Robert

MAP IV. ROBERT'S ROUTE
03.09.14 TO 11.10.14

© G Sayell

others wounded and about 250 of other ranks killed, wounded or missing. It is likely that Robert had served with some of the wounded or killed officers. 'Bootles' was the nickname given to Lieutenant Cresswell.

The Jocks: the 2/ Seaforth Highlanders, were, according to their War Diary, near Crécy at Magny-le-Hongre on September 4th.

In the OD Robert expressed his unhappiness with the Scottish soldiers- 'the Jocks have gone down many degrees in my estimation. No heart and always drunk and disorderly.'

Men throwing away everything: similar accounts can be found about units involved in the retreat from Mons. Soldiers discarded their belongings because of fatigue and so they could retreat more quickly.

The Scotch reinforcements are a disgrace to the army: the other Scottish regiment in the area at the time was the 2/ Argyll and Sutherland Highlanders. Robert felt they were like the Seaforth Highlanders, too often drunk and ill-disciplined.

Four hundred of the regiment: the BWD states that on September 4th 'a party of 14 officers and 402 men under Major Poole rejoined the Regt. from Le Mans.' On the 5th it was recorded that '1 Off. and 88 R and F joined 1st Reinforcement'; these must be Robert and his men.

September 5th

Marched off at 2 a.m. with the regiment, reinforced *to about a 1,000 strong.* Everybody wonders how it was done. Won't believe we did 34 miles to get up to them. Back the way we came through Crécy. Another long march in the heat and the dust. Men on their last legs, I am sorry for my men. We halted at a farm, presumably for the night, but on the sound of guns we marched on, and halted at another farm 6 miles further on. Here we had to take precautions against aeroplanes.

No news from Bob. Howling wind all night and day. Mrs. Driel came over at 12 o'clock and we discussed the vexed question of Mr. Whitwell in the parish. Driel came and had lunch and I unearthed whiskey for him. I went to see the Whitwells who took a peculiar view (at least he did) of the duties of a parish in a time like this.

September 6th

On again at daybreak. *Captured some skunking spies and shot them.* Women and children we passed told awful stories of their *atrocities.* They are only just in front.

Felt very sad all day. Went to Church in morning. Sermon about the maimed. Mr. Whitwell says it was very wrong that Mr. Tindall held services in the parish room without having communion, he says he should have got a licence from the Bishop. Mr. T. says Mr. W. should have got a licence from the Bishop to pull down the seats of the Church. Took dogs on the moor.

News was by now reaching Devon of casualties. *The Tavistock Gazette* reported the arrival of 100 wounded men from the Front at Plymouth. Ten wounded soldiers arrived in the town.

to about 1,000 strong: the Battalion was now back to normal strength.

In the OD he complains of having to march at 2.00 a.m. without any tea or anything to eat which he considered to be 'damned bad arrangements'.

Captured some skunking spies and shot them: peremptory shooting of spies was not unusual at the time. There is no mention of this in the BWD which states 'Army resumed the offensive, heavy fighting on our flanks, we did not get engaged.' ... 'the Allies stop their retreat and check the German advance before pushing them back' (at the first Battle of the Marne).

atrocities: much was made of atrocities in the British press which were used as propaganda. One of the most serious outrages against civilians occurred at Dinant in Belgium, south of Namur, where more than 630 civilians were shot. In eastern France, at Gerbéviller, about 23 miles south-east of Nancy, 60 civilians were shot, the Germans claiming that the locals had helped the French soldiers defend the town.

Montgomery: Left 2 a.m. Marched all day. Sore feet. Rode a horse. Bivouacked near Crécy at 5 p.m.

September 7th

Pushed on again and took up a position in an apple and grape garden. We remained here till 4 p.m. and then had a dirty, dusty ten miles to Les Fermières. Bivouacked at 10.30 p.m. Very tired. Plenty of clean straw, warm night. *Water* for the men a difficult question. But why only one water cart per battalion? What is the Quartermaster doing? A few shells landed near as we were getting in, but no notice was taken of them. First good sleep for days.

Still no news. Wire from Dr. Brydon to say he is beginning to believe the Russian report and that they are all at Tunbridge Wells waiting to go to war. S. and I practised bandaging collar bones with much success. Went to bed much happier.

September 8th: 'At Le Bois St. Jouaire…'- French locals at a Seaforth Highlander's grave, 'a friend of France' who was killed at Ferté-sous-Jouarre during the campaign in the Marne area　　　　Imperial War Museum Q53263

September 8th

Marched off at 3.30 a.m. and halted for breakfast at a neighbouring farm. Three German Aeroplanes. At *Le Bois Saint Jouaire* we got into battle formation, and advanced on the village over red hot fields, and in the heat of the day. When we got to within a few hundred yards, we heard that a whole regiment of Germans had been trapped by our mounted troops and captured. One sub was wounded and a Gunner Major killed. 'A' Company on outpost. An extraordinary show, and not off our feet till 11.30. Should not have thought Bentley would have been so jumpy. Dickie's birthday. Wood joined 'A' Company.

Dick's birthday. 3 years old. I gave him a tricycle horse which led to much quarrelling and falling about. Cynthia so selfish and masterful. I wish she would grow out of this. P.C. at last from Bob from La Jumeau. 'All well.' Great relief to me as I hadn't heard since the 29th. It is near Paris. Mrs. Driel (bless her) came up in the morning and drove me to the nursing class. Rather better than usual. My bandage roller keeps the party going alright. Scramble for figs.

Water: very important and a constant problem- Private William Tapp wrote in his diary on November 24th 'WATER- I am determined to get good water tomorrow if I have to go miles for it.'

Le Bois Saint Jouaire: should be Jouarre.

In the OD Robert records that at 11.15 pm there was a 'rum issue'.

September 9th

Stood to arms at 3.30 a.m. with aeroplanes flying about in all directions. Remained in the sun all day, while our guns shelled the German position in advance. 500 Germans are surrounded in a wood, and have been given till 4 a.m. tomorrow to surrender or be shelled to hell. We moved off at 4 p.m. and did six of the stiffest miles uphill I ever remember. Beds of straw. *In the Warwicks* one apparently does not ask, one does. If wrong you are for it. Little regard is paid to the comfort of the men outside their own company officers.

Letter and P.C. from Bob who says *the Warwick Regiment have suffered badly. In this morning's list* about 8 officers wounded or missing. *Michael John, Knight Bruce* and others I don't know. *The Col. Elkington is missing.* Miserable wet day. Dick's party fell through.

September 10th

Stood-to at 3.00 a.m. and moved off at 5.00 a.m. Halted while the guns opened fire, making a terrible din. *This is the hell.* We were never told anything more about it. *We crossed the Marne* without firing a shot. The poor old transport horses and mules had a fearful time, hauling their loads over the railway bridge, until some bright staff officer thought of derailing a regiment to help the poor animals, and of putting straw down between the deep sleepers. Everything over by 1.15 p.m. And then a race for the heights, and our first view of the *retreating Germans*. They fired a few shells but hadn't time to do more, as our guns were on them with direct hits first shot. We came across numerous dead Germans, and spies shot at any old wall. French farm girls came up with peaches and water. Halted just long enough not to drink the tea which would have been so welcome. Did another nine miles, and saw some of the results of our big guns. Awful sights. We all four, Bentley, Wasey, Wood and myself slept under the same straw and were very warm. Orders were continually being sent that we were to march at once.

In the Warwicks: he is comparing his experiences in the Warwicks with those in the Norfolks for whom he fought in the Boer War.

the Warwick Regiment have suffered badly/this morning's list: The BWD for August 26th refers to 'a loss of 7 officers wounded and 40 men killed, wounded and missing. We held our position under heavy gun fire for remainder of day with further casualties. 1 officer and 14 men wounded.'

Michael John: she must have heard the news verbally as she is referring to Major R. Meiklejohn who went missing on September 4th 1914 and was interned in Switzerland and repatriated in March 1918.

Knight Bruce: Captain J.H.W. Knight-Bruce went missing on October 1st 1914 and was repatriated on September 11th 1917.

The Col. Elkington is missing: Elkington and fellow Lieutenant-Colonel Mainwaring had allegedly surrendered at St. Quentin on August 27th (see p. 32-33 and 80).

This is the hell: His description of the horror of the warfare is echoed by Private William Tapp of 'C' Company who wrote in his diary on November 22nd- 'Once or twice I had a glimpse of hell.' Charlie Pratt recalled 'at times it is like living in hell.'

We crossed the Marne: The BWD mentions that they crossed on a railway bridge.

retreating Germans: The Germans were now in full retreat moving north towards the River Aisne; their Chief-of-Staff Helmut von Moltke was replaced by Erich von Falkenhayn.

September 10th

War news good. Allies taking the offensive all along the line. Austrian army nearly wiped out. *The Kaiser's* heart bleeds!

September 11th

After standing-to from 2 a.m. we eventually moved off at 5.30 a.m. with nothing to eat or drink, did a mile or so and halted. Moved on another mile and halted. Very weary and tired and hungry. Moved on again about three miles when men began to fall out. Very natural. We halted in the rain, and were shelled by some long distance guns. *Irish several casualties.* Warwicks none. We trekked on and on till dusk, too tired to speak. Bread which we hadn't seen for a week arrived, and bully. We could have eaten cat's meat. We had a good tuck in and some hot tea, and then slogged on again in torrents of rain, and roads like thick soup. The Warwicks billeted in a big farm about ten miles on. Part of this farm was burning furiously, by which we dried ourselves. The owner and his wife were burnt alive. The Germans taking good care that they could not escape. The children returned during the night, and were perfectly content to sleep with our Tommies anywhere. The name of this farm *Villers Le Petitfand*, the owner had left a lot of wine in the cellars. Bentley got hold of some and… he also filled both his flasks and water bottle. He had an awful nightmare during the night.

War news very good. Germans slowly retreating. We take the offensive everywhere. Wonderful despatch from *Sir J. French.*

War news good: the Germans were in retreat.

The Kaiser: The Emperor, Wilhelm II, King of Prussia and Emperor of Germany, was forced to abdicate on November 9th 1918, and went into exile in Holland where he died in 1941. He was the first grand child of Queen Victoria. It was ironic that despite the intermarriage between the British and German Royal families, War should have been conducted between the two countries.

Irish several casualties: The 1/ Royal Irish Fusiliers or the 2/ Royal Dublin Fusiliers- both were in the same brigade as the Warwicks.

Villers le Petitfand: Villers-le-Petit is approximately 11 miles south of Soissons. Since September 9th, the Warwicks had covered about 30 miles in difficult conditions. Some of the men in the B.E.F. had endured them since the Battle of Mons at the end of August; these professional soldiers described as a 'contemptible little army' by the Kaiser, showed great resilience and extraordinary commitment to the task at hand.

Sir J. French: Field Marshal Sir John French (1852-1925), was in command of the B.E.F. His early optimism evaporated after the retreat from Mons. Following a meeting with Lord Kitchener, the War Minister, he committed the B.E.F. to supporting the French counter attack on the Marne. He would eventually be blamed for the failure of the Loos offensive in Artois in September 1915 and was replaced by General Haig in December 1915. French was put in command of British Home Forces.

Montgomery: Left 4 a.m. Rations 6.30 a.m. Very wet. Billeted in farm.

September 12th

We moved off early. *Bentley as drunk as an owl.* The Coy. Sergt. Major was put in charge of him, and placed under arrest at the rear of the column. We expected to be in the thick of it at any moment. I took command of the company which was very much out of hand. We pushed on and on. Men and officers nearly sick with tiredness. We had had nothing to eat or drink and little sleep the night before. Lce. Cpl. *Tovey* was the only man who opened his mouth, nothing could daunt him. At Rozières we got one or two mouthfuls to help us on to the top of a hill above Septmonts. The Germans are reported retiring along their whole front. Wished to goodness they would stand a bit. Whenever we halted we were shelled. *The noise of gun fire this evening is terrific.* Few casualties among the Warwicks. More rain and wind, but in spite of both, the men and officers dropped down and went off to sleep. A battery of heavy guns were got up the hill and came into action about 100 yards from the regiment on to some fleeing Germans 6 miles off. When our 60 pounders opened fire the poor worn out Tommies sprung up as if they had been blown up. This caused much amusement amongst those who knew the guns were going to be fired. But down came the rain accompanied by thunder and lightning. A terrific thunderstorm which lasted for four hours. Down the hill again two miles long to billets. When the men heard they were going to get under cover they broke out into *Tipperary* and other songs. Indescribable confusion in the village. The order went out 'Get your men in anywhere you can.' 'A' Company got in somewhere in the pitch darkness. We soon had the dixies on, and had some hot tea and as everything was wet through they opened their *iron rations*. The officers had a good square meal prepared by the ladies of the farm, and afterwards had a good sleep. In the pandemonium that reigned in the village, the A & S Highlanders looted everything they could lay their hands on from the regimental transport. They stole all our cooking pots and even the doctor's instruments and everything the Quartermaster had. Disgraceful.

Bentley as drunk as an owl: Bentley continued to command his troops when drunk much to Robert and Montgomery's annoyance until he was put under arrest on October 23rd. Montgomery's diary entry for September 12th is just one word- 'Bentley'.

Tovey: Robert does mention him later as promised on December 13th (see p.103).

The noise of gunfire this evening is terrific: this was quite a baptism of fire for him as he takes over command of 'A' Company in place of Bentley. The rainy weather was in complete contrast to the sultry conditions experienced during the retreat from Mons. The BWD mentions that 'everyone wet through'.

Tipperary: 'It's a long way to Tipperary' was a popular marching song for British troops, written by music-hall entertainer Jack Judge of Oldbury in the Black Country and first introduced to the Army by the Galway based 7th Battalion of the Connaught Rangers Regiment. He wrote it in 1912 after a 5 shilling bet that he could not write a song to be performed within one day! It was first heard in public at the Grand Theatre, Stalybridge.

iron rations: emergency rations consisting of a tin of bully beef, biscuits, tea and sugar.

Sunday, September 13th

We marched up the hill again and halted on top till 9 p.m. Orders were issued to get tea made. This was done but, as it was too hot to drink, it had to be thrown away. We marched a mile and halted for three hours and where oh where was the tea? Guns are firing at us from all directions, and the Germans are still retiring. We held a section of the railway line near Soissons, and were given hot tea by the *African troops* of the French. They had just shot and burnt a spy. Heavy firing on our right. The 5th division heavily counter attacked. We marched through the night to reinforce. It poured with rain all night. The burning farms everywhere blazing made a wonderful sight. And thus we reached the Aisne.

September 13th: 'we reached the Aisne'- German troops along the river Aisne- the beginnings of trench warfare   British Newspaper Library, Colindale

Mrs. Driel went to church at Sourton with me. Big congregation owing to Mrs. Rich's death. *Whitwell's untactful allusion in his sermon.*

September 14th

We arrived at Venizel where there was a pontoon constructed by our *R.E.* in two hours, and over we went, but only just in time, for the Germans then opened a terrific fire on to it, and on us as we advanced to Bucy-le-Long. The men are miserably wet, but have plenty of rations. We pulled to pieces a rick of corn, and covered ourselves in it for the night. Bentley still under arrest.

Vile day. Splendid war news. *Germans retreating* like hell. All along the lines, leaving guns and prisoners. *Russia's crushing victory* over the Austrians. Susan and I practised bandaging. They say Jock Walford is back to the front again. Well done Jock.

———

African troops: French colonial troops included Algerians, Moroccans and Senegalese. The men Robert met were probably from the French Sixth Army.

Whitwell's… sermon: The vicar of Sourton and Renie were to cross swords on a regular basis in Robert's absence.

Montgomery: Left 7 a.m. Marched to top of hill. Artillery fire all day and crossed river at Venizel at 11 p.m. Marched all day to support 12th Brigade who had been heavily engaged. Slept in field. Bucy-le-Long.

R.E.: Royal Engineers were responsible for construction work (roads, railways, bridges, fortifications, accommodation etc.) and for demolition work; by 1918 there were 350,000 Royal Engineers.

Germans retreating: a reference to the First Battle of the Marne and the Battle of the Aisne.

Russia's crushing victory: in Galicia (central Europe) the Russian Army heavily defeated the Austro-Hungarians who lost 350,000 men, a third of their forces.

Montgomery: Woke up 3.30 a.m. Breakfast 5 a.m. under shelter of hill during heavy artillery fire. Went up to trenches with 'D' Company at 2 p.m. under heavy fire from enemy. *Bradford* killed. Letters.

Bradford: Montgomery is referring to 🔵 **Lieutenant-Colonel Sir Evelyn Ridley Bradford** aged 47, Commanding Officer of the Seaforth Highlanders. He left a widow, Elsie Clifton, Lady Bradford of Alton, Hampshire and was buried at the Crouy-Vauxrot French National Cemetery in the Aisne area near Soissons. He was mentioned in despatches.

September 15th

A finer morning spent mostly in sleep. The French guns are at it all day from the heights under which this pretty little Bucy-le-Long lies. *The Germans shelled* the road up from the river, and occasionally hit a wagon. It is wonderful the way the trench with their guns and wagons escaped untouched. They never do more than walk march, and yet shells drop within a few yards of them constantly. Another night in the straw.

Sourton sheep sale. Our 11 lambs fetched the record price of £2.6.6. each- £22.5/- the lot!! Top price of a very good sale. I bicycled to Lew for the nursing lesson, found only 8 people. Got on with my bandaging. On the way, an old man stopped me and asked whether *"they had murdered the mister"* as he had seen his name down in the paper.

September 16th

The Germans still shell the road, but otherwise we appear to be safe, as we are tucked into the hill. *(Promoted Captain).*

Very dull day. Wretched weather. No news from Bob. Mrs. Whitwell came up about the Harvest festival.

———

The Germans shelled: the mention of shelling in Robert's diary and the BWD becomes more common and already points to the fact that the War has become an 'industrial war' with artillery being the main killer of men rather than rifle fire.

"they had murdered the mister": rumours tended to spread quickly- in this instance that Robert had been killed at the Front.

Montgomery: Very heavy shrapnel fire. Rained hard all night.

(Promoted Captain): Robert was an ambitious soldier at this stage of the War and would have been greatly pleased by his promotion even if his report of the news plays down its importance. It was announced on this day in the *London Gazette*. However, he was not informed about this for almost six weeks as in his OD he wrote on October 29th that 'Piggott says he will ask the General if he may make me a Captain'. Piggott's enquiry led Robert to write on the 30th 'I was gazetted captain several days ago but count it from today when it was celebrated by a little dinner in my farm.'

Montgomery: Issued boots. Battalion split up at 1 p.m. 'C' and 'D' support to R.B. (Rifle Brigade) and King's Own. Bivouacked in rifle range.

September 17th

A most ghastly day. A huge shell dropped right in among the *Royal Irish* resting on the ground, and killed six outright, and wounded nine. It then occurred to somebody to move the regiments up the hill, and just as well. The Germans were firing at the village with their 90 pounders (280 pound shell). These guns were intended for the siege of Paris. They very soon found the range, something over thirteen miles, and literally blew the village to smithereens. I am afraid we have suffered some loss and here the *poor regimental transport* is no more. Houses simply went up. Hundreds of the villages were blown to atoms. The angle of descent of these huge shells must be very near perpendicular. At midnight we were told they were going to attack. We got right on top of the hill, and *dug trenches all night*, and stood to arms at 3.30 a.m. We were shelled all night by smaller shells but got an hour's sleep.

Dreadful weather- no news from Bob. Bandaged Cynthia's head. She and Dick very good.

September 18th

Bentley still with *S.M.* They were in the village through it all, and had some awful experiences to relate. We stood to arms at 3.30 in the trenches we had dug. Here we remained all day, and were well shelled. I was sent to reconnoitre in front, and got up into a hayrick. Was seen. One shell struck the rick full, and down I came quicker than when I went up. Cold and horrid all day. *Several men killed*. Ears buzzing as if they would burst. Marched off to occupy other trenches in the pouring rain. *The most miserable night* I ever remember spending. Mud and water, and well over our ankles. And an occasional shell just to keep us awake. Pitch dark and no dug outs. Bentley returned.

September 18th: 'trenches we had dug'- British troops in the Aisne area   Imperial War Museum Q51501

In the OD he describes this day as 'The most ghastly day ever known… hear there are some awful sights in the village.'

Royal Irish: 1/ Royal Irish Fusiliers' War Diary mentions that 5 were killed and 24 wounded.   **55** *poor regimental transport:* the BWD records 'lost 6 horses wounded but only water cart damaged.'

dug trenches all night: this is the first time Robert writes about digging trenches. Eventually the Western Front would stretch about 450 miles from Nieuport on the Belgian coast to the Franco-Swiss border.

Montgomery: Very wet. Bentley's Court Martial. Went into forward trenches 7 p.m. Worst night I have ever had. Listening patrols.

S.M: a Sergeant-Major was in charge of discipline. The word was often spelled with a 'j' at the time and on Memorials like the Menin Gate but Robert spells it throughout with a 'g'.

Several men killed: The BWD mentions 'a good many casualties from gunfire. Lieutenant Knapton and one man killed and 15 wounded.' **Lieutenant O.A. Knapton**, 21 year old son of a naval Captain of Rope Hill, Lymington, Hampshire, was buried at Vauxbuin French National Cemetery south of Soissons.

The most miserable night: having had a lucky escape in the hayrick and now with his ankles deep in mud, this must have been the worst day yet for Robert, his men and also Montgomery. The mud and the occasional shell would become standard features of the War.

September 18th
I went to Blackwells to see ponies for Dick and Cynthia. One old black thing of 14 he wanted £9 for; very fat through knees broken. Another nice black 12 years, he wanted £12 for and £15 for a bay pony. Too much. Went blackberrying got 7 pounds. Bandaged in the evening. Letter from Bob. All well. *Poor Wally Heath* died of wounds near Paris.

September 19th
We had something to eat in an *enormous cave*, which we wished we had discovered overnight. We explored it, but could not get to the end of it. Much used in the revolution. Shell fire still continues, which gives us no proper rest by day or night. Am quite sure I look fifty, I feel seventy. On watch tonight till 10.30 and then dropped off to sleep to dream the usual dream of masses of troops rushing about with no leader. Much noise of moving transport heard all night. *I wish I might command* this company or had a captain I could trust to keep sober.

Decorated for Harvest Festival which is very early this year. Winnie is to 'hold herself in readiness to go to the front as a despatch rider' for the 'Expedimentary' Force.

Sunday 20th September
More rain. In these awful *dug outs* with shells flying around all day. *Rum issue* twice a day. Wish I had my syringe. Moved up into the *firing line* trenches at 6.30 p.m. and at 7.30 a party of Germans crept up and *opened a heavy fire on us*, killing one and wounding two. With some difficulty, I got my platoon to cease fire as it was only wasting ammunition.

Poor Wally Heath: reference to **Lance-Corporal Wally Heath** whom Renie and Robert may have known from their Warwickshire days as he lived at 31 Court Street, Leamington Spa. He died on September 10th at the age of 26 when fighting with the King's Royal Rifle Corps. He was buried at Montreuil-aux-Lions Cemetery in the Aisne region.

enormous cave: the discovery of this large complex of caves must have been a godsend for the troops as they were to remain in the area until early October. The War is starting to become 'static'; the day's entry in the BWD mentions 'improved trenches during the night'.

I wish I might command: Bentley is back in command of 'A' Company. That Robert is prepared to commit his thoughts to paper reflects the level of his frustration with him.

Montgomery: Sat in trenches all day. Got parcel from home. Peppermint creams. Relieved by 'D' Company 7 p.m.

dug outs: these shelters for protection from shell burst and bad weather would become a feature of life on the front line. They ranged from basic and small holes dug into the sides of the trench to large rooms with a steep staircase from the trench floor.

Rum issue: rum was normally issued once a day, usually during stand to, for relaxing soldiers and to give them courage. It would also help to take the edge off the cold.

firing line: front line

opened a heavy fire on us: according to the BWD 'A' Coy 'opened a heavy fire on a party of enemy advancing on our front, only lasted a quarter of an hour…1 killed, 2 wounded.'

September 21st

Bitterly cold all day, and no means of warming ourselves. No matches and very little tobacco left. A postcard from Renie saying she had at last got one of my letters which was a great relief to me. Had a Times paper of September 8th which I read every word of, until the firing began again. The General sent an order for an officer and two men *to search for dead or wounded Germans*, I think the reply was "not in these trousers". I lit a fire in my dug out and had a really delicious cup of tea, and a *Tommy* gave me a bit of bacon in his fingers. Relieved at 6.30 and went down to Headquarters Cave, where they very reluctantly gave us liver and bacon. It was warm at any rate in the cave. Both ears gone, can't hear a word.

The Battle of the Aisne has now lasted a week. Schreiber and Walsh from the camp wounded. *The Pegasus* annihilated by the Germans.

to search for dead or wounded Germans: for intelligence gathering- e.g. which unit the German soldiers belonged to, troop movements and levels of morale. Robert's terse response suggests it would have been a dangerous occupation! The BWD does not refer to such an order, simply stating 'Few shells. Quiet day'.

Tommy: short for Thomas Atkins, a commonly used description of a British soldier, thought to have its origins in the 18th century. The exact first use of the term is unknown but it may have been chosen by the Duke of Wellington after the Battle of Boxtel in 1794 when he came across a badly wounded soldier of that name who is reputed to have said "It's all right, Sir. It's all in a day's work." He died soon after and in a War Office publication of 1815 Private Tommy Atkins was used as an example in instructions on how to fill out the Soldier's Pocket Book.

2nd Lieutenant Kenneth MacFarlane Gaunt formerly of the Queen's Westminster Rifles and now of the Warwicks wrote on this day with some prescience that 'It would be too awful to spend a winter where we are.' Nearly four months later on January 9th 1915 he bemoaned the fact that 'the weather is indescribable and the trenches are in an appalling condition.' He died on September 25th 1915 during the Battle of Loos- he is remembered on the Loos Memorial.

The Battle of the Aisne: operations along the River Aisne until the front stabilised on September 25th.

The Pegasus: on September 20th *H.M.S. Pegasus* was put out of action by the German cruiser *Königsberg* off the island of Zanzibar in the Indian Ocean.

Montgomery: Fine day. In support trenches. Cigarettes from Mrs. Briscoe. Omelette.

September 22nd

The Company spend the whole day in the cave. The town was shelled again. Went down to buy vegetables and eggs. We moved into the trenches near the other cave, where we had a good meal of *cold bully*, eggs and tea with rum in it. Ten till two, watch. *Two Germans surrendered*, and two were shot. Another hopeless *dream about Bentley*.

I went to Lew for a lecture by Dr. He lectured to us on bones and produced all sorts and sizes. Very difficult.

September 23rd: 'I can't understand why I should get all her letters…'- This envelope for a letter sent to Renie from the Plouvier sisters in December passed the censor (see p.107-108)

September 23rd

A sad letter from Renie. I can't understand why I should get all her letters, and she none of mine. Awful shelling going on. Taylor and I went into the town to *buy cooking pots and eatables*. Changed our trenches at night again.

Hopeful despatch from Sir J. French. Seward and Cooper wounded.

September 24th

We reinforced *Christie's Company* at dawn and stood to arms. A fine sunny morning. Our spirits rose accordingly. An issue of cigarettes, matches, chocolate, sardines and milk. At about 5 p.m. just when we were going to eat a stew of chicken and vegetables, the Germans opened all along the line, but did no damage. There is a rumour that peace was declared last night. Front line trenches for 24 hours.

---

cold bully: tinned corned beef, generally from Argentina, could be stewed or fried. Soldiers were often provided with the infamous Maconochie's stew of vegetables and some meat.

Two Germans surrendered: no mention of this in the BWD but 'one man killed in fire trench 'B' Coy. 7.30 p.m. when Coy. was being relieved.'

dream about Bentley: In the OD, Robert goes into greater detail about his frustration at being commanded by Bentley: 'Had another dream about men with no leader dashing everywhere and I was unable to do or say anything. Of course Bentley is the cause of it all.'

buy cooking pots and eatables: it was the job of the Army Service Corps (A.S.C.) to move and distribute food equipment and ammunition; the A.S.C. numbered over 6,000 in August 1914 but by November 1918 was over 320,000.

Montgomery: All day in forward trenches. Read 'Black Tulip'. Came out at 6.30 p.m.

Christie's Company: Major W.C. Christie of 'D' Company. He would be killed later on October 13th at the Battle of Méteren, when Lieutenant Montgomery was seriously wounded.

September 25th

The servants won't bring us up anything into the advanced trenches, so we sit and starve. The weather is most beautiful, especially the sunrises and sunsets, but infernally *cold in the damp clay* and one can't move about on account of shells and bullets. Back into Headquarter cave for the night. It is getting very foul in there, with about 300 men continually in it, smoking and sleeping.

September 26th
Another beautiful sun-rise, and very hot all day. I took my platoon down *to wash* at the village pump. My new underclothing has at last arrived.

Two postcards from Bob one dated 9th Sept. one dated 16th Sept. One was a Kitchener postcard. Mary had a wire from her brother who is passing Exeter on his way to the front from Egypt, so went off to meet him for a day or two.

Sunday September 27th
Gunning, gunning, gunning to no purpose whatever. It gives me an awful headache, and prevents any sort of exercise.

September 28th
In the advanced trenches again. Some Germans crept up and fired at us. We replied with some effect. One man killed and one wounded.

The servants: In the OD Robert was clearly annoyed by the servants: 'A day of much annoyance. The servants do nothing but eat and sleep and lose our things. Taylor has now allowed someone to steal our bottle of methylated spirits which cannot be replenished and so the little lamp is no good. They won't bring us anything into these advanced trenches and so we sit and starve.' It looks as though Taylor was living on borrowed time!

cold in the damp clay: much worse was to follow later in the clay of Flanders.

to wash: when trench life settled into some sort of routine, it would be difficult for men on front line duty to meet basic personal hygiene needs. Their tunics often became lice and flea infested.

Gunning, gunning, gunning: the stress caused by heavy and sporadic bombardment would result in many men suffering from shell shock. The BWD mentions that 'Enemy fired on us from 11.30 a.m. till 1 p.m. We did not reply. No casualties'.

September 28th: 'In the advanced trenches again'- a British sentry using a periscope in a more developed trench than those constructed near the Aisne   Imperial War Museum Q50687

In the OD: 'I was detailed to go to Paris by car tomorrow but at the last minute they sent Jackson.'

Montgomery: Forward trenches all day. Shelling began 8 a.m. Had breakfast 6 a.m. Generals came at 6.30 a.m. Thornhill came. To cave 6.30 p.m.

September 29th
A fine morning but cold. Improved our headcover, after having had bacon and eggs. Went down to get butter and nearly got caught by a shell returning. Another dream re. *Bentley*. Couldn't they find him a staff job?

September 30th: 'A long letter from Renie which I read by moonlight'-
Bruce Bairnsfather's cartoon captures the sadness of being parted…
Barbara Bruce Bairnsfather

Good lecture on treating fractures but far too much crammed in one time. Found Susan very frightened as a *mysterious letter* had come for me sent up by the Post Office. I had quite a turn but it was alright as it was 2 capital letters from Bob saying they were quite near the huge battle that was raging and that they were bivouacking in a cave.

September 30th

A long letter from Renie, which I read by moonlight. After a night in the *foul cave*, we enjoyed a good breakfast of bacon, eggs and fried potatoes. *All sorts of things are coming out for the men-* papers, chocolate, cigs, and tobacco. I walked about in the moonlight until driven in by German bullets.

Bentley: the continuing frustration with Bentley's drunkenness suggests that Robert was concerned about 'A' Company's safety and emphasises his anxiety that Bentley was unprofessional and failing in his military duties.

The BWD mentions the sighting of an airship and that 'General Rawlinson visited our position.' George Hewins, a Private in the Warwicks, recalling events later in the War, observed that 'you could smell the Top Brass when they came to the trenches…' Rawlinson's 4th Army struggled on the Somme in 1916 but it was successful at the Battle of Amiens in 1918 which helped pave the way for the German surrender.

mysterious letter: wives and mothers dreaded receipt of an 'official' envelope likely to contain bad news from the Front like the one received on October 2nd by Dorothy, the widow of **Captain G. H. Ker** of Whitchurch near Tavistock. She received a telegram from King George V and Queen Mary expressing sympathy for the loss of her 30 year old husband: 'The King and Queen deeply regret the loss you and the army have sustained by the death of your husband in the service of his country. Their Majesties truly sympathise with you in your sorrow.' Fighting with the Bedfordshire Regiment, he lost his life on September 15th and was buried at Vendresse British Cemetery.

foul cave: the conditions under foot were starting to deteriorate and the cave provided some shelter from the rain and mud and safety from German fire.

All sorts of things are coming out for the men: it was a great credit to the Army Postal Service that troops received letters and parcels often only two days after posting. By the middle of the War, over 10 million letters and 100,000 parcels were distributed every week.

October 1st

We reinforced the front firing trench at 4 a.m. A most glorious sunrise, but oh so cold. A warm and most beautiful sunny day. Company went down into the village to wash. Bought eggs and vegetables in exchange for bully of which we have dozens of tins in reserve. *Sacked Taylor* and took on Wilkes. Put up a gong made of shell cases. *The General and his A.D.C.* inspected and approved. *Sergt. Yates planted me a tree* to mark the best way up to the advanced trenches, through the long and wet grass. Sat in the moonlight till 11 p.m. reading Renie's letters.

Went on the moor with the Driels. Very jolly day. Got back late and found two letters from Bob, one written from the top of a hill saying the most awful battle was being waged that the world has ever known. The artillery fire was like rain coming down from the skies. The second letter was written from a cave 1 mile long. Nobody has ever got to the end of it yet. He is roughing it very much. Left all his baggage behind and all the necessaries of life. He is having a very hard time.

October 2nd

Had a bad go of cramp getting out of my dug out. Thick mist all day. A man of my platoon helped an old woman dig up and carry down to the village, many sacks of potatoes. The Germans shelling our advanced trenches at 4 p.m. Moved the Company up into them and had a most unexpected calm night. We then moved into the still further forward trenches which are not yet complete.

October 3rd

Private Baker and I set to work to make a new sort of dug out. Roof stout green branches. Twigs and straw, and covered over with 2'6" of earth and then cut into the bank behind it. Sergt. Pickering will *take a photo of it* if it is not blown down. *One man shot through both legs.*

Letter from Bob from Bucy-le-Long. He says they have no news at all of the campaign and that it was all deadly monotonous.

———

Sacked Taylor: Nine men called Taylor from the Warwicks were killed in action, three in 1914 and this may have been a ⚫ **Private C. Taylor** who later died on March 28th 1915 and was buried at Hazebrouck Cemetery. Robert received 'poor' Taylor's kit in England on October 19th 1915.

The General and his A.D.C: reference to the visit on September 29th of General Rawlinson and his Aide-de-Camp, an officer who acts as a secretary and carries the orders of a General.

Sergt. Yates planted me a tree: a good example of improvisation; soldiers on both sides became good at improvisation to react to new conditions and challenges. A Sergeant of the Warwicks, ⚫ **Thomas Yates**, fell at the Battle of the Somme in July 1916 at the age of 30 and is remembered on the Thiepval Memorial.

Private Baker: He became Robert's batman not long after October 12th.

take a photo of it: in several of his diary entries, Robert expresses pride in the quality of his dug outs. He writes more fully in his OD- 'Private Baker and I set to work to make a dug out as it should be made. We made the roof with stout green branches, twigs and straw, all covered over with 2' 6" of earth and then cut into the bank behind.' Baker was clearly making an impression as a potential batman. Later on Christmas Day, the quality of Robert's dug out attracted too many visitors for his liking!

One man shot through both legs: the BWD records 'One man in 'A' Company wounded by sniper' and there is another reference to 'a visit by General Rawlinson...at 6.30 a.m.' Three visits by a General in five days does not fit the standard view that the Generals stayed safely behind the lines in a comfortable chateau.

Sunday, October 4th

Shelling us again quite close. Bentley court martialled and given a chance and told that if his conduct was alright for the rest of the war, the entry would be washed off his records altogether. My *platoon* dug trenches in reliefs all through the night with the full moon and the stars. When I got back to our cave, I found *Bentley* very talkative. His views on religion are most extraordinary. He believes in there being an Almighty God thoroughly, but not in his Son, or in the story of the Cross and in the sacrifice. I am afraid his home life is not a happy one, and I feel sorry for him, but can never forgive him for the risks he runs when drunk. The men will not follow him, but nothing will induce him to believe this.

October 5th

In charge of a not worth the candle *route march*. We were badly shelled on our way back, but luckily had no casualties. We hear that the *Indian troops* and French are attacking on our left with our naval guns to help them. Rabbit and fresh meat stew and feel fit for anything. One *Young*, a good fellow with an eye-glass joined today. Tremendous 'wind-up' later. *Bannerman* came across from Headquarters shouting "Stand to, Stand to, the Germans are on you." We stood to and cursed B. all night.

---

platoon: Robert was in command of a platoon of about 50 men.

Bentley: Robert considered that Bentley's problems were caused by his home life although he may have been suffering from shell shock. Robert was a staunch Anglican who, when in Devon, would attend at least one Church of England service on a Sunday. For him, Bentley's Unitarian stance, that there was a God but no Son nor Holy Ghost, was 'quite extraordinary.'

Montgomery: Received four parcels from home, with shirt, socks, dated September 27th. To forward trenches 6.30. First parade service since war began. Quiet night. Sniping a lot.

route march: a march used for physical training; Robert is not impressed and rightly so. Was it Bentley's idea, a means to reassert his authority?

Indian troops: the first Indian troops to serve on the Western Front were known as Force A. They fought at the Battles of La Bassée in November 1914 and Neuve-Chapelle in 1915 before being posted to Egypt. A total of 1.3 million Indian troops served during the War; 72,000 were killed in action.

Young: in the BWD it is recorded that 'Lt. Young and one man joined the battalion.' The eye-glass or monocle would have been a talking point amongst other ranks. His arrival is also mentioned by Montgomery.

Bannerman: Major J. A. M. Bannerman received a D.S.O. (Distinguished Service Order awarded usually to the rank of Lieutenant and above for gallantry). As a Lieutenant-Colonel, Bannerman was in command of the 1/ Royal Warwicks from November 26th 1915 to June 14th 1916. By 1916, a photograph shows that he and Captain T. H. Harwood were the only officers remaining of the original B.E.F. still serving with the Warwicks after 21 months of warfare. Only 6 N.C.O.s were still serving in France. He was mentioned in a Report written in early January 1915 by Brigadier-General Charles Hull, Commander of the 10th Infantry Brigade, as having been commended for his untiring work by Lieutenant-Colonel Poole.

October 5th

Letter dated from Bob dated Sept 27th. I have a little cold. I went to the lecture. They are all quite over our heads, though the nice little Doctor does his best to explain things clearly. May talked most of the time and we all agreed that she ought to have a bandage put on her jaw. Tom bought 2 of my pigs at 16/- each, Mrs. Worden and Mrs. Ellis each bought one at £1 and Pope 2 at £1.

October 6th and 7th

Last night's scare was apparently a sniper or two. Bentley bet me a bottle of wine that at least 100 dead Germans would be found in our barbed wire. I bet there would not be one. It was nothing but a nervy scare. We had No.1 breakfast at 5.30 a.m. of bully and hard boiled eggs. No.2 at 9 a.m. of hot bully, potatoes, jam and cheese, lunch at 1.p.m. tea at 4, and dinner for which we were all quite ready at 7 p.m. consisting of chicken and rabbit stew, sardines and toast. The rest of the day we slept. After dinner we all four composed a rhyme *'The fate of the Pickelhauben patrol'* (which may or may not be found at the end of the diary) and then had another huge bully stew. And thus ended our occupation of Bucy-le-Long. We marched down to headquarters and eventually moved off at 1.30 a.m. a beautiful moonlight night, but so cold that I marched the eleven miles in my great coat, *carrying two haversacks*, water bottle and *rifle*. Fearfully sleepy just before dawn. We had to hide in a wood from aeroplanes all day, and so got a sleep. Two parcels arrive from Lady M. - a pound tin of Players Navy cut from George Bull, and many letters from different people. 'B' Company gave us a French cheese (Brie). We did about twelve miles and then 'A' Company billeted at a nice little farm. I had a spring bed. The occupants could not do enough for us. There were no men of course. Every male is fighting. *Rozet St.Albans* was the name of the village. The men were not very comfortable, I'm afraid.

Letter from Bob dated 30th and P.C. dated October 1st.

'The fate of the Pickelhauben patrol': is to be found written in purple crayon in the back of the original diary. The *pickelhaube* was the spiked helmet worn by the German soldiers. It lost its spike early in the War and the leather type was replaced by a steel helmet in 1916. The lyrics of the reworked nursery rhyme were written by Robert, Captains Bentley and Wasey and Lieutenant Wood (see p.130 for the lyrics in full).

carrying two haversacks: this emphasises the soldiers' strength and fitness carrying such heavy items on long marches.

rifle: the standard British rifle of the war was the S.M.L.E. (Short Magazine Lee Enfield) mark III firing .303-inch cartridges. Introduced to the British Army in 1907, the soldiers of the B.E.F. could fire 15 rounds a minute. The firing was so sustained that the Germans believed they were facing machine-guns.

Rozet St. Albans: he meant Rozet-St-Albin, south west of Villers-le-Petit. The Warwicks are moving away from the battle lines and are about to be sent to northern France. On October 6th, British troops of the Royal Naval Division landed at Ostend and Zeebrugge in Belgium. Amongst them was the poet, naval **Sub Lieutenant Rupert Brooke** who later died of septicaemia on the way to the Dardanelles in Turkey aged 27. He died on April 23rd 1915 on a hospital ship off the Greek island of Skyros and was buried in an olive grove on the island. He was born at 5, Hillmorton Road, Rugby and his father taught at Rugby School.

Montgomery: In wood till 10 p.m. Billeted in very nice French woman's house.

October 8th

All the farm girls lunched with us and we had great fun. We kissed them all. Bentley kissed them all twice. They didn't in the least mind, and only said *"Eh bien c'est la guerre"*. Grandpa amused us very much. He had been dressed in his best for three days and nights expecting to go to Paris. We moved off at 3.30 p.m. and halted for the night at Vauciennes; here 'A' Company had the pick of the billets again. My French is improving so I am asked to be company billeting officer.

A belated p.c. from Bob dated Sept.15th from 'Bucy-le-Long – Aisne'. No paper today. *Cicely and Winnie* still struggling to get to the front. They have found the *F.A.N.Y.* somewhat of a delusion.

October 9th

We started again at 6 a.m. and after a very long march arrived at Rully at 8 p.m. Men very footsore and weary, and nobody made any sort of arrangements for them. We were told to make the most of a large sort of American barn, but not to touch the straw. Beastly cold. By morning every bit of straw had been pulled down, and the regiment could hardly be found under it. I went out early and found a delicious cup of coffee and cognac, and took Bentley to breakfast there later. Many aeroplanes in sheds here. Could not get permission to fly. Moved off at 3.30 with *Lancaster in command* of 'A' Company. A special reserve officer just out and knew nothing. Great mistake. A Frenchman flew alongside us about 30 feet above our heads. Our feet are still bruised from the hard roads, and carrying of much kit. We arrived at *Lonquil St. Marie* where 'A' Company were billeted in a magnificent school, and the officers all had beds. Very tired indeed.

"Eh bien c'est la guerre"(oh well, that's war): a phrase often used by soldiers and the local population throughout the War as a way of shrugging off the unusual circumstances they faced. When commenting on the Christmas Truce in his diary, Captain Sir Morgan Crofton was to write: 'This is all very well but *ce n'est pas la guerre*'!

Cicely and Winnie: were Renie's sisters. In 1914 they were 23 and 25 years of age respectively. Winnie died in 1975 and Cicely in 1978 and both were buried in the churchyard of St. James's Church, Walton (see p.156).

F.A.N.Y: First Aid Nursing Yeomanry. Women worked as volunteers in hospitals and canteens and drove ambulances at the Front. Other women's voluntary organisations included the V.A.D. (Voluntary Aid Detachments) and the Q.A.I.M.N.S. (Queen Alexandra's Imperial Military Nursing Service).

Montgomery: Stayed in billets all day. Marched at 4.30 p.m. to Vauciennes and billeted in aeroplane shed. Very long march- 15 miles. Arrived 3.30 a.m. on 9th and very tired.

Lancaster in command: the BWD states that '3 p.m. Major Lancaster and Lt. Pilkington joined.'

Lonquil St. Marie: this should read Longueil-Ste-Marie.

Montgomery: Billeted with 'A' Company (Robert's Company) in big farm. Freeman came and I handed over 'C' to him. Billeted in splendid big house; Company in school.

October 10th

Marched off at 3.30 p.m. and arrived at   , where we were again made very welcome and had dinner in a big private house. Our host providing cigars and champagne. This town was practically untouched by the Germans, and so we were able to fill up with all sorts of luxuries. A friendly Frenchman gave me a tinder lighter, and most of the men got souvenirs of sorts.

Sunday, October 11th

We paraded at 3.30 a.m. to march three miles to the station at   , and were all entrained at 2.30 p.m. Everybody *very angry* at being robbed of their much needed sleep. Our destination was said to be *Étables*, and on and on we went all through the night. Saw the lights of Folkestone. We got something to eat at Amiens and then dropped off to sleep.

Fall of Antwerp. Fell on Friday after gallant resistance.

---

very angry: In the OD, Robert is more trenchant in his criticism: 'After parading at 3.30 am we managed by some superhuman effort to march three miles and entrain by 2.30 pm. This is how the officers and men are robbed of their much needed sleep.'

Étables: he means Étaples near Le Touquet on the Channel coast, 15 miles south of Boulogne. Étaples became the site of ten general hospitals, the notorious training ground known as the 'Bull Ring' and a number of infantry base depots. Étaples was pronounced 'Eat Apples' by troops. The British War Cemetery at Étaples is the second largest in France with nearly 11,000 burials. The largest is at St. Sever in Rouen. The town was the scene of rioting in September 1917. In 1918 when writing to his parents, Brigade Order Sergeant Charles William Nightingall wrote of disaffection amongst young soldiers there.

Winifred and Cicely Mordaunt, Robert's sisters-in-law contributed to the War effort in and around Étaples.

Fall of Antwerp: the northern Belgian port of Antwerp was defended by two rings of fortresses. The Germans started their siege on September 28th; the Belgian Army had withdrawn to Antwerp after the fall of Liège. Antwerp fell on October 9th but the German Army had been slowed down in their advance again.

Montgomery (October 10th): Entrained. Arrived Amiens 4 p.m., Boulogne 12 midnight, Calais 2 a.m., St. Omer 4 a.m.

October 12th

Arrived at *St.Omer* at 5 a.m. Some men elected to travel in open trucks and were stiff with the cold. We marched the men to some French barracks, and then set out to forage. A kindly Frenchman took me to a café, and gave me a capital lunch. A fine town with a beautiful cathedral in which troops were billeted, and services held all day. Wilkes got helplessly drunk. *The whole division* massed in the square, and wondered what was on. At about 3.30 p.m. a *German aeroplane* attempted to get over us and drop bombs, but up went two Frenchmen, *three bombs* were dropped short of the square but killed two women and a baby. The two Frenchmen attacked. A very pretty sight and down came the brute like a stone. Tremendous cheer from the division. Presently at the far end of the square was seen a *London omnibus* with all sorts of homely advertisements on it, and behind it, hundreds of others and cars of all descriptions. We then learnt we were going to push right up, and so thus began

October 12th: 'a London omnibus with all sorts of homely advertisements'- The 2/ Warwicks were transported in the London buses above on November 6th 1914 to Ypres via Dickebusch

Imperial War Museum Q57328

the great joy ride. I had secured a private car for the 'A' Company officers, but Bentley insisted on getting into a charabanc full of French officers. The roads were vile, and the men crowded together in these buses must have been anything but comfortable. The French officers gave us cigars and brandy at intervals during the night. They sang French songs, and we replied with English. It was great fun, but got very cold. The distance was *45 miles*, and not a single car broke down. We arrived at Caestre in the early hours of the morning.

More bombs dropped on Paris. They say they are going to invade by *airships* in a fortnight.

St. Omer: is about 20 miles south east of Calais and from this date until April 1916 was the base of the British General Headquarters and in 1917 the Headquarters of the Royal Flying Corps.

The whole division: it was in fact the Brigade.

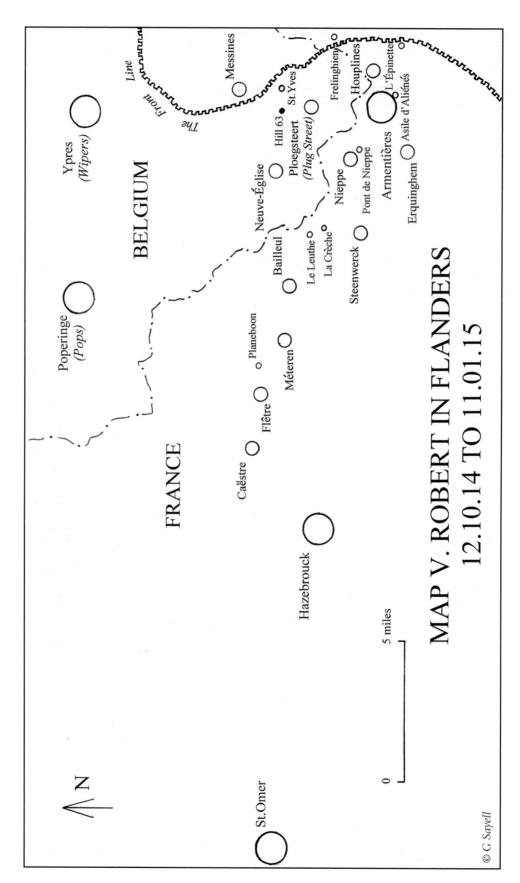

N

BELGIUM

FRANCE

St.Omer

Poperinge
(Pops)

Ypres
(Wipers)

The Front Line

Messines

Hazebrouck

Caëstre

Flêtre

Méteren

Planeboon

Neuve-Église

Bailleul

Le Leuthe

La Crèche

Steenwerck

Nieppe

Pont de Nieppe

Hill 63

Ploegsteert
(Plug Street)

St.Yves

Frelinghien

Houplines

Armentières

L'Épinette

Asile d'Aliénés

Erquinghem

5 miles

0

MAP V. ROBERT IN FLANDERS
12.10.14 TO 11.01.15

© G Sayell

66

German aeroplane…three bombs: only two bombs were dropped according to the BWD. By 1917, St. Omer would become a regular target for German air raids causing casualties amongst civilians and British nurses.

London omnibus: they would have been a remarkable sight on French roads. The situation is becoming critical; this date marks the start of the battle for Flanders- in effect the struggle for control of the coast.

45 miles: it should be no more than 15 miles so this was quite a detour, which suggests there was a lot of troop movement on the roads at the time.

More bombs dropped on Paris: during the War, there were 30 German air raids over Paris; the first was carried out on August 29th 1914. Some bombs were dropped from airships.

airships: were used for raids from the start of the War. The famous airships were the Zeppelins, named after their inventor Count Ferdinand von Zeppelin. The first airship raid in England was on January 19th 1915 over Norfolk, and caused great panic and chaos; 4 civilians were killed and 16 were wounded. Until June 1917, there were 51 airship raids over England causing 2,000 casualties which included more than 500 deaths.

Montgomery: Went into cavalry barracks at St. Omer. Breakfast 7 a.m. Shave, shampoo, hair cut and bath. Left 2 p.m. Waited by Town Hall till 6 p.m. for motor buses; went in buses to Caestre. Arrived there 3 a.m. Billeted.

October 13th

I got a most delicious omelette at a baker's. Here I met John Hayter who had been in action the day before with his battery. *The Germans were being pushed* as they never had been before, and now that we had arrived we were to push them out of Armentières. We bought honey and butter. The 6th division was in action and wanted reinforcements. They had routed the German cavalry, and killed the *Crown Prince of Hess* and captured a German General. With *'A' company advance guard* we started merrily at 8.30 to the sound of much gun fire. The men carrying loaves of bread and other provisions for the night's billet. 'A' company got into the thick of it at once, and had two killed and four wounded *as we lined out.* We advanced taking cover behind the only cover there was. (Cabbage leaves through which we counted the bullets.) Advancing on by short rushes and falling headlong down and hurriedly scraping earth up in front of our heads with our hands. On again to the top of the rise. Could go no further for a bit so signalled back for reinforcements. *Up came the Jocks* with their heads in the air, and singing some war cry. As they joined our line the whole of us advanced at the double with a rousing cheer and much shouting. We got into the German trenches but *found no men.* *'C' company on our right fared very badly.* Poor old Christie rushed his position, and was himself killed. *Gilliat* was hit on the head, and was not expected to live. *Thornton* and *Young* were both badly wounded. *The Irish* then reinforced and took the position. *Altogether we had* 95 wounded, 21 killed and 6 missing. The rain which began at about 2 p.m. continued till dark. Making things even more uncomfortable. We spent the night in the house by the side of the road just behind the battlefield. Poole very cut up about Christie, and thus the battle of Méteren.

Lecture on wounds, bruises, burns, scalds etc. We didn't believe them. Long letter from Bob saying they were in more advanced trenches and were taking pot shots at a German aeroplane. He had met John Hayter. Sent off a parcel of underwear to Bob.

The Germans were being pushed: in fact the Germans were advancing successfully into Belgium. Ostend and Zeebrugge were evacuated and Lille in France had been occupied.

Crown Prince of Hess: Maximilian, Prince of Hesse, born in 1894, was the Kaiser's nephew and great grand-child of Queen Victoria.

'A' Company advance guard: the BWD details that 'orders to move to Méteren' were given at 09.20 a.m. and ten minutes later 'A' and 'C' Companies 'formed advance guard under Major Poole with Divisional Cyclist Company and Cavalry in front.' The Cavalry was the divisional squadron of the 19th Hussars.

as we lined out: the BWD states that 'at 10 a.m. on reaching Flêtre, enemy were reported to be holding high ground along ridge in front of Méteren. 'A' and 'B' Coys were deployed... 'D' Coy under Major Christie was sent up behind 'C' Company in support- enemy retired into and just outside Méteren occupying trenches and houses.'

Up came the Jocks: The BWD records that at 11 a.m. 'Regiment ordered to push on and endeavour to drive them out.' At 1 p.m. 'gained outskirts of village but were held up and great need of supports' then the Warwicks were ordered to halt. The plan was for the 10th Brigade to

WILLIAM CHARLES CHRISTIE

attack north of Méteren, and the 12th Brigade from the south. The 12th Brigade 'attacked at 2 p.m. and an hour later the Seaforths attacked on our left and through 'A' Coy which withdrew at dusk to Planeboon.' The Jocks are the 2nd Seaforth Highlanders, now referred to by Robert in more complimentary terms than in previous diary entries! The Seaforths' War Diary records that the position was 'carried at the point of the bayonet at a cost of 4 officers wounded, 18 other ranks killed, 66 wounded and one missing.'

found no men: it is possible that Robert found a concertina in the trench, mentioned by his batman Sperry (see p.173).

'C' Company .... badly: 'C' and 'D' Coys under Captain Freeman and Major Christie were unable to withdraw until much later owing to heavy fire.

In the OD Robert records that 'Bentley and I dug ourselves in with our hands in a ploughed field. The Jocks and Irish did magnificently.'

*October 13th: 'Poor old Christie'
Major W.C. Christie of the
1/ Warwicks who was killed at
the Battle of Méteren* Rugby School

Poor old Christie: 🔴 **Major William Charles Christie** was buried after the War with the other Warwicks at Méteren Military Cemetery which contains more than 800 graves. In the pocket at the back of his diary, Robert had inserted a copy of a letter to *The Times* about Christie which may have been sent out to him by Renie. He was the son of John Robert and Margaret Christie, of Baynton House, Llandaff, Glamorgan and was the husband of Florence Violet Christie, of Somerset Lodge, Knowles Hill, Newton Abbot, Devon. He was educated at Rugby School- 800 old boys died in the Great War. He served in the Sudan Campaign in 1898 and was mentioned in Despatches. In the South African Campaign, 1899-1902, he was also commended in Despatches. In his OD, Robert wrote 'poor old Christie was hit in five places.'

*Major Christie's doleful charger tied up to a fence
surrounding his grave*
Royal Regiment of Fusiliers (Royal Warwickshire) Museum

In 1963, Sergeant J. Philpotts contributed to the BBC Great War T.V. series and wrote that on October 13th, 'suddenly a burst of machine-gun fire struck us from the rear. We soon located the gun in the Church tower. For sentimental, if not for religious reasons, we had always avoided using churches for cover, billets etc. and were sort of disgusted at the Germans for using the Tower as a gun emplacement. Our commander, Major Christie (a fine soldier) asked for volunteers to get the machine-gun. Before any could volunteer, he drew his pistol and dashed back to the church. He must have raced up the steps to the top of the tower and of course the Germans killed him and threw his body down to us as we rushed the church. This did not increase our love of the Germans needless to say.' This version of Christie's death is not corroborated anywhere else so Philpotts's story may have been embellished in the intervening 50 years.

Gilliat:  **Captain Cecil Glendower Percival Gilliat** died of his wounds the following day and is buried at Hazebrouck Communal Cemetery. He was 29, born in County Meath and attended Cheltenham College- 675 ex-pupils died in the War.

Thornton: **Colour Sergeant Philip Thornton** also died of wounds aged 33 and is buried at Méteren. He was awarded the D.C.M. (Distinguished Conduct Medal) for gallant conduct 'in endeavouring whilst wounded and accompanied only by a few men, to capture the enemy's machine-guns. In this attempt, he failed owing to there being no support at hand at the moment.' He was also awarded the French Médaille Militaire. He was son of the late Charles and Emma Mary Thornton, married Hilda in 1911, and lived at 36, Greenhill, Evesham, Worcs. His son Philip was one year old when his father died and a daughter Hilda had died on June 20th 1912. He was educated at Prince Henry's Grammar School, Evesham and served in the South African Campaign and on the North West Frontier of India with the Warwicks in 1908. A Colour Sergeant was a rank introduced during the Napoleonic Wars to reward long service amongst sergeants. Their role was to protect the regimental ensign. A prestigious rank, it was awarded to those who had shown courage in battle.

Other rank soldiers to die included **Private Arthur Taylor,** 26, son of Henry and Sarah Taylor, of 94, Miller St., Aston, Birmingham; husband of Emily Taylor, of 92, Great Colmore St., Edgbaston, Birmingham and **Private Harry Hales**, 22, of Rugby. Taylor is listed on the Ploegsteert Memorial and Hales was buried in the Méteren Cemetery.

The Irish: The 1/ Royal Irish Fusiliers.

Altogether we had...: The BWD recorded '42 killed, 85 wounded' and that it had been 'very wet all day. A perfect advance by Companies concerned & dash & spirit shown by all concerned.'

THE LATE MAJOR W. C. CHRISTIE.

...rdshire Regiment in July, 1913, and was 23 years old

" A Brother Officer " sends the following tribute to the late Major W. C. Christie, of the Royal Warwickshire Regiment, a brief biography of whom appeared in *The Times* of Monday last :—
He was a most gallant officer, a man who absolutely had no sense of fear. Under fire he was exactly the same as he was in the ordinary routine of regimental life. There are, of course, many such ; but somehow he stood out in his brave way as a model to officers and men serving with him. This I well know, as I was with him on August 23-26. For some time before the war he was an instructor for the O.T.C., and wrote a little book which was much used. I believe, in preparing for their examinations. Only on Sunday, little knowing I should see his death in Monday's paper, I was talking with the master of a public school who knew him and who spoke of his keenness and ability. He was the keenest of sportsmen, and some readers of *The Times* may remember him as a soldier rider under National Hunt Rules in the later nineties. He was also a splendid long-distance runner, and, I believe, held the record for the Crick at Rugby. Two years or so ago he ran a long-distance race with the men and officers of his company, finishing an easy first in spite of his 40 years. He could never have done anything small or petty, and in his regiment everyone loved him, and his influence was felt in all ranks.

October 13th: Newspaper cutting found in a pocket at the back of Robert's diary, likely to have been sent out to him by his wife Renie

October 13th: 'Thornton badly wounded'- Colour-Sergeant Thornton's grave on the battlefield- hop poles are in the background
Royal Regiment of Fusiliers (Royal Warwickshire) Museum

October 13th: '21 killed'- a mass grave for Warwicks and other Regiments killed at Méteren
Royal Regiment of Fusiliers (Royal Warwickshire) Museum

A row of Warwicks' graves- note the Antelope badge at the top of each. In the background are Planeboon hamlet and the area fought over during the Battle of Méteren. The Warwicks regrouped after the battle in the homesteads of Planeboon

A contemporary painting of the Battle of Méteren by an eye-witness Régina de Coninck   Daniel Fache

October 14th: 'Got into the village of Méteren at dusk'- a farm used as a billet in October and November 1914. It was from the top of the church that German snipers may have killed Major Christie   Imperial War Museum Q57346

Montgomery: among the names of the officer casualties is Lieutenant Montgomery who wrote in his diary- 'Company in empty houses, officers in nice houses opposite. Good breakfast, eggs, etc. at 5.30 a.m. Marched at 9 a.m. towards Fletre. 'A' and 'C' Companies vanguard. Deployed and attacked village. Captured trenches and houses. About 3 p.m. got hit in lung; five minutes later in knee. Lay in rain three hours. Carried back by four men. Christie and Gilliat'.

Montgomery was sent to the hospital in St. Omer; two days later he arrived at Boulogne by 'hospital train' and arrived at Southampton on October 18th. He was awarded the D.S.O 'for conspicuous gallantry on October 13th, during an attack at Méteren when he turned the enemy out of their trenches with the bayonet'. He was severely wounded.

October 14th

We marched off in rear of the division at 2.30 p.m. and halted on the road for hours. Several burning farms. Got into the village of Méteren at dusk and found a very superior house for our billet. The women of the house had been turned out of their beds at the point of the pistol, and treated disgracefully by German officers the previous night. *The language here is a mixture of French and Belgium,* and very difficult to understand. Wood declares that if he only had enough courage to talk to some of these 'preety' French girls, he would soon pick up enough to keep himself amused.

General Maritz has rebelled against us in S.Africa and stirred up a few *Boers* in Cape Colony to do the same. Horrid traitor. Sent off another parcel of jerseys and gloves. Nurse's brother is seriously wounded in the lung.

The language here is a mixture of French and Belgium: Robert means Flemish, spoken by the natives of Flanders.

Boers: they were defeated in 1902, so Britain's involvement in the War in Europe was an ideal

opportunity for the Boers led by Lieutenant-Colonel Maritz to continue their armed opposition to

British rule in South Africa. They were defeated on 24th October. Maritz fled to neighbouring German West Africa.

The BWD mentions that 'a good few prisoners were taken.'

Guerre Mondiale 1914-18   13 — BAILLEUL - Rue des Moulins et Rue de Cassel

ctober 15th: 'We then marched into Bailleul'. The road sign shows some of the villages on the Warwick's campaign route
ee map V on p.66)

Alan Reed Collection

October 15th

Stood to at 6 a.m.and had a hurried breakfast. Everybody's nerves very strained from yesterday. We did not get on the move till 7 p.m. In the meantime the Germans were being shelled and pushed out of *Armentières* the frontier town. We had a cheery and a much needed change in the shape of a tea party with 'La Grande Dame' as Bentley would call her, aged I would say about 28, Marie and Marcelline and two other girls from across the way. We all fell in love with Marcelline who sang and danced very prettily. The battle was quite forgotten. *M's rug and cake arrived*, also chocolates and tobacco from Renie. The cake of course we had for tea. We then marched into *Bailleul* amidst much public demonstration of joy. We again had most comfortable quarters, and had a hot bath. Les filles sewed up our tattered *khaki*, and mended all our socks.

The 'Expedimentary Force' leaves for the Front i.e. *Winnie and her car leave for Dieppe* in what capacity it is hard to gather.

Armentières: a town at the time with textile mills and breweries; later famous for the song 'Mademoiselle from Armentières' sung by British troops. There were several versions with varying degrees of coarseness but the last line was invariably 'Inky pinky parlez vous.'

Mademoiselle from Armentières

Two German officers crossed the line - parlez vous
Two German officers crossed the line - parlez vous
These German officers crossed the line
On the lookout for some women and some wine
Inky pinky parlez vous.

They came to an inn on top of a rise - parlez vous
A famous inn of bloody great size - parlez vous
They saw a maid all dimples and sighs
They both agreed she'd lovely eyes
Inky pinky parlez vous.

Oh landlord you've a daughter fair - parlez vous
Oh landlord you've a daughter fair - parlez vous
Oh landlord you've a daughter fair
With lily white tits and golden hair
Inky pinky parlez vous.

Nein, nein mein Herr she's much too young - parlez vous
Nein, nein mein Herr she's much too young - parlez vous
Mais non, mon père, I'm not too young
I've often slept with the parson's son
Inky pinky parlez vous.

The rest of the tale I can't relate - parlez vous
It's a very old story but up to date - parlez vous
The story of a man seducing a maid
It could offend - you're too sedate
Inky pinky parlez vous.

M's rug and cake arrived: sent to the Front by his mother.

Bailleul: known to British troops as 'Baloo' or 'Berloo', Bailleul is a small town east of Méteren with at that time several textile mills. It became a forward base and the large asylum was used as a major hospital by the British Army. From 1915, it became a popular behind the lines town for British troops like Poperinge ('Pop' or 'Pops') west of Ypres, where the 'Toc H' movement was started at Talbot House run by a remarkable priest 'Tubby' Clayton who helped men to relax and become 'human' again. His humour helped to keep their spirits up with quips such as 'do not judge a man by his umbrella- it might not be his.'

khaki: Hindustani for dusty, the colour of the British Army field uniforms.

Winnie and her car leave for Dieppe: not many young female members of the V.A.D. would have had their own vehicle but it was not unusual for a number to take their car to the continent.

October 16th
More papers arrived with letters from Renie in all of them. We had a *miserable billet* tonight, and slept on the stone floor. Only an old man, his wife and a screamer. We heard of some awful things done by Germans here to young girls. *Belgian dogs* turned the mill wheel.

October 17th
Marched off at 6 a.m.for Armentières. *The Irish Fusiliers* with their bayonets have been busy all day. *The Germans levied a tax* of 200,000 pounds on the town which was paid on the condition

that it would not be shelled. I went across some fields to a farm and got eggs, butter, coffee and cigarettes. While there the son of the house returned, having been captured by Germans, but owing to their hurried retreat, they could not guard their prisoners. Read Renie's letters again, and at last we marched in. The wild joy of the inhabitants knew no bounds, and the whole triumphal entry was, to say the least of it, a little embarrassing for the officers. I had at one time two girls hanging on to my neck. Old women would seize your hand and kiss it. Children crying for joy. Red wine and water at every street corner, and anything

October 16th: 'Belgian dogs' were used by the Belgians for a variety of tasks- the Army used them for pulling machine guns
British Newspaper Library, Colindale- War Budget 29/8/1914 p.23

the poor people had, that the Germans had left, they gave away, and above all was heard Tommy singing "It's a long way etc." This is *one of the larger towns of Belgium* with some very fine buildings and private houses. The Warwicks were given an area for billeting, and I was sent to find one for 'A' company. A dear little girl led me to the Mayor's house, who said we might occupy a big empty swimming bath, which would have been very comfortable; as there was stacks of clean straw in it. She then led me back to where I had left the company, to find they

had gone. Bentley having marched off to some *railway sheds*. We were inlying picket for the night. The officers assembled at a big hotel for a feed. Here we enjoyed ourselves very much, but am sorry to say Master B. was at his old games again, and did not rejoin the company till well after midnight. At about 2 a.m. there was a wild alarm with shells dropping everywhere, nothing could wake Bentley until the *adjutant* came down to see why we were not standing to. Bentley was once more allowed to get off.

October 17th: 'some very fine buildings'- Armentières Railway Station in 1914   Source: Archives Communales d'Armentières

miserable billet: according to the BWD, they were billeted in farms at Le Leuthe, a hamlet on the Franco-Belgian border.

Belgian dogs: the Belgian Army used dogs to pull equipment such as machine-guns.

The Irish Fusiliers: the BWD records that 'Irish Fusiliers got into touch with the Germans & took the town with a little street fighting.'

The Germans levied a tax: this was not an uncommon practice. It is clear from the diary that the German invasion had been most unpopular amongst the local inhabitants.

one of the larger towns of Belgium: Armentières is actually in France!

railway sheds: confirmed by the BWD which mentions the battalion was 'near the station'.

adjutant: an officer, usually a Captain, who assists the Lieutenant-Colonel in his duties.

October 18th: 'He was shot through his head poor fellow'- the gravestone of Private F. Batchelor at Houplines Cemetery

Sunday October 18th

Left the sheds at 4.30 p.m. and halted on a railway crossing near the lunatic asylum, and had some nice hot coffee given us. Part of the *brigade* advanced and took up a position, and then the shelling began. I was sent to reconnoitre 'A' company's position. Got back and brought the company up, and then returned to the cemetery to report we were in touch with 'C' company on our right and 'B' on our left. The Germans completely wrecked the church. Wrote to M. to thank her for the magnificent pair of glasses she sent me, and a postcard to Renie. During the shelling at the cross roads, some of the men played football with a cap comforter rolled up. Whilst reconnoitring 'A' Company's position, and crawling along a ditch alongside the road, one of our dispatch motor riders passed me at about 50 miles an hour. He was shot through his head poor fellow, and fell twenty yards from where his machine, which was wrecked and remained there for weeks after. He was buried close to his machine.

Sent off parcel to Bob- 200 cigarettes, some stationery and a slab of chocolate.

October 19th

Major Piggott took command of the regiment. Such a mistake after all *Poole* had done, and seen with them. *We remained in our dug outs* on the road all day sleeping and eating. Crawled up into the advanced trenches at 6.30 p.m. and spent the night digging ourselves in. A quiet night.

Commoners meeting held at Sourton to vote £5 for materials at £5 or possibly £10 to provide for a Belgian refugee family in the village.

October 20th: 'The Jocks charged'- one of the Celtic regiments, on the right, marching through Armentières after it was liberated
Source: Archives Communales d'Armentières

brigade: the BWD mentions that the Brigade gained ground and took up position near Houplines, on the eastern outskirts of Armentières. It also records that there was 'heavy firing till 11 p.m.' and that 'Capt. Tomes & 6 men wounded. 1 killed.' The dead despatch rider was probably **Private F. Batchelor**, age unknown, who was buried in the Houplines Communal Cemetery Extension.

Poole: Robert had great respect for his commanding officer Major A.J. Poole who was to rise to the rank of Brigadier-General and received a Companion of the Order of St. Michael and St. George (C.M.G.)

We remained in our dug outs: meanwhile the Seaforth Highlanders attacked Frelinghien, north of the Warwicks' position, supported by the Irish Fusiliers.

October 20th

At about 9 a.m. when the mist had risen, the Germans started shelling us with every description of shell. *One man was killed* close to me, and in the rear trench *my poor servant* was killed by a shell. I had a capital sleep for about two hours. Later on *the Jocks charged* and got home with the bayonet, and we gained a little ground. At about 8 p.m. when quite dark it was possible to move about a bit, *a black cat* came from somewhere and rubbed itself against my legs. 'C' company did not relieve us until after 9 p.m. which was not quite playing the game. We got back to the road and found an old deserted cottage in which we slept.

5th lecture on Nervous System. More of the Expedimentary Force leave for Dieppe including Cicely and Norma. Really it is preposterous these ignorant bumptious girls going out.

October 21st

Cold day in the trenches on the road. All sorts of clothes and eatables came out for the men. I got a good letter from Renie dated October 10th. Mrs. Kendall of Stratford-on-Avon sent me some things too. Went across with a man to milk a cow. In the middle of the operation, a shell pitched right into the farm. Got a nice drop all the same. Just before marching off, we heard a German cheer followed by furious firing. We lined up and were just going to advance to reinforce the company in the advanced trench, when a salvo of shells landed right in our midst, *killing three and wounding five*. There was a lull for about an hour when I got my two platoons safely up into the advanced trenches, when there began a most terrific shelling. Some Germans charged us and were driven back by our rifle fire. The Royal Irish did likewise.

Bob's promotion to Captain is in the *Morning Post!*

one man was killed / my poor servant: according to the Commonwealth War Graves Commission, a
⬤ **Private Tom Crump** died on October 20th and was buried at Boulogne East Cemetery.
⬤ **Private John Albert Baker**, Robert's batman, also died and is remembered on the Ploegsteert Memorial.

the Jocks charged: their WD records that 'C' Company 'attacked and occupied several houses held by enemy snipers' at a cost of 1 officer wounded, 4 other ranks killed and 6 wounded.

a black cat: later named by Robert as Epinette after L'Epinette the hamlet beyond Robert's position on the front line.

killing three and wounding five: there is no mention of these in the BWD which refers to 'Battles raging all round- heavy shelling'.

Morning Post: a conservative daily newspaper published in London from 1772 to 1937, when it was acquired by *The Daily Telegraph*. The news of Robert's promotion was published in the paper over a month after the event and Robert himself did not receive the news until late October.

October 22nd

The shelling began again at daybreak, and continued all day. We had a more or less quiet night, and made use of it by *digging excellent trenches* from 5.30 p.m. till 4 a.m. *My new servant* brought me out some excellent rabbit stew. *Bentley was drunk again*, and had to be taken back to the trench by two N.C.O.s.

Mr. Ellis sent up to know if I would hold a meeting of the committee which I agreed to do. We had a business-like little meeting. Mr. Ellis, Mr. Elstone, Mr. Webber, Mrs. Parsons who I can't stick, Miss Butter and myself followed by port wine and plum cake. Settled about materials and discussed the general situation. I invited the Whitwells to my meeting- they didn't come but called just before and abused the Chapel people hotly and said the Sourton folk wouldn't contribute a penny towards keeping the Belgian refugees.

digging excellent trenches: as static warfare took hold, the hours of darkness would be the time for repair of trenches and for work on defensive barbed wire entanglements.

My new servant: was Private Nobby Hall.

Bentley was drunk again: this was the last time that Bentley behaved unprofessionally when on duty.

October 23rd: 'a shell landed…killing Bentley'- the gravestone of Captain C.A.C. Bentley at Cité Bonjean Cemetery, Armentières

October 23rd

Stood to arms at 4.30. The battle began again shortly after. They charged us again with the same result. Several of the 'C' company's men were hit. *Jack Johnsons* and *coal boxes* started at 11 a.m. and when our big guns began, the noise was terrific, and I thought every minute my ears would burst. Bannerman had heard about Bentley, and went along to put him under arrest. B. saw him coming and staggered out of the trench to meet him when a shell landed between them, killing Bentley and wounded Bannerman. So that was the end of *poor Bentley,* and I took complete command of 'A' Company, much to my joy. I *relieved a company of Leinsters* at 9 p.m. in another section of the line. A most complicated business made all the harder because they did not know where their men were. I shall always consider this one of the luckiest nights of my life. There was the whole company standing above the parapet waiting to be told where to go to. The other company would not get out of the trench. If the Germans had opened fire on us they must have killed a great number. The captain led us down and said his men were ready to file out of the trenches as we filed in. They were not. They were not even dressed, then one of his platoons were lost. The whole relief took three hours to accomplish. During most of this time all my men were fully exposed and waiting in the rear of the trench. My subs and myself crept up and down trying to get this company on the move. If the Germans had opened fire on us we would have had many casualties, as it was not a shot was fired, and I always consider this night the *luckiest of my life.* Then the rations had to be fetched from the cross roads and distributed amongst the company. When the company was finally fixed up, I returned to a large farm which had been used as a company headquarters. There we were given something to eat and drink, and told it was the safest spot in the whole line. They milked the cows, had eggs and bacon every day, and the farm was never shelled. I don't think any of the officers ever went near the trenches. They were deplorable ones, dead bodies everywhere, and *not a single communication trench.* The officers left there about 12 p.m. At 2.30 a.m. Bum crack, wiz bang. Every minute I expected to be our last.

This diary entry includes details for 24th. The two days mark one of the critical moments for the British Front Line.

Jack Johnsons: name given to the burst of a German 15 cm. shell giving out a cloud of black smoke. Jack Johnson was a black American boxer who won the world heavyweight championship in 1908.

coal boxes: another description of a heavy shell that produced black smoke on impact.

poor Bentley: ⬤ **Captain Charles Arthur Campbell Bentley** was aged 35 and his grave is at Cité Bonjean Cemetery in Armentières. He graduated from Edinburgh University and went into the medical profession before joining the Army. He had three children- Charles who was seven when his father died, Sybil six and Hester two.

relieved a company of Leinsters: The 2/ Prince of Wales's Leinster Regiment (also known as Royal Canadians) were part of the 17th Brigade.

luckiest of my life: on a number of occasions during the diary, Robert counts his blessings and was clearly anxious during these long three hours considering the intensity of the rifle-fire and shelling before and after this.

not a single communication trench: this shows his concern for the safety of his men; a communication trench would provide some safety for soldiers on the way to or from the front line trenches.

October 24th

The noise was deafening. Bullets and shells striking everywhere, and *star shells* lit the whole road. To leave the farm as this was going on was certain death. Collected what men I could, fixed bayonets and prepared to charge any Germans advancing down the road. After 40 minutes of this it suddenly fizzled out as quickly as it began. I went down to the trenches to find poor Taylor hit between eyes. Gave him an arm up to the farm, and down towards hospital. Two other men were killed and two wounded. We buried our two and two of the 1st Royal Fusiliers at dawn, and then sat down to a huge bully stew. *Several Germans were seen carrying their dead in.* I retired to my dug out, on the side of the road, and slept most of the day. Everything seemed fairly quiet at night, so three of the servants and myself had an excellent rubber of whist with the cards sent out by M.

2 Post cards from Bob saying he had got some of the parcels and a beauty from Mama- shirt pipe, socks, blanket, and rug. Capital long letter too saying that they were in the middle of a lovely forest when the parcels arrived and were going off on a 4 day journey, *Antwerp he thought.*

Sunday 25th October

As usual the Germans chose Sunday to bombard peaceful farm houses and churches. *They blew my farm* and the farm next door pretty well down, and then started on more distant ones.

Miserable wet day. Good sermon. Nothing to record.

---

star shells: a 'star shell' was a form of artillery used as a means of illuminating the battlefield during the hours of darkness, and also as a means of passing signals (see front cover of the book).

Several Germans were seen carrying their dead in: at this stage of the War and at Christmas time, an unwritten agreement prevailed allowing both sides to bury their dead. However, this became less common when attitudes hardened later.

Antwerp he thought: Antwerp surrendered to the Germans on October 9th. Robert was thinking of a possible link up with three British naval brigades there.

They blew my farm: in the BWD it is recorded that there was 'heavy shelling all day. 'A' Company's farm demolished and burnt'. Robert would not be lucky again with his 'farms'.

October 26th

Thornhill and I had a good sleep in my dug out. Shelling everywhere. I went over to Headquarters to arrange *about cutting up a cow*, which had been killed by a shell, also about making our own tea in *'Leafy Lane'. Black* joined the company. The battle on the left at midnight. *The Seaforths* were driven out, but rallied and charged and retook their trenches. Another battle at dawn, chiefly artillery. 'A' company 2 wounded, 'C' company 15.

Mrs. Driel looked in on her way to Exeter and brought me a wild duck. Driel laughed at me for calling the snipe, woodcock. They were going to Exeter to see about letting Bidlake- how dreadful- what shall I do when they are gone? I don't dare think about it. Painted palings all day. Getting tired of this job. Stubborn *battle raging round Ostende*. Germans determined to get to Calais.

---

about cutting up a cow: the shelling and sniping do not appear to deter Robert from the unending task of finding provisions.

'Leafy Lane': as the War increasingly centred on trenches, troops gave names to their trenches or places where they stayed; names could be descriptive, humorous or reminders of places back home.

Black: BWD mentions on the 25th that 'draft of 1 officer and 113 men arrived' as reinforcements after losses at the Battle of Méteren. The new officer was Captain Frank Henry Black who was killed during the 2nd Battle of Ypres (see p.133).

The Seaforths: are experiencing heavy fighting again; their BWD records that 'enemy later attacked and reoccupied the brewery and several other buildings. Casualties 23 killed, 37 wounded, 3 missing.'

battle raging round Ostende: on October 23rd Ostend harbour was shelled by a French and British flotilla; by the 26th the Germans had been halted at the Yser, the Belgian Army having flooded the area from Nieuport to Dixmude. The Germans used Ostend and Zeebrugge as submarine bases. The British would attempt in 1918 to block these harbours on St. George's Day April 23rd and on May 10th, with little success, although these operations acted as morale boosters at home.

October 27th
Shelling and sniping all day but otherwise quiet. Had some nice liver off the cow, and bacon from a pig we killed at the same time. At 5.30 p.m. they sent a salvo right into the trench, and only wounded one man. Two alarms of heavy firing during the night.

P.C. from Bob dated 19th. All well. Mrs. Driel drove me to the last lecture on Drowning and Poisons, very complicated.

October 28th
Very quiet all day, except for a continuous stream of lead from snipers. *Private Hales* one of my best men, and a great pal of Lce. Cpl. Tovey was hit rather badly, (he died in hospital two days later) but he had just *accounted for* an officer and one man on the barricade guard. Very cold at night. *Freeman* and other officers kept turning into my farm to read the Morning Post, which had been sent out by Renie, and to get warm at my fire.

Susan and I did some splendid shopping in Plymouth and spent £5 on flannel, wool and linen, made up socks, gloves and mufflers. I bought 2 hats, 3 blouses and 4 ties.

October 29th
Nothing doing all day. Getting on well with *the new trench* and dug outs, and communication trench. Men very cheery. *A shell killed one of my men* during the night. Sounds of much firing well on our right. Another game of whist.

October 28th: 'Private Hales one of my best men'- gravestone of Private S. Hale at Cité Bonjean Cemetery, Armentières

October 30th

They shelled our trench badly all day, killing one, and wounding three. *An airship flying five balloons* passed over our trenches. A little dinner at my farm to celebrate my taking command of 'A' company. They drank my health in *rum*. Some kind person (my father) sent me out 500 Russian cigs, and my field glasses and compass, a gift from my kind M-in-law, arrived this evening.

———

Private Hales: a **Private Sidney Hale** died of wounds on October 31st and is buried at Cité Bonjean Cemetery. He was the son of John and Sarah Hale and was born at St. Paul's, Leamington Spa. The family later moved to the Infirmary in Warwick.

accounted for: BWD records that 'we got 1 officer and 3 Germans at sniping and they got only one of ours (so we finished 3 up). Fine!'

Freeman: Captain H.P. Williams-Freeman was in charge of 'C' Company. He was mentioned in Montgomery's diary on October 9th.

the new trench: a standard British trench system would consist of the front line or fire trench, the support line and the reserve line, all linked by communication trenches.

A shell killed one of my men: **Private Herbert Bonham** who is commemorated on the Ploegsteert Memorial. He was married to Ethel Norah of 6 Athelstan Road, Folkestone.

An airship flying five balloons: did Robert see an airship or an observation balloon? If it had been the latter, it probably would have had five parachute-like devices inflated by the wind to keep it pointing in the right direction.

rum: in this instance to celebrate Robert's promotion to captain, news of which took about six weeks to reach him after being gazetted on September 16th. Rum for soldiers on the Front Line was distributed from large jars with the initials S.R.D. (Service Rum Dilute) and was referred to by the troops as *Seldom Reaches Destination* or *Soon Runs Dry*.

October 30th

Sourton Commoners 2nd meeting, rather a violent meeting. Mr. Whitwell dead against the Belgian refugee scheme so they are going to carry it out without him. Mr. Elstone made himself rather objectionable about the *Belgians not working*. The Parish lives for meetings these days.

October 31st

Two men wounded. Thornhill and I walked over to Headquarters during the night to get some butter. Worked on *No.4 platoon* trenches, making *traverses and recesses* till 1.30 a.m. Had another look at them at 5 a.m. before going down into the town to attend a Field General Court Martial.

Hear *the Elk* did something very cowardly and has been cashiered- dreadful.

October 31st: 'Worked on No.4 platoon trenches'
British soldiers trench digging south of Armentières
Imperial War Museum Q57380

———

Belgians not working: it is interesting that this debate was being held in view of the propaganda in the press about 'gallant little Belgium'.

Two men wounded: the BWD- 'A' Coy 'shelled during the day. Sniping incessant, 3 casualties'.

No. 4 platoon: there were 4 platoons in a Company each commanded by a Lieutenant or 2nd Lieutenant.

traverses and recesses: a trench was a series of straight lengths and bays.

the Elk: One of the strangest stories of the Great War and one with an unusually happy ending is that of Lieutenant-Colonel John Elkington who arrived in France in August 1914 as Commanding Officer of the 1/Royal Warwicks. On September 12th he and his colleague, Lieutenant-Colonel Arthur Mainwaring of the Royal Dublin Fusiliers were found guilty by a Field General Court Martial of 'behaving in a scandalous manner unbecoming the character of an officer and gentleman in that they, at St. Quentin, on August 27th, during a retirement following upon an engagement at Ligny, without due cause, agreed together to surrender themselves and the troops under their respective command' to the Mayor of St. Quentin. The defence of their surrender was that it had been motivated solely by their desire to prevent unnecessary loss of life amongst the local population at the hands of the Germans and to secure food and rest for their exhausted and starving men. They did at least avoid conviction for cowardice which could have resulted in the death sentence but were instead cashiered.

Mainwaring was physically and mentally a spent force but Elkington was determined to win back his former rank and respect. Two weeks after his court martial, he joined the Foreign Legion as 'an English gentleman who had made a mistake'. He fought with great courage and received the Médaille Militaire and the coveted Croix de Guerre. They were presented to him when in hospital recovering from a badly shattered leg, suffered when he had single-handedly taken out a German machine-gun after which he lay bleeding in a German trench for twelve hours until rescued. In an interview in the *Daily Sketch* on September 8th 1916, Elkington modestly insisted that 'I did nothing of note. I was with the others in the trenches. I did what everybody else did. We all fought as hard as we could.'

The happy ending? On his return to England, Elkington was granted a full pardon, his former rank was reinstated and he was awarded the Distinguished Service Order by King George V 'in consequence of gallant conduct while serving in the ranks of the Foreign Legion of the French Army'.

The Daily Sketch reported that the Lieutenant-Colonel returned to the Royal Warwickshire Regiment.

Sunday November 1st
Had breakfast at Headquarters and then on to the F.G.C.M. One of the accused was a Munster Fusilier and the other a *Seaforth Highlander,* and it was as much as we could do to understand what they said. Wrote several letters when I got back. *One man wounded in the shoulder.*

Church at Sourton, usual pouring wet day. Felt distracted about Bob all day.

November 2nd
Had a good wash and shave in my farm, and then took the dogs for a walk before dawn. Very fond of these two big *fawn coloured Belgian dogs,* which follow me everywhere. My men killed five sheep and cut them up. Letter from young Winnie who is doing chauffeur to some doctor in Dieppe. Too light to attempt to go down to the trenches tonight.

November 3rd
After going round the trenches before dawn, I made my way into Armentières, and got the shoemaker to make me a new sort of equipment, made of webbing. Went to see my friends of the first night. Had a good meal, sleep and wash and then the little French girl and I *explored a magnificent house* belonging to a millionaire with a palm court in it. The Germans began shelling the town. No casualties today.

The Elk is cashiered. Letter from Bob. *His captain is killed* and he now commands 'A' Company and part of the outpost. They had a hot time holding a farm. 5 of them drive back the Huns. He has 2 dogs besides a cat now. Mrs. Whitwell came in the morning to run down the Belgian refugee scheme. Packed her off with 5 balls of wool to knit. We attend a fracture class which the kind little Dr. gives us. And I bandage his bald head and put his thigh in splints. Hope I get on as well on the exam day.

F.G.C.M.: Field General Court Martial: one of four types of court martial; it consisted of a three man panel chaired by a major or officer of higher rank. The death penalty was the maximum sentence. No soldier from the Regiments of the 10th Brigade was 'shot at dawn' in 1914. However, five Warwicks were executed from 1915-1918 (see p.123-124).

Seaforth Highlander: Private T. McSorley was sentenced to three months Field Punishment No. 1 for drunkenness and a Royal Munster Private M. Molloy was given the same punishment for drunkenness and 'losing by neglect' an article of his equipment- a waterproof sheet. Field Punishment No. 1 entailed being tied to a post or wheel for two hours a day for up to three months, known as 'crucifixion', followed for the rest of the day by hard labour.

One man wounded in the shoulder: BWD reported 'A' Coy 'shelled for most of the day- no casualties from shell fire- sniping incessant. Lt. Bamber and 1 man wounded.'

On a medal sheet, Bamber is recorded as having inflicted an injury on himself- strange, therefore, that he should have received a medal. His wedding was recorded by Robert in 1920.

fawn coloured Belgian dogs: on a number of occasions Robert was adopted by dogs and cats who sensed his good nature towards them.

explored a magnificent house: by now some of the locals would have fled from their homes; the well-to-do would go well behind the lines for the rest of the War. Houses hit by shells would be open to any inquisitive 'visitor' who wished to explore.

his captain is killed: she is referring to Captain Bentley.

November 4th
Guy Cave joined 'A' company at dawn. One man killed and one wounded. The shelling over 1 and 2 platoons was one of the worst we have had. The men counted the shells and had bets among themselves as to who would be the nearest *the total* by 5 p.m. *The total was 378.* We were very alarmed to find two bullet holes clean through our room at the farm. Veal for dinner, and a rubber of bridge after. Renie's parcel of two good shirts and tobacco were most welcome.

November 5th
We both went round the trenches at 4.30 a.m. A man only out yesterday wanted to kill a sniper, but *got one through the head instead.* I had a *very close shave* while I was picking up part of a man's

So Obvious.
The Young and Talkative One: "Who made that 'ole?"
The Fed-up One: "Mice."

November 4th: 'alarmed to find two bullet holes'
Barbara Bruce Bairnsfather

81

equipment near the farm. More shelling everywhere. A pretty aeroplane fight this afternoon. M's glasses were the only ones it was visible with. Moon makes all movements along the trenches dangerous.

Rode Rhon to the meet at Chillaton. Extraordinary gossip put about, about Bob being cashiered!! *Never felt so furious* about anything in my life. I went with Susan to run the mischief to ground, first to the Parsons, then to Mrs. Ellis, then to old Bull. And finally to Mr. Whitwell. The whole thing originated from Mr. W. saying to Bull that the Lieut. Colonel of Mr. Hamilton's Regiment had been cashiered, meaning the Elk, and so the tale flew from one public to another to Bridestowe and everywhere.

Guy Cave: Lieutenants Cave and Bairnsfather would be hospitalised later, suffering from shell shock after the terrible day for the 1/ Warwicks on 25th April 1915 when officer casualties totalled 18 north of Ypres.

the total: the men having bets on the number of shells underlines the spirit within the B.E.F. at the time, reinforcing the 'contemptible indomitable little army' re. Kaiser Wilhelm's description.

The total was 378: a remarkable figure for a small area of conflict.

got one through the head instead: not an uncommon occurrence as men new to the front line and not used to the conditions would take risks or forget about the dangers.

very close shave: another lucky escape for Robert especially after the two bullet holes mentioned in the previous day's diary entry.

Never felt so furious: understandably Renie was upset that Robert had been falsely rumoured to have been cashiered- a punishment that brought disgrace on Elkington.

November 6th
A heavy mist till 8 a.m. *Went round* earlier this morning and then had our breakfast so that the smoke from the chimney by daylight should not give us away. The look out man on my farm threw an awful fit at 9.30 p.m. Had to hold him down and put a spoon between his teeth and send for the doctor.

Glorious weather. Wrote out the exam paper 28 questions set by the little Doctor.

November 7th
Usual round. Breakfast 5.30. Thick mist. *Piggott*, Poole and Freeman strolled round my trenches at about 8 p.m. when all was quiet. Suddenly and without the slightest warning, a *salvo* of six shells landed as we thought on us. Piggott declared his hair was singed. Being more used to this sort of treatment, I was the first to recover from the shock, and went to see if all was well with the others who had mysteriously disappeared. Poole and Piggott were huddled up in two dug outs. *The sentries were amused* and just 'carrying on.' Freeman was off back to his own trench, and *Jackson* full of cheap chat as usual. Germans sending up star shells and *singing all night*. One casualty tonight.

2 long letters from Bob saying he is between Lille and Armentières. His ears splendid.

Sunday November 8th
A disastrous day for my company and myself. One killed and three wounded by a shell at 8 a.m. Breakfast late. Nobby Hall my servant who went to the farm to get us some water was shot in the arm. Three men who were in the machine-gun section were hit. When I got back to the farm after my round, I found it full of wounded. Thick mist, so got them all off to hospital, and then

went down again to hold a little service in the trenches. On returning was told there had been a fire in my dug out, and that my precious field glasses and compass were utterly ruined. Wood held a service in Leafy Lane also.

Went to Church at Bridestowe. Rather a silly sermon.

Went round (the trenches): to check on his men on the front line.

The BWD mentioned that 'Lt-Col. Piggott went sick'- Major Poole took command of the Battalion.

Piggott: if Robert was right, Piggott has made a swift recovery!

salvo: corroborated by the BWD: 'some shelling of 'A' Company in afternoon- one casualty'.

The sentries were amused: it would not be the first time that the 'other ranks' would be amused by the reaction of some officers (especially newly-arrived ones) to heavy shelling.

Jackson: Lieutenant, later Captain, A.H.K. Jackson received a D.S.O and an M.C. and Brigadier-General Hull reported in January 1915 that he 'has been brought to my notice before- on this occasion by skilful leading he established himself within 100 yards of the enemy's trenches where he held out until ordered to retire. I recommend him for mention in despatches.'

singing all night: the opposing trenches were close enough to hear the enemy singing: a precursor to the Christmas Truce.

A disastrous day: 'A' Company is still under sustained German shelling; the BWD does mention 'usual sustained shelling and sniping- 1 killed and 5 wounded.'

November 9th
A party of snipers in a shattered building in front were continually killing and wounding my men, so I got permission to find the gunner responsible for this area. Having pointed out the building to him, from a tower in the middle of the town, he directed his battery by telephone, one and a half miles in rear, and his first shot landed clean into the building, having repeated this nine times, we were never again bothered with them. The men were delighted. I could not get back till dusk, and so went into Armentières. And had lunch and tea with a very nice French family. Germaine being very concerned about my cold and deafness. As I was getting back, I saw *my farm* and the one next to it in flames. Evidently a little reprisal for my gunner's work this morning. Freeman called round and had a chat in my dug out, about Warwickshire people.

November 10th
Went round before daylight and had a talk to Poole who I like very much. Young Jackson as giddy as ever, and had secured two shot guns from the Mayor of the town, and meant to shoot partridges. Quite a change. Went on to 'A' company and found them about to turn in for the day after a hard night's work *on their parapets,* so went back to Headquarters and on into the town and had breakfast with Madame and her pretty daughter Germaine who said my French was becoming perfect. I of course replied that that was due to her perfect teaching. A mixed up rumour of the capture of 20,000 Germans, 66 guns and a convoy. *Sperry* had an awful nightmare and when awake insisted on seeing a full blown German coming down the steps into the dug out. As he went out to make sure, a tin of bully fell off the shelf and hit him on the head, then he was quite sure the Germans were on us.

Letter from Bob. Willie went out with the Harriers. I think this hunting is altogether too footling. Mrs. Driel walked back with me and we visited the Bridestowe Belgians.

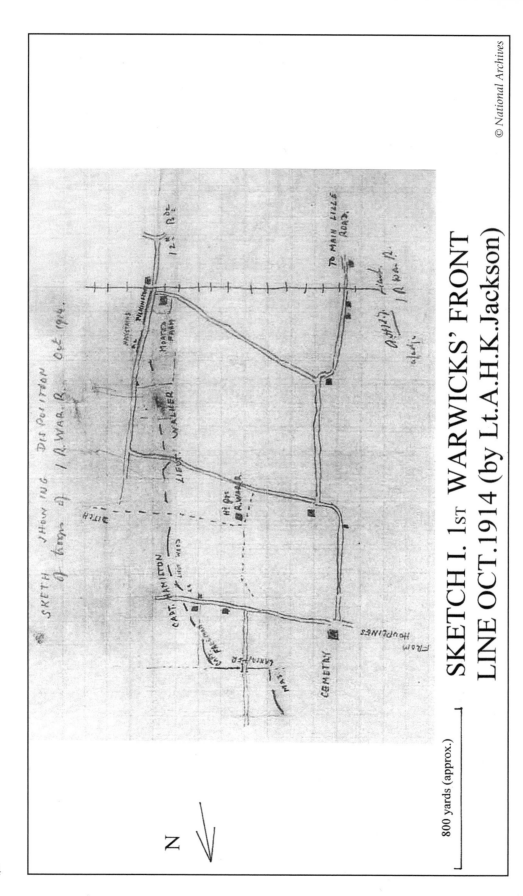

SKETCH I. 1st WARWICKS' FRONT LINE OCT.1914 (by Lt.A.H.K.Jackson)

800 yards (approx.)

N

84

my farm: the BWD records that 'Hamilton's farm shelled and burnt'- Robert was unlucky with 'his' farms! Lieutenant Jackson drew a sketch of the Warwicks' position near Houplines (see sketch I opposite). It shows Robert's 'A' Company position east of Houplines cemetery and one of the dark squares just behind his line would have been 'Hamilton's farm'.

On this day Winston Churchill spoke at the Guildhall, in London and said that the British people had taken for themselves the motto- 'Business carried on as usual during alterations on the map of Europe'.

on their parapets: the side of the trench facing No Man's Land; the rear wall was called the *parados.*

Sperry: Robert's new batman who would keep in touch and reappear when Robert was in the Isle of Wight in 1915. This amusing incident would help to steady the nerves following a long and stressful spell on duty; humour often provided some welcome relief to all concerned.

November 11th
The rains have set in. Rifle and cannonading all day. We made up our minds we would just dine in the farm, and then sleep in the dug out. We were just going to start dinner when the second bombardment of my farm started. Every gun, rifle, and maxim opened on it. The noise was indescribable, bullets fizzed in from every angle. Shells burst on the road just in front and altogether it was *most unpleasant. Poor Black and Thornhill* who were with me thought the end had really come. I pushed them into the stable and *began to whistle.* I had been through this sort of thing before. The whistling had the effect of quietening them down. Nothing else could be heard. I dashed across to the room where Cave and his servant had remained and found they had both said their prayers. It lasted three quarters of an hour and then once more fizzled out, when we all went down to the trenches to see how the men had fared and found they had had an awful time of it, but nobody touched. Reported to Headquarters and then we all sat down to an enormous bully stew, and a good game of bridge and then turned into our dug outs.

5 letters from Bob!

November 12th
I slept the whole day, and then went down to the company after dark, and got caught again with shrapnel and heavies. My poor old ears didn't get a chance. Remained in Wood's dug out till 9 p.m. and then dodged the snipers and searchlights up to my dug out. Sperry and *Greening* have brought the stove out of the farm, and we propose occupying the dug out only in future.

November 13th
We slept most of the day after working on the dug out till 3 a.m. Our trenches are *in an awful condition,* but the men are still quite cheerful.

November 14th
Poured with rain all day. Something must be done to make the roof of our dug out waterproof. Over *three hundred shells* were fired over our dug out and landed in a field just the other side. No damage. We slept through most of it.

---

most unpleasant: in the circumstances an understatement.

Poor Black and Thornhill: For Black see p.133. ⚫ **Geoffrey Holland Thornhill** died on May 10th 1917 and was buried at Chorleywood Road Cemetery. He was 28.

began to whistle: a method quite often used to calm nerves.

Greening: may be the same **Private Arthur Greening** who died on April 26th 1915 during the 2nd Battle of Ypres and is remembered on the Menin Gate Memorial at Ypres (see p.35).

in an awful condition: the BWD reinforces this remark- 'incessant shelling all day. Heavy incessant rain. Discomfort indescribable.' The men now had to cope with another 'enemy'- the mud.

three hundred shells: the men are now getting used to the daily shelling; even the BWD states that there was 'nothing of importance'. Private William Tapp mentions in his diary that there were '2 shells a minute'.

At a Field General Court Martial on November 13th, Private Hill of the Warwicks was convicted of drunkenness and sentenced to three months of Field Punishment No. 1. Private Ward received the same sentence for drunkenness in the field and Private Boyne of the Royal Dublin Fusiliers had 'gone to hospital and was not available for trial having wilfully injured himself with intent to render himself unfit for service.'

The Fatalist.

" I'm sure they'll 'ear this damn thing squeakin'."

November 15th: 'The blooming barrow made a noise'- the problem of noise alerting the enemy is captured by Bairnsfather's cartoon   Barbara Bruce Bairnsfather

Sunday November 15th

Went down to see about a railway wagon tarpaulin for our roof. When it was dark the servants and I set off to fetch it. This was very exciting. We had to cut it up at the siding to get it into the barrow, and then *the blooming barrow* made a noise loud enough for any German to hear. We got it back at last, and then I had another lucky second. *A shrapnel burst* right across the road not ten yards from where Freeman and I were standing. After working all night on it we completed the job and put two feet of earth on top so that *aeroplanes* could not spot it.

Mercy and I biked to Paignton. A fearful thunderstorm came on but we kept pretty dry and had lunch on the sands. We saw over the *American hospital* a wonderful place and had talks with the soldiers. I saw 3 Warwicks men. *Chappell* who knew Bob well and said he had been with him in Africa and India. Kelsey and Luton declared Bob was a prisoner of war. Couldn't persuade him otherwise and he gave me an address to find out about him, so I wrote to Col. Clyne.

the blooming barrow: an incident that is reminiscent of the Bairnsfather cartoon on this page.

A shrapnel burst: a shell filled with small lead balls named after General Henry Shrapnel who was Inspector of Artillery in the early 19th century. A time fuse would ignite a charge of explosives above ground so that the lead balls would rain on troops in open ground.

aeroplanes: in 1914 they were used mostly for observation and reconnaissance. Germany had about 250, France 150 and Britain 60. The Royal Flying Corps was established in 1912 by Minister of War Richard Haldane who was also instrumental in the creation of the Territorial Force and the B.E.F. as a continental task force. The R.F.C. became the Royal Air Force on April 1st 1918. By the end of the War the number of aircraft had increased dramatically from 60 to 22,000 with over 290,000 personnel.

American hospital: In September 1914, 'Oldway' House near Paignton in Devon, described by the locals as 'little Versailles' was converted by Paris Singer, third son of New York-based Isaac Singer the inventor of the sewing machine. It was known as the American Women's War Relief Hospital. Every available space was utilised to house rows of beds for the wounded soldiers being brought back to England from the trenches of France and Belgium. In November 1914, Queen Mary visited the hospital.

Chappell: a **Private Stanley Chappell** died in action on April 15th 1918 and is commemorated on the Ploegsteert Memorial.

November 16th

The bottom of the dug out is *below the level of the ditch* so there is two feet of water under us. We lie on a thick bedding of straw which is on a big board. But something must be done as the dug out is beginning to smell. We decide to have another night on it. At about 2 a.m. when we had got rid of most of the stinking rotten straw underneath and were having a well earned smoke, a coal box landed exactly six feet in rear of the dug out. It shook the ground like a jelly and knocked down everything on the shelves, but *did not explode,* or naturally this diary would never have been found. One more piece of extraordinary luck. Orders came up shortly after and we hear we are to move. About time. *Some say Ypres,* and some say Egypt, but in any case I think we are in for some pretty dirty work.

6 letters from Bob. And 2 P. Cards. He has had a hot time of it and has been through the battle of Méteren. His lovely glasses and compass got spoiled by *someone leaving a candle* in the dugout. Rotten luck. Letter from Miss Ratallie actually ordering me to send her clothes for the Bridestowe refugees. I replied that I was keeping them for mine.

" Where did that one go to ? "

November 16th: 'one more piece of extraordinary luck'- the kind of incident that might have inspired this cartoon   Barbara Bruce Bairnsfather

November 17th

Freeman and I got down before light into the town to say good bye to all our good friends. We could not find a café for a long time, as most of the inhabitants had been shelled out of the town. We eventually found my little girl and her mother of the first night who were still quite cheery and bright. They gave us a nice breakfast and let us wash and shave in their bedrooms. We then turned into another large house where the owners were even more kind, and gave us more eggs and coffee and cognac, and *a comfortable fire* to sit by. A very pleasant day. Got back to the dug out to find a huge mail from home with another change sent out by Renie.

Saw Mrs. Ellis, Mrs. Parsons and Mrs.Ball about the refugees and Miss Hamlyn's interference has made a great stir in Sourton.

below the level of the ditch: this would become a major problem for troops fighting in the trenches in Flanders which is low lying. In some areas water would be encountered after a couple of feet of digging.

did not explode: another lucky escape; a shell that failed to explode was called a 'dud'.

Some say Ypres: the Battalion would move from the area on November 21st and go across the border into Belgium and become engaged in trench warfare in the Ploegsteert area or 'Plug Street' as it was affectionately known by the British troops.

someone leaving a candle: the reason for the fire in Robert's dug out as recorded in his diary on November 8th.

November 18th: 'Sat in the dug out all day'-
British officer relaxing in 1914
Imperial War Museum Q53502

a comfortable fire: in Armentières, some of the locals fled for safety. Those who did remain, continued to show their gratitude towards the British troops.

November 18th
Sat in the dug out all day till 6 p.m. when *the Leinster regiment* relieved us. I don't envy them their job in these trenches, but believe they have had a very soft time lately. Fine and sunny all day. *Tyler* and Cave with old Sperry went into the town. We had no orders and no rendezvous, and just got out of the firing line, *ecce dum* and marched slap for *Pont Dieppe* where we billeted very comfortably in a huge *brasserie*.

Sweet letter from Bob- he says 20,000 prisoners taken- 66 guns and a whole convoy.

November 19th
We rested all day and watched the snow. Cave, who speaks the language like a native, went out and bought all kinds of delicious things for our supper. We celebrated the termination of our stay at Armentières in good old English style and *enjoyed ourselves* very much.

November 18th: 'huge brasserie'- Brasserie (brewery) l'Espérance
at Pont de Nieppe is the tallest building on the left where soldiers
had longed-for and welcome baths in large wooden beer vats
Musée de Nieppe

the Leinster regiment: it was their first battalion, part of the 17th Brigade, that billeted in the lunatic asylum at Armentières; their BWD mentions L'Epinette when relieving the Warwicks.

Tyler: probably not the same man but a
🔵 **Private Albert Tyler** of the Royal Warwickshire Regiment died on September 4th 1918 and his name is on the Loos Memorial.

ecce dum: Robert's Latin at Trinity College, Glenalmond coming to the fore here- 'just as quickly as we could'.

Pont Dieppe: he means Pont de Nieppe.

brasserie: French and Belgian towns had their own local breweries and their large rooms were ideal to billet troops. In some cases the vats were used as communal baths and it is said that some brewers, having had soldiers washing in their vats during the day, would make beer in the same vats at night! This was the Brasserie l'Espérance (Hope) destroyed during the War and never rebuilt (see photo opposite).

enjoyed ourselves: quite a relief after such a sustained and testing time on the Front Line.

November 20th

I marched the company down to a *huge linen factory* for a real wash. We arrived at it at 7.30 a.m. Bitterly cold and deep snow, the ground floor of the factory had been divided by a match board partition. On one side were 200 women and girls, and on the other 200 stark naked Tommies in huge tubs, each of which held ten men. Beautiful hot water, plenty of soap, hot towels and brand new shirts, pants, vests and socks for each man to put on when clean and dry. By the time they had these on, their trousers, jackets and *puttees* had been thoroughly shaken,

At the Brewery Baths
" You chuck another sardine at me, my lad, and you'll hear from my solicitors "

November 20th: 'a real wash'- Robert's 'A' Company took their baths in the linen factory in Pont de Nieppe. Some may have had baths in the 'Brasserie' with Bairnsfather's 'C' Company, the inspiration for this cartoon
Barbara Bruce Bairnsfather

brushed and ironed by the women next door. The men were delighted with the whole thing, and *the A.S.C.* which arranged it all are to be congratulated for their well thought out scheme. We then marched off to clean billets nearer Armentières. 'A' company officers once more secured *the best billets* to be had, chiefly due to guide Cave and his persuasive eloquence. The other company officers became rather jealous about it, so we decided to hand it over to them and look for others. Cave succeeded and we had a most cheery supper party with a French girl each. We played écarté with them later and then sang songs in most wonderful French, and then I took on an old Belgian refugee, who fought all *through 1870*, in a game of piquet in French. The dear old fellow was much too polite to beat me, so I beat him, much to his delight. Bruce *Bairnsfather*, now of *Bystander* fame, joined the regiment and is given the machine-gun.

huge linen factory: in Pont de Nieppe it was the factory 'Jeanson' known by the troops as the 'blue factory'. On December 3rd it was inspected by King George V and the Prince of Wales. On December 16th 1914, during Sunday Mass, the local priest and a British Army chaplain delivered a sermon in their respective languages. The subject was the supposed goings-on between the soldiers and French women in the 'blue factory'; the result being that 'in order to avoid any temptation' the soldiers in the baths would be separated from the 'washer women' by a row of small trucks. A corporal would guard over the soldiers and 'deux contre-dames très sérieuses' would watch over the French girls!

puttees: long strips of cloth wound round the leg from ankle to knee for protection and support - from the Hindu word for 'bandage'.

the A.S.C.: the Army Service Corps worked wonders in trying circumstances. This system of looking after the hygiene of the troops who had just had a tour of duty on the front line would become standard procedure; one method of delousing garments was to oven bake them!

the best billets: good fortune in finding the most comfortable accommodation seems to follow Robert wherever he goes- his improving command of French also helped.

through 1870: a reference to the Franco-Prussian war of 1870-71 which concluded with the ignominious defeat of the armies of Emperor Napoleon III and the annexation of Alsace and most of Lorraine by the Prussians. Hence the general French desire for revenge or 'esprit revanchard'. It is not the first time that Robert incorrectly thinks he is in Belgium.

Bairnsfather: the first mention of Bruce Bairnsfather in the diary. He was in charge of the Battalion's machine-gun section which consisted in 1914 of two teams of six men in each; each team had a Maxim gun, introduced in 1890 and capable of firing 400 rounds per minute or a Vickers gun, first used in 1912 (450 rounds per minute). Bruce 'rejoined' the Warwicks after the start of the War. On September 12th he was commissioned as a 2nd Lieutenant into the 3rd Battalion and moved to the barracks on the Isle of Wight before being allocated to the 1st Battalion as a Machine-Gun Officer.

Bystander: was a British weekly magazine which featured reviews, topical sketches and short stories. Fleet Street-based, it was established by William Comyns Beaumont in 1903. Bairnsfather sent a sketch to the magazine entitled 'Where did that one go to?' (see p.87). To his surprise, a few weeks later, he received a cheque for it and it was published in 1915. It became the first of a running series of cartoons known as 'Fragments from France'.

A British position north of Plugstreet Wood
Imperial War Museum Q50688

Plugstreet Wood in 1918 when captured by the Germans- photographed by Leutnant Kurt Zehmisch
In Flanders Fields Museum, Ypres

November 20th
2 letters from Bob, one very exciting about the blowing up of the farm and the fright of the young subs. Pellow came up to see 3 calves and valued them at £21.10 so have offered them to Palmer for this. Very busy day. Children awfully noisy.

November 21st
'M. Guy Cave' as he is now called and I walked into *Nieppe* to get company pay, but finding *the cashier* away for the day, walked back. We ('A' company warriors) had a most excellent lunch at our private house, while all the other officers had to be content on bully stew. The regiment moved off at 3 p.m. for our new trenches near *the famous Plugstreet Wood*. We arrived at our respective rest billets behind the advanced trenches at about 6 p.m. Once again 'A' company fell on their feet in the

way of farm billets. The men had good barns with lots of straw, and the officers had two very nice farm houses. We four with the Sergt. Major and *Q.M.S.* sat round our roaring fire till after 11 p.m. yarning. (We are all out of France now.)

———◆———

Nieppe: described by Bairnsfather as 'a dirty red-brick town with a good sprinkling of factory chimneys and strange feel; rather the same as one of the Potteries towns'.

the cashier: 'The Field Service Pocket Book 1914' states that 'funds required for all services will be drawn on imprest from the base cashier or a field cashier.' As a Captain, Robert was responsible for issuing the pay to the soldiers in his Company.

the famous Plugstreet Wood: By 1916, when this version of the diary was written, the wood north of the Belgian village of Ploegsteert had become 'famous'. The British soldiers had their own inimitable way of adapting the spelling and pronunciation of French and Belgian towns; e.g. Ypres became 'Wipers'.
The wood became well known as it would be used to familiarise newly-arrived units to trench warfare and conditions. After 1914 it was a relatively quiet sector but, during the German final push in April 1918, the wood and Ploegsteert village were captured, only to be liberated in September 1918.

The area round the wood is famous for the personalities who served there:

- **Winston Churchill**: commanded the 6/ Royal Scots Fusiliers south of the wood. He painted Laurence Farm which was his advanced H.Q.

- **Anthony Eden:** Churchill's Foreign Secretary in the Second World War and Prime Minister 1955-57, served in the Plug Street area in April 1916 as a subaltern in 21/ King's Royal Rifle Corps.

- **Adof Hitler:** was in the 16th Bavarian Reserve Infantry Regiment on the front line north-east of Messines during the winter of 1914-15 and when he was wounded in the arm, he was treated in the crypt of Messines Church which is north of the wood. Like his future adversary Churchill, Hitler was a painter and the ruins of the church were a subject for one of his studies.

Q.M.S.: Quarter Master Sergeant

November 21st: 'our trenches near the famous Plugstreet Wood'- bread for the troops was regularly provided by the Belgian baker with his dogs and cart in the Plug Street area in November and December 1914
Imperial War Museum Q56167

November 21st: 'Hyde Park Corner' in Plugstreet Wood before destruction by shelling. The track on the left goes to Hill 63 and the road to the right to Messines
Claude Verhaeghe

Winston Churchill was based in Ploegsteert in 1916- the plaque on the Town Hall depicts a 2nd World War Churchill surveying a Great War trench!

THE ETERNAL QUESTION
"When the 'ell is it goin' to be strawberry?"

November 23rd: 'Rations came up at 7.30 p.m.'-
Bairnsfather's 'eternal question', inevitably
unanswered, was 'when will it NOT be plum and
apple jam?'! Barbara Bruce Bairnsfather

Sunday November 22nd

Woken at 7 a.m.by much dripping from the ceiling.
The R.F.A. will no longer occupy the room above.
The adjutant and others as usual seemed to prefer
our farm to others. *Major Poole* went home on leave.
A nice gunner major came in to have tea and a chat,
and to tell us about his children as he calls his
battery of six inch guns. We relieved the Dublin
Fusiliers in their front line trenches (they all appear
to be front line trenches and very much front line
too)- a bad relief. The men could not be persuaded
to come out of their dug outs. Getting up to the
trenches appeared the most dangerous thing we had
done yet. Bullets seemed to be fired at you from
about ten yards distance. One could not help an
occasional 'duck.' Going between the two ruined
farms the noise of the *snipers'* bullets made one
wonder what it was like in the actual trenches. These
were in a shocking way. Dead bodies everywhere
and the stink was awful. Black, Cave and self in dug
outs on *the sunken road* with our line of trenches a
few yards above us. Wood had No.1 platoon with
the Sergt. Major on our left. A quiet night on the
whole.

Very cold again. Went to Church at Sourton. Spent
the afternoon looking up my Red Cross.

November 23rd

Very sleepy all day after the anxiety of the relief last
night. *I would sooner do* a great many things before
relieve a company for the first time in
unknown trenches and under a hot fire
the whole time. Snipers from all directions
all day and night. *Rations came up at 7.30
p.m.* and I was thankful when they were all
safely distributed without any casualties.
On watch till 2 a.m.

———

The R.F.A.: the Royal Field Artillery was
one of three branches of the Royal
Regiment of Artillery. It operated field
guns like the 18 pounder. The other
branches were the Royal Horse Artillery
which supported cavalry with lighter guns
and the Royal Garrison Artillery for heavier
guns such as the 60 pounder.

*November 22nd: 'We relieved the Dublin Fusiliers'- Royal
Dublin Fusiliers in Plugstreet Wood* Imperial War Museum Q50690

Major Poole: was replaced by Major Lancaster according to the BWD.

snipers: the BWD confirms this incident- 'incessant sniping all day from all sides- very little
shelling- 2 killed- 2 wounded'. ● **Private G. Bradley** and ● **Private G.R. Jackson** aged 25 and
a native of Bermondsey London were the two killed that day and were buried at Prowse Point
Cemetery. The Warwickshire line, north of Plugstreet Wood, was in the hamlet of St.Yves, also
referred to as St. Yvon. The Germans opposite occupied ground which gradually rises to become

the Messines ridge; from ruined buildings the Germans could easily snipe at the British coming down from La Hutte and Hill 63.

the sunken road: see photo on p.120.

I would sooner do: Robert showing his attention to detail and to the safety of his men. Battalions would have an officer whose duties included reconnaissance of advanced positions before his unit moved up to the line; one such officer was the poet Edmund Blunden who served in the Royal Sussex Regiment.

Rations came up at 7.30 p.m: it was normally the time when hot food was brought in from behind the lines if circumstances allowed.

November 24th

We had to set-to in earnest to build up our parapets which had been knocked down during the day. Came across *several dead bodies* buried in the trench.

Very cold again. Went to Church at Sourton. Spent the afternoon looking up my Red Cross. I rode and met Sylvia and Mrs Driel. Mrs Driel walked back with me and stopped to lunch. I felt horribly upset at having to kill a poor thrush who was very badly hurt as I did it so clumsily. We worked hard at looking up Red Cross.

November 25th

Poor old Sperry was hit by shrapnel while bringing me my breakfast. This makes my fifth servant, one dismissed for being drunk, two killed and two wounded. He went off on a stretcher by night. I gave him a letter for Renie. *Epinette, my trench cat* is very amusing in the straw. Turned in at 3.15 a.m. for a sleep.

I rode over to Driels and she drove me to the school at Lew where the exam was to be held. We had three very simple questions about Bleeding, Fractures and Artificial Respiration and nearly an hour to do it in while the others were being examined in practical work and *Viva Voce*

"**There goes our blinkin' parapet again.**"

November 24th: 'We had to set-to in earnest to build up our parapets'- the soldiers could never relax and constant shelling meant that repairs had to be carried out regularly
Barbara Bruce Bairnsfather

questions. Miss Miller who I was questioned with, was a treat. When asked to find the femeral artery on a wretched little boy she fumbled for 10 minutes without finding it and when the Dr. asked what she would do after showing her where it was, she said she would pull the leg out to stop the bleeding and apply a broomstick for a tourniquet.

November 26th

My new servant *Pte. Gregory* ('double ginger' of truce fame) cannot make tea or anything approaching the taste of it. Our guns nearly shelled *the Somersets* out of their trenches in mistake for the Germans. Some of our batteries are said to be commanded by officers with queer sounding names. We got *back to our farm* where our cook Jimmy Long presented me with a foaming glass of beer. 500 more cigarettes from father. Long letter from Renie and also one from M, Father and many others.

several dead bodies: of the 2nd Seaforth Highlanders whom the Warwicks had relieved.

Poor old Sperry: whilst lucky with the quality of his billets, Robert was not so fortunate with his batmen. Sperry returned to England and was transported by train to the Royal Aberdeen Hospital to recuperate.

Epinette, my trench cat: when the Battalion had been on the Front Line east of Armentières, L'Epinette hamlet was beyond their line.

Viva Voce: by oral examination (Latin for 'living voice').

Pte. Gregory: was to play a major role in the Christmas Truce. A ⚫ **Private Ronald Christopher Gregory** died on September 8th 1918 and was buried at the Abbeville Communal Cemetery Extension but was 19 when he died which would have made him 15 in 1914- so unlikely to have been the same 'double ginger'.

the Somersets: 1/ Somerset Light Infantry were on the right flank of the Warwicks, east of the wood.

back to our farm: the BWD records that they were relieved by the Royal Dublin Fusiliers and were back in billets at Hill 63 which would become the place for the reserve Battalion to the Brigade. From now on, a routine is established whereby the Warwicks and the Dublin Fusiliers take turns on the Front Line. Four or five days on duty and four to six days in reserve or in billets at Pont de Nieppe, then La Crèche.

The WARWICKS are "holding their own."

November 27th: Renie received a postcard from Robert but one assumes not this one…   Alan Reed Collection

November 27th

First shave for eight days. In reply to *'mother and baby'*- the Germans put a shell right through our farm. We were furious. I took charge of 'A and 'B' companies and marched them *back to Nieppe* for their rest. Jackson's job as Adjutant seems to have swollen his head.

P.C. from Bob. *'The Bulwark'* was blown up by accident with a loss of 700.

November 28th

'A' and 'B' companies did a *route march*.

Good news in Poland. 2 German Army Corps wiped out. Kitty, Hilda and Evelyn have lost their husbands poor little souls.

Dear ————
"At present we are staying at a farm . . . . "

November 27th: 'the Germans put a shell right through our farm'- an experience shared by Bairnsfather and other Warwicks officers at this time

Sunday November 29th

Church service at 11 a.m. *Marched back* to our farm for the night (5 miles) before going into the trenches again. Met a gun team returning for a rest. It was stuck in the mud and expected us to wait until it was dug out. It was pitch dark.

Heard from Coutts that Cox had paid in £50.4 for Bob's kit allowance and mobilisation and £68.6.10 for pay from August 5th to November 30th jolly good pay. Have written to them to tell them to pay off the debt. Vile weather, church at Sourton.

'mother and baby': 'mother' was the name given to the prototype of the 9.2 inch Mark I heavy siege howitzer, weighing 15 tons with a range of 10,000 yards. Following trials in July 1914, these heavy guns were sent to the Western Front in November. 'Baby' refers to the shells.

back to Nieppe: the Warwicks were relieved by the Seaforth Highlanders at Hill 63 and moved to billets at the brewery L'Espérance at Pont de Nieppe- a popular resting place with the men, it is safe to assume.

The Battalion Diary for the Royal Dublin Fusiliers recorded that 'trenches owing to thaw are in many places in a very bad condition.'

'The Bulwark': H.M.S. Bulwark was built in 1902 and was a pre-dreadnought battleship accidentally destroyed by an explosion in its ammunition store at Sheerness in the Medway on November 26th with only a dozen survivors.

route march: seems odd that they should be doing a route march- energy conservation might have been more appropriate.

Good news in Poland: on November 22nd the Russians defeated the Austrians in southern Poland around Krakow with about 6,000 prisoners taken but on November 23rd the Germans broke through the Russian line near Lodz.

Marched back: to relieve Seaforth Highlanders at Hill 63.

November 30th: 'our guns knocked out ...'-British Artillery 6" Howitzer in Plugstreet Wood   Imperial War Museum Q56162

November 30th

Went round to see the Jocks and got some coke from them. They have had a bad shelling this time until our guns knocked out two German trench mortars. We arrived at the trenches at 7 p.m. and relieved the Dublins. We were lucky in getting a dull and windy night when we could neither be seen nor heard. It is a marvel to me we are not hit along this track to the sunken road. My orderly arrived at 2.30 a.m. to say that 20 more men are to be sent to me tomorrow. Where can I put them? There are only a dozen dug outs standing and they are half full of water.

November 30th: 'We arrived at the trenches'- a typical reinforced wooden track used for troop, equipment and supply movement around Plugstreet Wood Claude Verhaeghe

Blowing a gale and pouring in torrents. Day too bad for hunting.

December 1st
Felt in a very bad temper today as the Dublin officer who has been living in my dug out has left it in a filthy condition. *Thirty men* of the draft arrived at dusk in a hail of bullets. Felt very *sorry for them*, but distributed them amongst the older hands. Worked all night on our parapets, and turned in at 5.30 a.m. *One man killed and buried at night, and one wounded.*

December 2nd
One man killed and one man wounded. Good work by night again. Made my dug out more comfortable. The full moon over these desolate shattered remains of buildings is a very sad sight.

Vile vile vile day. Too bad to do anything but stop indoors.

---

thirty men: according to the BWD altogether 89 men- Captain Rigg and 2nd Lieutenant Nicolai arrived as reinforcements. **Lieutenant Ronald Claud Nicolai**, 22, would later be killed on the fateful day April 25th 1915 near Ypres and is remembered on the Menin Gate (see p.35). He was son of Adolfo and Claudia Nicolai of Cranbrook, Kent. The panels on the Menin Gate commemorate more than 54,000 soldiers who have no known grave and who died up to August 15th 1917. The others, more than 34,000, who died in the final 15 months of the War, are recorded on the back wall of Tyne Cot Cemetery. With nearly 12,000 graves, Tyne Cot is the largest British Military Cemetery in the world, situated near the village of Passchendaele.

sorry for them: it would have been quite a baptism of fire for the new arrivals and Robert was sensitive to their situation.

One man killed and buried at night, and one wounded: recorded in the Brigade but not the Battalion War Diary. **Private Arthur Henry Ashford** died on that day, but his grave was lost. He is remembered on the Ploegsteert Memorial at Hyde Park Corner at the western end of Mud Lane. The memorial bears the names of more than 11,000 soldiers who have no known graves and who were killed in nearby battles.

In his OD Robert recorded that 'General Wilson gave me a lift back from H.Q. in his car.' Wilson was liaison officer to the French Army.

According to the Brigade War Diary, King George V and the Prince of Wales visited Headquarters at Nieppe, inspected the troops and presented Distinguished Conduct Medals to Privates James and Darlow for 'gallantry on 13th October. Volunteered to go forward to a place where the greatest danger was to be expected and helped to bring in Major Christie who was dangerously wounded.' It was also recorded that the Warwicks' communication trench was pumped out by Royal Engineers. The BWD records that Major Poole returned and reassumed command.

December 3rd
Quiet day. 80 batteries of French and English played the devil with *Messines*, Cave said it was the sight of his life. Fearful row. We shall hear later what the target was. More plum pudding arrives. Shall have to get rid of Gregory as a servant.

December 4th
The Dubs relieved us at 7 p.m. We implored them to do some more work on the parapets, and to leave the trenches clean. They are a fearful lot. Marched to our farm, where we found a roaring fire, sacked Gregory. Took on *Casswell*.

December 5th

Get the men shaved and washed and divided the men of the draft equally among the platoons. We *marched back* on our own as no orders were forthcoming. Dined together in a baker's shop, and had a game of bridge.

Robert wrote in his OD- 'The full moon at midnight over these shattered buildings is a most sad sight'. Gregory's dismissal was because 'he couldn't find any straw to lie on because he couldn't be bothered.'

Quiet day: the BWD mentions 'sniping rather less than usual' and 'one section under Capt. Freeman paraded in Nieppe to meet the King.' King George V issued a Special Order after the parade- 'I am very glad to have seen my Army in the Field. I much wished to do so in order to gain a slight experience of the life you are leading. By your discipline, pluck and endurance, inspired by the indomitable regimental spirit, you have not only upheld the tradition of the British Army, but added fresh lustre to its history. I cannot share in your trials, dangers and successes but I can assure you of the proud confidence and gratitude of myself and of your fellow countrymen.'

Messines: Mesen in Flemish, was 1¼ miles north of the Warwicks' line.

The Dubs relieved us: after which the Warwicks marched up to Hill 63. The Brigade War Diary mentioned that 'an officer who went forward from our front line last night met a German who ran away'!

Casswell: Robert's last batman before leaving the Western Front on January 12th, 1915.

marched back: to Pont de Nieppe having been relieved by the Seaforth Highlanders.

The 2/ Royal Dublin Fusiliers enquired at Brigade Headquarters if 'an armistice could be arranged for both sides to bail (sic) out their trenches.'

Sunday December 6th

Found another nice little private house to have our meals. Church parade at 11 a.m. Met *Shelley* who has composed a most amusing parody entitled *'A little grey louse in my vest'*.

Two letters from Bob who is having a nice rest and thinks he may get leave Jan 21st or even at Xmas!! Church at Sourton. Finished off my fairy play and sent it off next day to be typed.

Shelley: Captain E.V.M. Shelley.

louse: lice and fleas were the bane of all soldiers on the Front Line and why the baths arranged for them after their tour of duty were much appreciated. The 1/ Somerset Light Infantry from 11th Brigade were also resting at Pont de Nieppe and one of their lieutenants wrote that the baths- 15 large vats (10 men to a vat) were in a linen factory and that the men, having removed their jackets and trousers, tied their garments with their identity disc. The uniforms were then taken away for fumigation, washing, repair and ironing while undergarments were boiled in disinfectant. In the trenches, cigarettes were used to remove lice and fleas. Private Harry Morgan of the Warwicks' 'C' Company complained of having lice after just one night spent in a barn.

'A little grey louse in my vest': when on the march in 1915, troops sang their version of 'My little grey house in the west'. Shelley's earlier version would have been on the same lines as:

I've a little wet hole in a trench,
Where the rainstorms continually drench,
There are star shells that shine,
Every night at nine,
And a lot of things you civvies miss;
There are whizz bangs and five-nines galore,
And the mice and the rats I adore;
Sure, with a bomb from the air,
Why, no place can compare,
With my little wet home in the trench.

December 7th

Soaking wet day and *alas the trenches tonight.* Wood and I managed, by making ourselves charming to a S.M. of the A.S.C. to get a little paraffin. All the 'A' company officers had a most excellent lunch at an *estaminet.* I determined to get a conveyance of sorts to carry some of the men's extra blankets and odds and ends of things that make life bearable in these saddened trenches, and to have if possible something dry when we get there after a four mile march in a drenching downpour, with mud over our ankles all the way. Commandeer an old horse and if possible an older brougham. The springs on one side were broken, likewise both windows. A Belgian boy as a driver. Ten minutes after it arrived at the billet, it was loaded sky high. Frying pans and pots were tied on to the handles of the doors, neither of which would open. Inside were blankets and sacks, a lusty cockerel or two, and some rabbits or Belgian hares, and the whole in charge of Jimmy Long, Wood's servant and also the company wit. They were loudly cheered going through the village. They started 3 hours in advance and got there half an hour before us, after one of the most thrilling adventures (as told by Jimmy Long) ever recorded. *The crazy cart* tipped over once and blocked the narrow lane against a battery of artillery returning to their snug billets for the night. Long seems to have given the officer in charge a good piece of his mind under cover of the darkness. The cocks crowed all the way, and the pots and pans, banging against each other were sufficient warning for miles. Long

In and Out (I)

That last half-hour before "going in" to the same trenches for the 200th time

December 7th: 'alas the trenches tonight'- Bairnsfather's cartoon reflects the melancholy at the prospect of returning to the trenches
Barbara Bruce Bairnsfather

December 7th: 'had a most excellent lunch at an estaminet'- like the 'Aux Trois Amis' in Ploegsteert

was much more mud than clothes, but cheery as a lark. The horse 'A company pet' as Long christened him, was none the worse and was found later having a good meal on the company *ration biscuits*.

alas the trenches tonight: the strain is starting to show.

S.M. of the A.S.C.: Sergeant-Major of the Army Service Corps which was responsible for feeding the troops on the Front Line.

estaminet: restaurant/café ideal for soldiers' relaxation behind the lines.

The crazy cart: this whole episode would have made a good subject for one of Bruce Bairnsfather's cartoons. It shows there was much morale boosting laughter about the episode amongst the officers and men.

ration biscuits: 'hard tack' biscuits were not always appreciated by the men; sometimes they were used to keep a fire burning but the horse obviously relished them! Bruce Bairnsfather wrote in 'Bullets and Billets'- 'coke was scarce and always wet and it was by no means uncommon to overhear the remark "chuck us the biscuits Bill, the fire wants mending."'

The Brigade Diary records that the strength of the Brigade was 3,488 and the number of officers 78. The numbers remained constant for the rest of the month.

December 8th: 'Poor British Tommy but one and all'- 'Bills', 'Berts', and 'Alfs' in their Warwicks' trench with, on the right, ● **Lance-Corporal Thomas Henry 'Pat' Rafferty**, *for some, the inspiration for Bairnsfather's 'Old Bill'. From Handsworth, Birmingham, he died on April 25th 1915 and is remembered on the Menin Gate (see p.35)*   Tonie and Valmai Holt

December 8th

The trenches were in the most deplorable condition. Everyone was over the ankles *in liquid mud,* and the communication trenches *over the knees.* Most of the dug outs had fallen in. Those that hadn't were full of water. Poor British Tommy but one and all declared that *if the germans could stand it,* surely they could. Major Poole came round and was very pleased to see their good spirits, and the way they had already begun to do what was possible. I spent the night with them (a quiet one luckily) and was rewarded next day by half a dozen of *'my Black Hat gang'* volunteering to put my dug out right. Wood was *by no means well* and several of the men would have liked to have seen the doctor, but ended as usual by *sticking it.*

in liquid mud: The mud suffered by soldiers in the Great War evokes thoughts of the Battle of Passchendaele in 1917, when the mud was so deep that men would disappear in it and drown. Robert's description indicates that such conditions existed from the first winter of the War. Pumping water out of the trenches was a constant problem as the BWD records: 'tried to drain trenches but found it useless'. Private William Tapp recorded on this day that 'it will take boats to relieve us.'

The New Submarine Danger
" They'll be torpedoin' us if we stick 'ere much longer, Bill"

December 8th: 'Everyone was over their ankles in liquid mud'- Bairnsfather's take on the situation!
Barbara Bruce Bairnsfather

My Dug-Out: A lay of the trenches.

December 8th: 'Dug outs that hadn't fallen in were full of water' Barbara Bruce Bairnsfather

'Old Bill': Bruce Bairnsfather's portrayal of a 'Tommy'
Barbara Bruce Bairnsfather

over the knees: the fighting conditions caused new ailments, one of the worst being 'trench foot' caused by prolonged exposure to cold and wet conditions. It could become very painful and in the worst cases, required amputation of toes; at first it was a punishable offence to catch 'trench foot' and Private Harry Morgan received 14 days Field Punishment No. 2 which was similar to No. 1 but without 'crucifixion', for taking his boot off because he was suffering from trench foot. 'Any hard or dirty work came my way.' Advice given in the 1914 'Field Service Pocket Book' to 'preserve the feet' was to wash them with soap and then smear them over with a greasy substance such as unsalted grease, kerosene etc. Eventually the men were instructed how to look after their feet with frequent changes of socks and constant use of foot powder and as a result 'trench foot' casualties decreased; an officer would be in charge of 'foot inspection'.

if the germans could stand it: an early sign that the enemies have a shared experience and suffer the same privations which were motivating factors for the Christmas fraternisation. Note the lack of a capital letter for mention of the Germans!

'my Black Hat gang': was probably at this stage Lieutenants Black, Wood, Cave, Thornhill and Captain Wasey.

by no means well: another ailment which troops in the trenches suffered from was 'trench fever': an infectious disease spread by lice with similar symptoms to influenza. In severe cases, those affected would be hospitalised for several weeks.

sticking it: the 'Old Contemptibles' are showing the enduring spirit that was commented on by other armies. Some of these men have endured the retreat from Mons, have suffered sleep deprivation, long route marches in miserable weather and have been subjected to shelling and sniping. Now, four months after landing in France, they are fighting the mud and the cold.

Private William Tapp noted in his diary that he received a birthday card from 'my sonny' and that 'we were to attack the next day, I felt excited, waited for the time and longed for the glory of it, but for some reason it was cancelled.'

December 9th
More rain and so *more misery*, and am afraid there will be a lot of sickness. It is quite impossible to do anything whatever to the trenches or parapets. Planks, boards and sandbags are sent up each night to the *cross roads in Plugstreet Wood*, and needless to say they don't remain there long. Cave's dug out is almost

impossible, so I hope Black does not return from his *charcoal course* just yet. Star shells all night. Wood's dug out came down with a crash and buried poor *Long*. I went across to see him as he seemed pretty bad, ordered him back to the farm billet to see the doctor. He declared he wasn't going to leave us just when things looked their blackest and an hour later he was still there doing his best to pretend he was alright. I had to be very stern with him, and at last got him out. The doctor's report next day was two ribs and an arm broken, he will be a great loss to the company in every way. Two men were killed and three wounded.

Bob thinks he may get Xmas leave!! Working tea party. Sourton Parish has made 40 *garments* and bought 18.

December 9th: 'Two men were killed'- one was Private H.T. Davis who was buried at Prowse Point Cemetery

more misery: the battle against the conditions is getting desperate. BWD- 'trenches in a very bad state. Work all night trying to make them habitable- 2 killed, 8 wounded.' One of those killed was ● **Private Henry Thomas Davis**, aged 35 of 3 Victoria Terrace, Stratford-on-Avon and husband of Leah. He was buried at Prowse Point Cemetery.

cross roads in Plugstreet Wood: tracks made of wooden duckboards were built by Royal Engineers inside the wood for the movement of troops. Tracks were given names by the London Rifle Brigade who were in the front line, east of the wood such as 'The Strand', 'Regent Street', 'Oxford Circus', 'Piccadilly Circus' and 'Charing Cross'.

charcoal course: charcoal was burnt on the Front Line probably because it was smokeless and didn't alert the enemy to soldiers' whereabouts. It may have been used for water purification. It seems odd that an officer should go on a course...

Long: may have secured a 'Blighty' as a result of his accident, a wound serious enough to get him sent home, from the Hindustani word 'Belati', originally used by British troops posted to India to mean 'home'.

garments: probably for the local Belgian refugees.

December 10th
More rain. The more it rains the more the men whistle. I wonder what they think of to whistle. All the planks in the trenches which rested on piles of sandbags have disappeared beneath the mud. Oh dear! At midnight, an orderly came round to say

The Conscientious Exhilarator
" *Every encouragement should be given for singing and whistling.*"
That painstaking fellow, Lieut. Orpheus, does his best, but finds it uphill work at times

December 10th: 'The more it rains, the more the men whistle'- Bairnsfather's Lieutenant Orpheus found his men less keen on whistling than Robert's
Barbara Bruce Bairnsfather

December 10th: 'down on my luck at losing so many of my splendid men'- Lance-Corporal Mole, and Privates R.H. Taylor and F. Yates are commemorated on the Ploegsteert Memorial

poor *Wood* was hit rather badly. Should have liked to have seen him but did not like to leave for a minute while things were as they were. He sent me a cheery message, and said he would be home for Christmas. One man killed and two wounded. Felt very down on my luck at losing my best subaltern and so many of *my splendid men*.

Mrs. Whitwell writes a very disagreeable note and declines invitation to tea and to inspect work. Because I didn't invite her to party.

German Cemetery at Steenwerck- a stark contrast to a British Cemetery. There are less German cemeteries in the area because the French and Belgians were not keen to grant land to the Germans even on a leasehold agreement. However, they donated land to the British

December 11th

It rained all night and the whole of today. When I went round the sentries I found them quite resigned to *another flood*. They were amused. One Pte. Carter said "it will *lay the dust, sir*, won't it?" at which I laughed heartily and so did they. But poor fellows they were on their last legs for this trench trip. Cave had to spend the day and night in my dug out as his was flooded. Thanks to my Black Hat gang of the deepest drinkers and worst of characters (in peace time) in the company, my dug out was the only one dry. The men are trying to build dug outs with sandbags only.

Sylvia drove me to Grace's where I dined and played poker winning 2/3 this time. Idiotic game all the same. Grace smokes into my face all the time. Disgusting. Dr. Young tells me I did exceedingly well in Exam and got top marks.

December 11th: 'It will lay the dust, Sir!' - Lieutenant R.C. Money, 1/ Cameronians, would have enjoyed Private Carter's comment as he tries to pump water out of a trench. Imperial War Museum Q51568

Wood: a 'Blighty' for one of Robert's officers and member of his 'Black Hat Gang'. Brigadier-General Hull reported in January 1915 that 2nd Lieutenant Wood's work 'has been consistently good and he showed admirable example and fortitude under trying circumstances.'

my splendid men: a camaraderie born out of the shared conditions in the trenches would develop between many of the officers and men, cutting across wide social divisions (see p.173-174 re. Private Sperry's relationship with Robert). One of his 'splendid men' was 29 year old ⚫ **Corporal Benjamin Mole**, son of Henry and Isabel Mole of Charlecote, Warwickshire. Also killed were ⚫ **Private R.H. Taylor**, husband of Ada of 218, Heneage Street, Ashted, Birmingham and ⚫ **Private Frederick F. Yates** aged 25. They are remembered on the Ploegsteert Memorial.

Mrs Whitwell: Parochial politics were getting quite heated!

another flood: reference to mud and flooding is the subject matter of many of the early Bairnsfather cartoons. His first book, 'Bullets and Billets' published in December 1916, was dedicated to 'my old pals, Bill, Bert and Alf who have sat in the mud with me!' They were the subjects of many of his cartoons. Unlike Robert, Bairnsfather rarely mentioned his fellow soldiers by their correct name in his writings. Quite a coincidence but in the Lieutenant Frank Black file at the Imperial War Museum, there is a letter to A.H. Seaman, which started 'Dear Alf' and refers to the 'mass of mud up to our thighs- one wants to be a lion to stand all the hardship out here'. It is signed 'Bert'!

'lay the dust sir': a wonderful riposte that couldn't have been bettered by Bairnsfather himself. Referring to 'Old Bills' in his interview with Canadian T.V. in November 1958, he said that they just accepted the conditions with 'humorous grousing'.

December 12th

Our last day for this trip. Everybody cheered at the prospects of getting down to billets. Still raining. The Jack Johnson and coal box holes are like young lakes. One man hit in the hand and hip, the

December 12th: 'well into Plugstreet Wood': 'Plugstreet Hall' was not far from the southern edge of the wood- note the Warwicks' Antelope badge to the left of the door   David Vaux

Dubs relieved us at 6.30 p.m. and we implored them to try and do something to the trenches and dug outs when it stopped raining. Every german sniper seemed to know we were being relieved (or perhaps they are relieving companies themselves) a perfect hail of bullets the whole time we were getting out of the communication trenches and until we were well into Plugstreet Wood, but only two men hit. We got to our farm and lit a fire and ate, and after a game of baccarat for the extra lot of rum, we turned in for the first real sleep for four days and nights. There is a rumour that all leave stopped. I hope this is not true, and wish now I had said nothing about it to Renie.

Sunday December 13th

Recommended *Lce. Cpl. Tovey* for the D.C.M. and spoke to Poole about Sergt. Harvey who had also done very well. Church service at 12 noon. Marched off at 5 p.m. for our new billets at La Crèche which were very comfortable and clean. 'A' Company's proverbial luck in the matter of billets. A howling bad night. Thought for tonight the 'trenches'.

December 14th

A bright and sunny morning, so ordered *my charger* and went for a ride. Cave went off to Armentières. In the afternoon Black and I walked into the village of *Staenweck* and had a pleasing *bottle of the boy* in a wine tavern, run by a couple of enterprising dark eyed French girls. We brought back another to help the plum pudding and mince pies down. The gay Guy elected to remain in Armentières which was heavily shelled all night, so we drank the bottle ourselves and slept like tops.

December 14th: 'walked into the village of Staenweck'- Steenwerck Town Hall was where a large number of the Warwicks were inoculated and went, according to the BWD, to a 'cinematograph show'
Musée de la Vie Rurale de Steenwerck

103

young lakes: any crater made by an exploding shell would quickly be filled with mud. One of the famous photographs of Bairnsfather shows him wearing a Balaclava helmet and standing in front of a hole made by a 'Jack Johnson' shell (see p.113).

Lce. Cpl. Tovey: having built two saps (trenches dug outwards from an existing one) towards the German lines on December 10th, a reconnaissance of the German trench was carried out by Lance-Corporal Samuel Tovey. The BWD records that '5 dead Germans found in it.' The Distinguished Conduct Medal was awarded to non-officer ranks for distinguished service or gallantry but despite Robert's recommendation, the 30 year old Tovey nor Harvey appear to have received a medal.

⬤ **Lance-Corporal Samuel Tovey** born in Leamington Spa died on January 1st 1915 of wounds received and was buried at Boulogne East Cemetery. Brigadier-General Hull commended Tovey for assisting in the burial of three dead Somerset Light Infantry found lying outside an empty German trench but getting wounded in the process. 'He was always the first to volunteer for any risky work.'

my charger: war horse

Staenweck: the correct spelling is Steenwerck, a large village south of La Crèche. Robert's spelling of such names, particularly Flemish, is often inaccurate but he was writing in his private diary!

bottle of the boy: his description of a bottle of champagne.

December 15th
I was detailed for a *court of enquiry* in Staenweck and so instead of going up to the farm, rode into the town. Had a shave and then hunted for a house to sleep in. Struck oil. *The sisters of mercy,* by name Flouvière, were most kind to me and gave me everything of their best, including a feather bed. I talked more French that night than ever before in my life.

All our kind gifts to the soldiers are still reposing in the Exeter cloakroom- wrote Linen League a piece of my mind. Mr. Whitwell wrote me a *rude letter* signed Truly Yours.

December 16th
Walked back to our farm and found the Company just starting for the trenches. These dirty Dublin Fusiliers have done nothing but pull down anything of wood to burn. I reported that a certain portion of the trench was *waist high*, no matter we occupied it. Miserable night. The germans must have been more so, as very little came our way. The orderly arrived at midnight to say I was to attend the court of enquiry again.

Wrote to Mr Whitwell signed *Yrs. Sincerely.*

December 17th
Set off at dawn. My horse met me. Rode in. Finished the enquiry at 6.30 p.m. The sisters introduced me to their brother and his family, who lived in a big house, where all sorts of amusements took place. *Had tea with the family.* La petite Elizabeth, aged six, fell in love with me and went to sleep in my arms. More French with 'Les Soeurs' and another good night's rest.

---

court of enquiry: it was the first step to investigate failures in discipline (absenteeism, loss of equipment etc.) Dependent on the court's findings, the soldier could then be sent for a court martial.

The sisters of mercy: Renie received two letters from the Plouvier (not Flouvière) sisters on December 19th 1914 and on June 15th 1915 which were passed by the censor (see p.58, 107-108 and 146).

rude letter: Renie is fighting her own battles too! And fights back...

waist high: more problems with flooded trenches.

In his OD Robert recalled that 'I reported a certain portion of the trench was untenable but Major Poole insisted on it being held.'

Yrs. Sincerely: Renie was not a lady to be trifled with!

Had tea with the family: the French were welcoming to the British as many in the area had suffered bad experiences at the hands of the Germans.

Brigade War Diary- 'New pumps sent up to the trenches last night proved a great success. 20 Other Rank soldiers arrive for the Warks.'

December 17th
Letter from *Lady H.* saying that it would suit her best if Bob gets his leave later as they want to spend Xmas with dear *Ida* who cannot be left alone. *Whitby, Scarborough and Hartlepool bombarded* by the Huns who shelled them from the sea and after inflicting much damage and considerable loss of life got off Scott free!

December 17th: 'Scarborough bombarded by Huns'-Scarborough was shelled by a German cruiser squadron on December 16th
British Newspaper Library, Colindale- War Budget 2/1/15 p.209

Lady H: Robert's mother.

Ida: was Robert's sister photographed at Robert's wedding whose husband Captain Alec Campbell died in 1917 (see p.160).

Whitby, Scarborough and Hartlepool bombarded: the north eastern towns were bombarded on December 16th by a cruiser squadron commanded by Rear-Admiral Franz von Hipper. More than 1000 German shells were fired and caused significant damage. Wendy Godfrey, the mother of Ruth Smith who designed this book, wrote:

'On December 16th, 1914, a German battleship had sailed into Scarborough's South Bay between the trawlers and the shore and trained its guns on them.

"We warn you! If you raise the alarm, we will blow you out of the water!"

Dad's trawler, at that time the 'Morning Star', had to look on while Scarborough was shelled. Explosives rained down on the bewildered town, ripping into homes and boarding houses. Panic seized people. Crowds took off for the countryside to the West. My mother took her deep pram with the two girls Ada and Madge in it and Cis by the hand and made for Scalby Road and Lady Edith's Drive where Raincliffe Woods would provide the illusion of safety. If nothing else, she could save her children. By evening, when the bombardment was deemed to be at an end, a nervous return began. What would they find? Commercial Street had been hit and Gladstone Road Bridge, but not our house. Dad's safe return, his fury about the event and relief at the family's safety was mirrored through all Scarborough. War had moved to our very doorsteps! My mother and sisters never forgot this terror and frequently rehearsed it for my benefit.'

There was public outrage that 130 lives were lost and nearly 600 wounded. Winston Churchill, then First Lord of the Admiralty, referred to the Germans as the 'Scarborough Baby Killers'.

December 18th

Wrote letters all morning, and then went to say goodbye to the brother's family before riding out. Found *Hart* and *Wasey* at the transport. After getting back to my dug out, was sent for to headquarters to have *the morrow's scheme* explained. Went on with it to number one platoon to explain it there. Had to cross a field of mud. Several bright star shells being sent up, had to flatten myself in it each time. The snipers are only *eighty yards from us.*

———◆———

Hart: the only mention of Captain H.C. Hart in the diary. He was with the Battalion in France from the start and wrote a 'Narrative of the Retreat from Mons'.

Wasey:  **Captain Cyril Walter Carleton Wasey** was the son of George and Jane Wasey of Marlborough, Wiltshire. He was hit in the arm by a bullet in March 1915 and was wounded during the Battle of the Somme in 1916. Wasey left the Warwicks and joined the 16th Squadron of the Royal Flying Corps and is recorded as killed in action over Northern France on October 28th 1917 aged 24. He was buried at the Aubigny Communal Cemetery Extension. He is mentioned in C.L. Kingsford's 'The Story of the Royal Warwickshire Regiment'- 'Aug 25 north to St. Python. Haldane sent out Lieutenant Wasey of RW whom he knew to be an exceptionally good and resourceful scout to bring back such news as he could get...'

That Evening Star-shell.
"Oh, star of eve, whose tender beam
Falls on my spirit's troubled dream."
—*Wolfram's Aria in "Tannhäuser."*

December 18th: 'star shells being sent up'-
Bairnsfather's 'Alf' or 'Bert' has been caught in the
spotlight having overdone the jar of rum!
Barbara Bruce Bairnsfather

Captain Wasey was described after the War by one of his men, Private Henry Morgan, as 'a chancer with a total disregard for his own life or anyone else's, a real daredevil. There wasn't much of him, 5'4" but he was more than a little reckless.' At one stage he had decided that he had 'had enough of Captain Wasey for the time being, I could never stand his Douglas Fairbanks attitude.'

In a glass case at the Royal Regiment of Fusiliers Museum in Warwick there is a statuette presented to the Regiment in memory of Wasey by his fellow officers. Throughout the final version of the diary, his name is incorrectly typed as 'Wassy'.

the morrow's scheme: the Warwicks' 'B' Company were to provide heavy fire 'half right' from rifles and machine-guns to support the 11th Brigade's attack to the east of the Wood on the right flank of the Warwicks. That night Bairnsfather and Sergeant Rea went on 'our Sherlock Holmes excursion' to find and fortify a position for the machine-gun.' On his sketch map of Christmas 1914, Bairnsfather shows the exact spot 'where a friend and myself fired the machine-gun on a sewing machine table'! (see p.136)

eighty yards from us: not a usual width for No Man's Land, although there was never a defined distance between the two front lines. The opposing armies tended to be about 200 yards from each other although it could be as little as 50 yards and as much as 700 yards. Much depended on the terrain.

In and Out (II)

That first half-hour after " coming out " of those same trenches

December 20th: 'gifts from home waiting us'- the Officers have broken into their Fortnum and Mason hamper. The concertina is an interesting inclusion because Renie received a letter dated December 3rd which quoted Robert's batman Sperry who was recovering from wounds in Aberdeen Hospital. Sperry recalled that 'your husband had a concertina he found in the German trenches and he used to amuse them all by playing it!'   Barbara Bruce Bairnsfather

December 19th
The scheme lasted all day. Awful din. *The Bedfords* advanced on our right, and took some trenches, but finding them full of water had to retire and lost heavily.

2 letters from Bob and a funny one from two French ladies who put him up for the night and treated him like a Prince, *dear old things!* His leave is cancelled- too bad! "Damn- there, I've said it" as Cynthia would say.

Sunday December 20th
We were heavily shelled all day, but had no casualties. The Dubs relieved us at 6.30 p.m. and we marched off under much sniping *to our farm*, where we found plum puddings, chocolates, cigarettes and all sorts of other Xmas gifts from home waiting us. We set to and ate, drank and were merry.

———

The scheme: the aim was to 'straighten out the line' east of the Wood; it proved a costly attack for the 11th Brigade as the 1/ Rifle Brigade lost 3 officers and 23 other ranks and 3 officers and 42 other ranks were wounded. The 1/ Somerset Light Infantry had 6 officers and 27 other ranks killed and 52 other ranks wounded and 30 were reported missing. The 1/ Hampshire had one Major and 15 other ranks killed and 25 were wounded. Some troops of the 1/ Rifle Brigade managed to enter German trenches but were forced to retreat because of shelling from their own side. The Warwicks' War Diary in an understated way records that 'we suffered some casualties from our own gunners.'

The Bedfords: Robert is confused here- there was no battalion from the Bedfordshire Regiment in Plugstreet Wood at the time.

dear old things!: we're not convinced that they were 'dear old things'! On December 16th they wrote to Renie: 'You will doubtless be surprised to receive a letter from us who don't have the honour of knowing you but we have had the honour of giving our hospitality to your dear husband Captain Hamilton. Believe us Madam, we are doing our very best to ensure that he finds here the rest he needs after the fatigue of the trenches.' They asked for a photograph of her children and to save any envelopes she received with 'censor stamps' which they were collecting for charity. The letter concluded by commending Robert on the improving standard of his French.

to our farm: at Hill 63, before being relieved by the Royal Dublin Fusiliers, the BWD records that 2 were killed. ● **Private J. Goodhead**, aged 18 from Aston Brook Street, Birmingham and ● **Private W. Crumpton** were buried at Prowse Point Cemetery.

December 21st
My horse came up so I went for a ride, and came across one of our aeroplanes struggling to rise from a ploughed field our useless *anti-aircraft guns* ripping away at the clouds. Mud and filth perfectly appalling. Marched back to La Crèche and to a new billet which was even more comfortable than the last. Milk and butter, and quantities of fowls.

Had a wire from *Adela* from Marseilles saying she would like to come here from Plymouth Sat 26th. Very exciting and so thankful that *the wire wasn't bad news.* Was very afraid for a minute.

December 22nd
Wasey rejoined (away since Méteren). We all four found horses. I produced my French horn, and away we galloped, and fondly imagined we were having a day with the hounds. Wasey was good on the tally-ho. We rolled up at Staenweck and I introduced my subs to the tavern. We had a very lively time with *the dear things* and drank as much champagne as was good for us. After which young Thornhill turned up and played the piano, and so we all danced with the French girls and forgot the mud and the trenches. Got back to our billets and after another merry dinner turned in.

December 23rd
Went round to see the *young Plovers* and of course young Guy Cave must needs lose his heart to the elder one, because she could sing and dance. The officers and men of 'A' company all in the best of spirits marched off to our farm behind the trenches. We were told it had been blown to blazes, and we were to billet at another much distressed and expected our luck in billets had at last turned. But not so. We found our new resting place a palace, and were most comfortable, and had even coal for our fire.

Decorated the Church. Mrs. Whitwell polite and me amiable.

———

anti-aircraft guns: in 1914, the British Army had a few 3-inch guns mounted at the back of three ton lorries. The gun had a vertical range of 18,000 feet and a rate of fire of 15 rounds per minute.

Adela: was Renie's older sister.

the wire wasn't bad news: Renie like thousands of wives on the Home Front were fearful of receiving a telegram with the worst of news about their husbands on the Front Line.

The Brigade War Diary commented that the River Douve was in flood and 40 feet wide in one place.

the dear things: maybe they were not as old as Renie might have thought. A relation, maybe a brother, is remembered on the war memorial in Steenwerck.

On this day, the Brigade War Diary mentions that 'a notice was put up by the enemy stating that prisoners would be kindly treated. A suitable reply will be put up by the 2nd R.D.F. (Royal Dublin Fusiliers) tonight.'

young Plovers: it is unlikely that Robert was using the old English slang for a prostitute!

December 24th

I rode about in the morning but the mud and slosh made it most unenjoyable. We set off *for the trenches at 6.30 p.m. a little sad* at spending Xmas day in them. Crossing the well worn danger zone to our consternation not a shot was fired at us. The Dubs told us as we relieved them that the germans *wanted to talk to us.* When we were settled down, we heard them shouting, *"Are you the Warwicks?"* To which our men replied *"Come and see".* They said "You come half way, and we will come half way, and bring you some cigars." This went on for some time, when *Pte.Gregory,* Double Ginger, my late servant came and asked if he might go out half way. I said "Yes, *at your own risk."* (Note Readers of this diary please remember that up to this date there had been no *Lusitania outrage,* nor any of the *other fiendish crimes,* which have since put the huns beyond the pale, and which have forfeited to that nation's soldiers, for ever the honourable battlefield liberties, indulged in all previous great wars between fighting men and fighting men.)

Pte. Gregory stepped over the parapet, and got half way, and was heard saying, "Well here I am, where are you?" "Come half way" they said, so on went Gregory, until he came upon two unarmed germans, and one fully armed, lying down just behind, with his rifle pointed at him, *typically german.* Gregory was unarmed and alone. *Typically British.* He got his cigar and spun them some magnificent yarns about the strength of his company, which amused us all very much when he told us later. They wanted me *to meet their officer,* and after a great deal of shouting across, I said I would meet him at dawn, *unarmed.*

Wire saying Medina arrives at 8 a.m. Drove Rhone down to fetch corn in afternoon. 4 geese fetched 18/- we are £8 out of pocket over them. Biddy made £20. Feel very tired and unwell.

In the Seaforth Highlanders' Battalion War Diary it was recorded that 'Germans ceased hostilities after dark and commenced Xmas by singing and shouting...Some of our men went right up to their trenches and obtained a certain amount of information- we put up a lot of wire during the night.'

for the trenches at 6.30 p.m: half an hour earlier, Leutnant Kurt Zehmisch of the 11th Company of the 134th Infantry Regiment made his way to the German Front line opposite St. Yves, having ordered his men not to fire that evening or on Christmas Day.

a little sad: this feeling of sadness would not last long as Robert and the Warwicks were about to participate in one of the momentous events of the 20th Century: the Christmas Truce of 1914, an armistice which Bruce Bairnsfather believed 'put a little human punctuation mark in our lives of cold and humid hate.' Two years later Sir Arthur Conan Doyle described the Truce as 'an amazing spectacle...one human episode amid all the atrocities which have stained the memory of the war.' The unofficial armistice held in the St. Yves area is well documented with eleven accounts: ten from the Warwicks and one from 2nd Lieutenant Cyril Drummond of the Royal Field Artillery. The Warwicks' evidence for the occasion was provided by a Captain (Hamilton), three lieutenants (Bairnsfather, Black and one 'unknown'), a sergeant (Philpotts), one corporal

(Judd) and four privates (Mattey, Morgan, Pratt and Tapp). The 'unknown' officer told his story to an American journalist, Alexander Woollcott, when they met in the autumn of 1930 'across a lobster stew at Billy the Oysterman's in New York'! The 'unknown officer' mentioned later in *The American Legion Magazine* turned out to be Bruce Bairnsfather!

Taking into consideration that time may have blurred the accuracy of some of the accounts recalled many years after the event, it has nonetheless been possible to recreate a composite picture of what the Warwicks experienced during these incredible days in chapter 11 entitled 'A Day Unique in the World's History.' Leutnant Kurt Zehmisch's description of the events told from a German perspective adds authenticity to the account.

wanted to talk to us: from the majority of witnesses in the St.Yves area and elsewhere along the line of trenches, it tended to be the Germans who tried first to attract attention from the other side of No Man's Land. Some shouted and some sang; Private Tapp heard singing coming from the German trenches, Philpotts was impressed by the quality of their singing, mentioning that 'our line was only 70 yards from the Germans with turnips growing between the wire' and on the Warwicks' left flank the Seaforths heard the Germans singing carols and sang some in return. On the Warwicks' right flank, Frank and Maurice Wray attached to the 11th Infantry Brigade, remembered that the Germans had brought up a band to their trenches and upon hearing 'hymns and tunes common to both nations, quite understandably a wave of nostalgia passed over us.' Charlie Pratt also heard a German band that 'gave us a few selections which we appreciated very much'. Interestingly, the Germans used Berlin time which was one hour ahead of British time.

"Are you the Warwicks?": The Germans would have known which troops they were facing. The two front lines were so close in places that men occasionally shouted across to each other, threw things and even had shooting matches with bottles as targets. General Sir Horace Smith-Dorrien, Commander of II Corps had heard about such goings-on and was concerned that troops could become over friendly; accordingly at the beginning of December, Brigadier-General G.T. Forestier-Walker, Smith-Dorrien's Chief-of-Staff issued his superior's orders: 'Troops in trenches in close proximity to the enemy slide very easily, if permitted to do so, into a 'live and let live' theory of life...such an attitude is, however, most dangerous, for it discourages initiative in commanders and destroys the offensive spirit in all ranks...friendly intercourse with the enemy, unofficial armistices and the exchange of tobacco and other comforts, however tempting and occasionally amusing they may be, are absolutely prohibited.' These proved to be prophetic words but it was an order that was qualified by what appears to modern readers as the remarkable thought that 'the attitude of our troops can be readily understood and to a certain extent commands sympathy'- a surprisingly considered reaction from the men at the top, who have been described as 'donkeys' by their critics.

"Come and see": this account of the first exchanges that led to the Truce differs to other Warwicks' accounts. It is safe to conclude that at least two attempts were made to arrange an armistice along the line of trenches held by the Warwicks. The other one, recounted by Lieutenant Black and Privates Pratt and Tapp involved Sergeant Rea meeting two Germans, exchanging gifts and lighting cigarettes. One of several of Bruce Bairnsfather's accounts is precise as to the location of the early meetings- 'the remnants of a hedge and ditch ran out at right angles from our trenches to the Germans,' a description corroborated by Leutnant Zehmisch who referred to a natural field ditch 'from which one Englishman emerged and met two of my men.'

Pte.Gregory: had been sacked as his servant by Robert for his inability to make a decent cup of tea (see entries for November 26th on p.93 and December 4th on p.96).

at your own risk: although not prepared to go out into No Man's Land himself, it was a brave decision in view of what could have happened to Gregory.

Lusitania outrage: Robert's rant was inserted into his 2nd and 3rd versions of the diary- the sinking of the *Lusitania* did not occur until May 1915. The 32,000 ton Cunard liner, sailing from New York, was sunk by a German U-20 submarine near the western coast of Ireland. It sank with the loss of 1,200 lives, including 124 U.S. citizens and was thus a propaganda coup for the

Allies and was a factor in the United States' involvement in the War; some Americans were so incensed by the outrage that they went to Canada and joined the British Army.

other fiendish crimes: one of these would be the first use of poison gas by the Germans when chlorine gas was released from cylinders at the start of the 2nd Battle of Ypres on April 22nd 1915; French troops bore the brunt of the initial attack and soon retreated. The 1st Canadian Brigade counter-attacked while waiting for more support to arrive. The 10th Brigade which included the 1/ Warwicks was sent to help and on April 25th was involved in a fierce and bloody battle near the village of St. Juliaan. The Warwicks suffered many casualties amongst officers and other ranks- Lieutenants Maclagan and Nicolai were killed, and the bodies of Captain Black and Lieutenant Tillyer were never recovered. Captain Tomes was wounded, Lieutenants Cave and Bairnsfather were hospitalised suffering from shell shock. The Warwicks were part of the 4th Division which suffered 11,000 casualties during the 2nd Battle of Ypres and there were nearly 60,000 in total for the British Army.

typically german...Typically British: note the use of lower case for german and upper case for British! Not surprisingly, Robert's view of the Germans is unfavourable and in his 'Bullets and Billets' Bairnsfather's contrast between the two sets of soldiers who met in No Man's Land on Christmas Day is similarly biased: 'Our men in their scratch costumes of dirty, muddy khaki, with their various assorted head-dresses of woollen helmets, mufflers and battered hats, were a light hearted, open, humorous collection as opposed to the sombre demeanour and stolid appearance of the Huns in their grey-green faded uniforms, top-boots and pork pie hats.' Kurt Zehmisch's account of the truce is strikingly impartial in comparison.

to meet their officer: in the original version of the diary, Robert had written 'to come and parley'.

unarmed: Robert again highlighting his perception of the differences between the Germans and British and what constituted 'fair play'. For an officer to agree to meet the enemy in such a way was unquestionably a punishable offence and was like Gregory's earlier, a risk he was prepared to take. There appeared to be a spontaneous decision on both sides that, as Lieutenant Black explained, it was safe enough 'to stroll about outside the trenches as though there were no war going on.'

If the author of the Brigade War Diary was aware of the happenings after 6.30 p.m. on Christmas Eve, he chose not to elaborate- 'R. Dubs reported a quiet day. They announce Germans were singing and seemed cheerful. When our artillery shelled La Petite Douve, no movement of men was observed.' The Battalion War Diary was even more succinct: 'Quiet day. Relieved the R. Dub. Fus. in the trenches in the evening.'

'Xmas Day'

I went out and found a Saxon officer of the 134th Saxon corps, who was fully armed. I pointed to his revolver and pouch. He smiled and said seeing I was unarmed, "Alright now." We shook hands, and said what we could *in double Dutch*, arranged a local armistice for 48 hours, and returned to our trenches. This was *the signal* for the respective

A MEMORY OF CHRISTMAS, 1914: "LOOK AT THIS BLOKE'S BUTTONS, 'ARRY. I SHOULD RECKON 'E 'AS A MAID TO DRESS 'IM"

Christmas Day 1914: 'exchanged greetings and gifts'- similar exchanges took place along the lines although the Commanding Officer of the Seaforth Highlanders banned any fraternisation
Barbara Bruce Bairnsfather **111**

Christmas Day : How it dawned for many

Dawn on Christmas Day 1914 as captured by Bairnsfather   Barbara Bruce Bairnsfather

soldiers to come out. As far as I can make out, this effort of ours *extended itself* on either side for some considerable distance. The soldiers on both sides met in their hundreds, and *exchanged greetings and gifts. We buried many germans,* and they did the same to ours. *The chef of the Trocadero* was among the Saxons in front of us, and he seemed quite delighted to meet some of his former clients. They told us quite frankly that *Russia with her nine million soldiers* was washed out, when Lieut. Campbell of the Irish Fusiliers, who came out with me and who had heard, but did not believe that, we went out and talked with the enemy, came along with his magnificent black beard. I took him out and said *"What about this Russian?"* They looked distinctly disappointed. They said they knew that Ireland was fighting against us (I now presume *Casement* had told them this). *The French* they laughed at. (*Verdun,* they don't know I presume.) Wasey and *I went to a concert in 'D' company's trench,* and at about midnight, we attended another in our own. The Black Hat gang had rigged up an enormous dug out, and had plastered

Front cover of The Illustrated London News for January 9th 1915. Christmas trees were more important culturally in the celebration of Christmas for the Germans than the British in 1914   *British Newspaper Library, Colindale 9/1/15 p.1*

the walls with Tatler pictures of all the latest girls. They had a stove with a teapot singing away, and altogether was *a most enjoyable evening.* A very merry Xmas and *a most extraordinary one,* but *I doubled the sentries* after midnight.

In his original hand written diary Robert heads the page for Friday December 25th with 'A day unique in the world's history' .

in double Dutch: unlike Zehmisch, a modern language teacher, this Saxon officer is not an English speaker. Interestingly, the two officers agree a 48 hour armistice whereas most others along the line of trenches arranged truces for 24 hours.

the signal: in this instance the other ranks waited for the officers to make the truce in some way official; on the Warwicks' right flank, the Wray brothers with the Rifle Brigade heard a voice from the German trench: "we good, we no shoot" and for them 'was born an unofficial armistice'. On the Warwicks' left flank, the Seaforth Highlanders' commanding officer would have nothing of it. He had not heard that some of his men, including Lance Corporal Ferguson and three others had met some Bavarians on Christmas Eve and reacted furiously when he saw them waving at each other and ordered his Major to send the Germans back to their trenches. The Seaforths were ordered not to fire unless the Germans left their trench. When Sergeant Philpotts of the Warwicks' 'C' Company recalled seeing a German standing on the parapet, shouting and waving his arms, and promptly being 'shot down', he may well have witnessed the carrying out of the order to the Seaforths.

Bruce Bairnsfather is enjoying his favourite cigarette- a Gold Flake at Christmas time in front of a crater caused by a coal box or 'Jack Johnson' Barbara Bruce Bairnsfather

extended itself: Robert claimed he initiated the armistices that sprung up throughout the line of trenches. He may have been right but they were more likely to have happened spontaneously when soldiers on both sides started to mill around peacefully in No Man's Land. Private William Tapp described it as 'a strange sight, unbelievable, we are all mixed up together' and Bairnsfather wrote about 'soldiers everywhere in disorder' just like a football crowd. In his article written in 1931, about 'an unknown officer' the American Alexander Woollcott mentioned 'mischievous laughter' and pointedly observed that 'the monstrous disobedience involving the colossal defiance of the high and mighty, imparted to the whole proceedings the larky air of an escapade.' Bruce Bairnsfather, 'the unknown officer' wrote in his own book 'Bullets and Billets' that the Christmas morning with its cloudless sky and snow on the ground was perfect- 'just the sort of day for Peace to be declared'.

Leutnant Kurt Zehmisch (seated) wrote a detailed description of the Truce. On the reverse of this photograph he recorded 'March 1915 in a fire trench. Next to me Leimbach (now Leutnant Leimbach), behind him, my shelter. Between them are filled sand bags. By my head are fire slits. The bench is there so that we can see over and shoot over the parapet' In Flanders Fields Museum, Ypres

exchanged greetings and gifts: Lieutenant Frank Black chatted to some German officers who promised that, if they received orders to fire, 'they would fire high to warn us'- Tapp swapped buttons with a Saxon; Pratt saw badges changing hands; a Private and a German were seen toasting each other with mugs of rum;

Bairnsfather used his barbed wire cutting pliers to swap buttons with a German officer. A mutual trust he wrote, established itself in No Man's Land of the type that 'forms itself between companions in misfortune'. Meanwhile Leutnant Zehmisch was conversing with two or three officers in English, French and German.

we buried many Germans: Sergeant Philpotts recalled a mass burial of British and German bodies and a military funeral on the edge of Plugstreet Wood.

The Brigade War Diary noted 'A quiet day, no firing. The Germans appear to think that an armistice exists for Christmas Day. An informal interchange of courtesies took place between troops in the fire trenches of both belligerents. Some valuable information was gleaned during the intercourse. The trenches seemed fairly strongly held, the enemy cheerful and well fed. 3 men of the Somerset Light Infantry, 3 Germans of the 134th Saxons, 7 of the Hampshires, a Prussian and an Uhlan were all buried. The Germans helped in the digging, the 1/ Warwicks supplied the tools, the Germans stating they had no spades'! Leutnant Zehmisch similarly noted that 'my people buried the fallen English and Germans whose bodies were already completely decomposed.'

Bairnsfather recalled a German taking photographs including one of himself. Woollcott wrote that 'my friend, the lieutenant, was photographed squatting arm in arm with a German officer, the while a pleasing cluster of Fritzies and Tommies framed this unexpected duo.' The German photographer was, according to Zehmisch, N.C.O. Holland who took three photographs 'showing us in groups with the English.' A remarkable photograph to have survived is the one taken by Lieutenant Drummond who was attached to the Warwicks showing a group of British and German soldiers. Drummond stated in reminiscences recorded in 1976, that his photograph shows Royal Dublin Fusiliers fraternising with Germans. This cannot be the case because they were not present- the Dubs relieved the Warwicks on December 28th which is corroborated by the War Diaries and Robert's entry for Christmas Eve (see photo on p.140).

The chef of the Trocadero: see Chapter 5. It is a delicious irony that Robert should have met the Chef of the Trocadero who had created such an excellent meal for the Norfolks in 1912!

Russia with her nine million soldiers: Corroborating Robert's diary entry, the Brigade WD claimed that the Germans 'believed Russia was already defeated, but that all taken together, the Germans had undertaken too great a task.' It is possible, of course, that Robert may have passed this intelligence on to Headquarters.

"What about this Russian?": that Robert should have played a joke on the Germans underlines the cordial atmosphere that existed between the two sides.

Casement: see chapter 13 diary entry for April 26th 1916 on p.151.

The French: had suffered heavy losses in 1914 but stopped the German advance along the river Marne.

Verdun: was a fortress town about 170 miles east of Paris. It held a symbolic significance for the French who believed that if Verdun fell there would be open ground to Paris. By the end of 1914, Verdun formed a salient on the Western Front; it would become the scene of the longest battle of the War from February to November 1916 ending in stalemate with a staggering combined total of one million casualties for the German and French Armies.

I went to a concert in 'D' Company's trench: see chapter 11. There was much jollity, Music Hall favourites, parodies of old 'chestnuts' orchestrated by Bruce Bairnsfather who would have been in his element, having produced pantomimes before the War at Compton Verney, seat of the Willoughby de Broke family. There had been other 'goings-on' that day. Woollcott records that some men had gathered from abandoned houses some finery, hats and parasols and 'these masqueradors' proceeded to behave like 'fools'.

More remarkable was the game of football. According to Bairnsfather, at about noon, 'a football match was suggested…someone had evidently received a deflated football as a Christmas present.' Despite the frozen and pitted surface and the surviving turnips, a football was kicked about and in an interview with Canadian Television in November 1958, Bairnsfather was adamant that 'one of ours brought up a football, blew it up, to kick about.'

Zehmisch is as definite- 'a couple of English brought a football out of their trench and a vigorous football match began. This was all so marvellous and strange. The English officers thought so too…towards evening the officers asked whether a big football match could be held on the following day between the two positions.' The Wray brothers on the Warwicks right flank recalled- 'a battalion of the 10th Brigade on our left arranged a football match against a German team, one of their number having contacted in the opposing unit a fellow member of his local football club in Liverpool'! Zehmisch, however, was unable 'to definitely agree' to a Boxing Day fixture because he was about to be relieved by another company. That appeared to knock the idea of a 'big match' firmly on the head.

In his book written in 1921 on 'The History of the London Rifle Brigade' Major-General Sir Frederick Maurice made clear his view of the event: 'Concerning visits to enemy trenches by adventurous spirits and rumours of a proposed football match, the authorities frowned upon ideas of this sort and stopped them- quite rightly.'

a most enjoyable evening: Corporal Samuel Judd agreed that it had been 'an enjoyable day.' Zehmisch concluded- 'so after all, the Christmas festival, the festival of love, caused the hated enemies to be friends for a short time.'

a most extraordinary one: a more effusive reaction than that of the author of the BWD: 'A local truce. British and Germans intermingle between the trenches. Dead in front of trenches buried. No shot fired all day. No casualties.'

The Brigade War Diary reported that the Germans were 'well fed in the trenches, with plenty of tea, cocoa and Swiss chocolate. However, they were seen to almost fight for a tin of bully. Their letters were 4 or 5 days old. They cooked in trenches in company kitchens. They stop in advanced trenches only one night. Barbed wire is of only one kind…some 150 to 200 yards behind advanced trenches, 2nd and 3rd line were observed…snipers wore distinctive uniform, they carry an electric lamp on their chest…snipers do not get up trees.'

The Brigade powers-that-be have put a positive spin, therefore, on the Christmas Truce- they saw it as a useful intelligence gathering exercise and no mention was made of the treasonable nature of the armistices.

Private Mattey claimed that some of the men went into German trenches whereas fellow Private, Harry Morgan was of the opinion that 'the English officers used the pretext of getting the men back again, or going out to meet Germans half way to prevent the enemy seeing our trench system.'

I doubled the sentries: more experienced and older than many of his colleagues, Robert was not prepared to take any chances and played safe and thus ended, as agreed by all concerned, a 'remarkable' and 'extraordinary day' when humanity and decency overcame the horrors of war. For Lieutenant Bairnsfather and Private Mattey, the day ended bizarrely with the sight of one of Bairnsfather's machine-gunners cutting the hair of 'a docile Boche, who was patiently kneeling on the ground'.

December 26th
The truce continues. Our guns opened fire on the second line german trenches, but *not a rifle shot was fired* all day. Such a relief to get one's morning duties done in peace and comfort. It all seemed strangely quiet at night and I hope they are not cooking some devilish plot. Wrote a long letter to Renie. The gang boarded the floor of my dug out, and put me in a stove and altogether made it so comfortable that all my subs seemed to think they are entitled to it. The Xmas mail came out with stacks of good things for everybody. We all *smoked german cigars.*

Down at the docks at 8.30. Waited till 2.30 for the *Medina* scorning the policeman's offer to go out in the tender and meet Adela. At last she came looking thin and older. We rushed across to North Rd. missed the 3 train and had to wait till 7. Home at 9 o'clock.

The truce continues: in his original diary Robert wrote 'we talk with the Germans at half-way.' Tapp observed that 'it's too ridiculous for words, we are all mixing up again.' As part of his duty as Forward Officer of the Royal Field Artillery, 2nd Lieutenant Drummond set off for his observation post at St.Yves after breakfast. He was met by his Sergeant-Major who excitedly reported that 'I have shaken hands with a German.' As Drummond approached the trenches it was 'just like Earl's Court Exhibition.' He and his telephonist walked down to the sunken road just 70 yards from the German trench. He and a Warwicks' officer met some Germans who 'were nice fellows to look at, they looked more like university students than soldiers.' Talking mostly in French, Drummond received some cigars and one of the Germans commented to him- 'we don't want to kill you, and you don't want to kill us, so why shoot?'

not a rifle shot was fired: from the Warwicks and Saxons opposite. This entry is at odds with the BWD which states that 'Truce ended owing to our opening fire. German light guns reply on 'D' Coy trenches. 2 wounded.'

In the OD, Robert recorded that 'I am told the General and staff are furious but powerless to stop it.' Significantly, he chose to omit the observation in his final version. Others were also thinking about the situation- William Tapp expressed his concern- 'I don't know what our General would say if he knew about this' and Harry Morgan later mused- 'If all the troops along the line had refused to fight on both sides, would the War have ended there and then?' Bairnsfather commented that 'With hate and all the propaganda that is used to inflame soldiers gone from the war, it would be hard to get the thing started again' and 2nd Lieutenant Drummond considered that 'the war was becoming a farce and the high-ups decided that this truce must stop.' The Generals did indeed react swiftly and General Smith-Dorrien was, on Boxing Day, seeking details of officers and units who had taken part in the Christmas Truce 'with a view to disciplinary action.' Few officers were brought to account; at worst they were given a reprimand. Meanwhile on the Warwicks' right flank the Wray brothers heard a voice calling out from the German trenches- 'want to speak to an officer…yesterday I gave my hat for bully beef…I have grand inspection tomorrow…you lend me and I bring it back to you'; the loan was made and the pact kept, sealed with a tin of bully!

smoked german cigars: in his original version they were described as 'jolly good german cigars'! The BWD noted that 'in the evening German star shells show large party of 'B' Company putting up wire. No shots were fired.'

Medina: it was a P. and O. ship torpedoed on February 1st 1917 off the coast of Devon.

Brigade WD - 'Left section shelled as usual, about 100 shells. No sniping.'

Sunday December 27th
The truce continues, so we all walk about as if there was no enemy within a hundred miles of us. We have dug more trenches, made *new parapets,* and put up miles of entanglements, and at night we hear them doing the same. Can't turn these talkative young subs out of my warm dug out with its fire. Shall have to detail a *fatigue party* to make them each, one of their own. Jackson and Lancaster called and left cards. I like Jackson, but can't make much of Lancaster.

My birthday which fact I actually forgot till Adela reminded me. Nice presents from Mama. We went to Bridestowe Church. Best sermon old F. ever preached with a birthday allusion strange to say and something for Adela rather to the point. We stayed in as it was a beast of a day.

December 28th

It rained all day, and we were thankful we were going to be relieved tonight. I suddenly resolved to make myself another large dug out, with the assistance of two of the Black Hat gang. They fetched a *table and chair* and a lamp from somewhere, and completed the dug out to their and my complete satisfaction. They said they would get me a bed and a cottage piano if I would like them. We were *relieved by the Dubs,* and got down to our farm when an order came for a fatigue party of forty men to clear mud away tomorrow.

The truce continues…walk about: according to Lieutenant Drummond it lasted for a week. Mutual trust still continued to the extent that Bairnsfather was able to explore the ruins of St. Yves and in the village he found a cottage, almost intact, in which he would fortify a room, a real 'luxury' after his damp dug out and where his 'Fragments from France' would take shape.

new parapets: both sides used these quiet days to improve their defensive systems, realistically accepting that the Truce could not last. On this day, Winston Churchill, First Lord of the Admiralty, wrote to Prime Minister Asquith- 'Are there not other alternatives than sending our armies to chew barbed wire in Flanders?' Later in the War he strongly supported the use of tanks in the hope they would limit the loss of lives.

fatigue party: men chosen to do chores, mostly heavy ones. From the French for 'tiredness', troops humorously pronounced it 'fattygew'.

In the OD Robert wrote 'hear that German aeroplanes have dropped bombs on Dover, Folkestone and the Thames.' On December 24th a German aeroplane made one of the first air raids on England- the bombs were dropped in the Channel near Dover and on Christmas Day the same plane, FF29, returned to drop two bombs in Kent.

table and chair: were likely to have been found in destroyed houses in the area.

relieved by the Dubs: this took place in the evening without incident and the Warwicks, after their Christmas in the trenches, moved to billets at Hill 63. There was evidence that the truce was still in operation- during the Dubs' tour of duty orders came to Drummond's battery behind the line 'that fire was to be opened on a certain farm behind the German support line.' He knew through his observations that Germans would be having coffee at that time so he went to see Loveband, commanding officer of the Dubs, who then 'sent someone over to tell the Boches'. The farmhouse was shelled and 'of course there wasn't anybody there'. **Lieutenant-Colonel Arthur Loveband** died on May 25th 1915 and is commemorated on the Menin Gate, Ypres.

December 29th

We marched over *to La Crèche* in oceans of mud, and found our billet most comfortable and warm. More parcels and letters for everybody. *The men in excellent spirits.* Thirty per cent are allowed *passes into the town.*

I hunted at Wrescham. Rotten day which should have been a capital one. Lots of foxes, quite good scent, wretched hunting.

December 30th

Rode over to Bailleul and ran up against old Archer, who told me the Norfolk regiment were in billets there. I went to their headquarters and there found *Done commanding, Johnnie Bagwell. Megaw, Brudenell-Bruce just the same.* Filgate, I was surprised to see, and Field, they all enquired after Renie, which I liked them for (Done married in November 1916 and became Brigadier-General).

THE BIRTH OF "FRAGMENTS": SCRIBBLES ON THE FARMHOUSE WALLS

December 31st: 'Bruce Bairnsfather dined with us…and showed us some of his sketches.' Robert and fellow officers had a preview of the first 'Fragments from France'   Barbara Bruce Bairnsfather

THE BYSTANDER'S
FRAGMENTS *from* FRANCE

"Well, If you knows of a better 'ole. Go to it."

By
Capt. Bruce Bairnsfather   1/- NET

The 1916 first edition of The Bystander's 'Fragments from France', a collection of
118   *41 cartoons*   Barbara Bruce Bairnsfather

to La Crèche: the BWD confirms that in the evening 'A' Company provided fatigue parties for the Royal Engineers.

The men in excellent spirits: not surprising after their experiences of the previous five days and they would have been keen to exchange individual stories with men from other Battalions.

In his OD he wrote' Before marching off, I had to address the Company on their behaviour lately. In spite of my giving them more liberty and many more privileges than any other Coy there were no less than nine cases of either drunkenness or absence. I warned them all beforehand and now they will have to suffer for it.'

passes into the town: the first mention of this- officers were more free to go where they wanted.

Done…just the same: Four of those mentioned were at the Royal Norfolk's Regimental Dinner at the Trocadero in 1912- Major H.R. Done who was in command of 'A' Coy when the 1/ Norfolks arrived in France on August 16th with Captains R.H. Brudenell-Bruce, Bagwell and W.C.K. Megaw who fell at the 2nd Battle of Ypres on April 25th (see p.19 and 22). Robert was pleased to meet his officer friends from the 1/ Norfolks who were in the 15th Brigade in the 5th Division. They had been involved in the retreat from Le Cateau in August, fought in the Battle of the Marne in September, were then sent north and joined the fighting along La Bassée Canal. At Christmas and New Year they were holding the line in the Wulverghem sector, west of Messines.

The BWD notes that the Battalion was sent to Nieppe to wash and a 'large number of men were inoculated.'

December 31st
Rain and wind all day. Cold a little better but still very deaf. The men are sending *Princess Mary's gift boxes home*. It is greatly appreciated. A nice letter from Renie, and a most flattering one from Fan. *Bruce Bairnsfather dined* with us, sang us some of his songs, and showed us some of his sketches, and we all saw the New Year in. *O dear!*

Princess Mary's gift boxes home: officers and men behind the lines were catching up with their mail and many sent their Princess Mary Christmas boxes home for safe keeping. It was an embossed box, containing accoutrements for smokers, and a card with a photo of the Princess and the King. All soldiers yearned for home- Lieutenant Black wrote in a letter on this day 'the Germans are just as tired of the war as we are, and said they would not fire again until we did.' Both sides had been confident that the War would be finished by Christmas. They could not have imagined that three more Christmas Days would pass before the War came to an end.

The Wray brothers, east of Plugstreet Wood, found a drunk German in the barbed wire and had to extricate him.

Little did 'A' Company know that there was a German cartoonist on the loose in nearby Messines! The cartoon on the wall shows, from the right, German soldiers cheering, Germans shooting and the French soldiers in retreat. The caption reads 'The fright of the French'   In Flanders Fields Museum, Ypres

Bruce Bainsfather dined:
Robert and the celebrating officers would have been some of the first to see the early 'Fragments from France' cartoons. Bainsfather claimed that he drew his sketches 'for entertainment at first' and that 'I always had this complaint in my blood.'

O dear: not a great idea to be returning to the trenches with raging hangovers! The BWD recorded that it was a 'miserably wet day' and recorded that Major Poole was to take over the 2nd Battalion of the Warwicks to replace Lieutenant-Colonel R.H.W. Brewis who was killed on December 18th south of Armentières when at least 9 officers were killed and 363 other ranks were casualties. The 2nd Warwicks arrived at Zeebrugge on October 6th and helped Belgian and French troops stem the advance of the Germans. W.L. Loring the Battalion's Lieutenant-Colonel at the time was killed on October 24th during an attempt to recapture lost trenches at Polygon Wood east of Ypres. Robert was sorry to lose Poole whose leadership he commended on a number of occasions.

 Lieutenant-Colonel Robert Henry Watkin Brewis died at the age of 41, fought in the Sudan, was mentioned in despatches and was buried in the Sailly-sur-la-Lys churchyard.

January 1st 1915
We marched up from La Crèche *straight into the trenches.* It poured in torrents the whole way, and we arrived drenched to the skin. I got a fire lit in my dug out, and we did the best we could to get dry, and it was a poor New Year's Day. *The Saxons* are very quiet in their trenches. Have been round

January 1st: Private William Tapp recorded in his diary that a dog was sent over to the British trenches with a message- this dog in 1917 was returning from a German advanced trench. Note the steel helmets which had by 1916 superseded the pickelhauben
Imperial War Museum Q50649

the sentries and warned them against surprise. We are all glad we have not got *the treacherous Prussians* opposite us. The three subs and young Jackson rolled up to my dug out at midnight, and there was just a tot for all.

119

January 2nd

We saw the germans *patching up* their barbed wire so we did a bit more to ours. Our guns and theirs were firing most of the day, and we watched them exploding, but no rifle shots were fired. We had our meals at a table placed in the sunken road. Cave recounts his numerous love affairs. In the middle of one, *Poole turned up* and finding us all convulsed with laughter remarked we were the happiest lot of company officers he had.

———

January 2nd: 'we had our meals at a table placed in the sunken road'- it was on the north/south road east of St.Yves. The British front line was over the embankment to the right and the Germans were in front of the trees, a mere 80 yards, the distance from a cricket pitch to the boundary! Broken Tree House(s) can be seen on the left (see p.135 and 140)   Alan Reed

straight into the trenches: William Tapp wrote that 'the Germans sent a little dog with a message reading "how are you nicey Englishmen, we are all well, please send the dog back.' The dog was given some bully beef and refused to return- fed up perhaps with German sausages!

The Saxons: were also happy not to resume hostilities.

the treacherous Prussians: not an unusual reaction from the British- the Warwicks and others were much better disposed towards the Saxons than towards the Prussians who were considered as less civilised and more aggressive. Even the Saxons blamed the Prussians for the resumption of hostilities!

patching up: according to the BWD there was 'no sniping all day' which allowed both sides to patch up their defences and dig new trenches. According to William Tapp, a German found drunk on the wire said that 'they all wanted to give in, but were afraid to come over'!

Poole turned up: he should have gone to take up his command of the 2nd Battalion by now; it is possible he dropped in to say his farewells.

The BWD registered that '2nd Lieutenant Maclagan and 50 other ranks join the Battalion.'

Sniper and Observer at Anton's Farm: Bairnsfather recalls that in the New Year he was sniping at the enemy from Anton's Farm- he escaped just before shelling started which was the inspiration for the cartoon 'They've evidently seen me' (see cartoon p.2 and maps p.134, 136 and 139)
Imperial War Museum Q50690

🔵 **2nd Lieutenant Gilchrist Stanley Maclagan** shared a dug out with Bruce Bairnsfather and moved into the cottage at St.Yves where Bairnsfather drew his first drawings on bullet-ridden walls in January 1915. Maclagan was described by Bairnsfather as 'an excellent fellow ...one of the best chaps I ever knew'. He was known as 'Hudson' in 'Bullets and Billets' and his true identity was uncovered by the detective work of Mark Warby, the Editor of *The Old Bill Newsletter*.

Educated at Eton and Oxford, Maclagan was a stock broker before the War. He was one of few Olympic gold medallists to die in the conflict- he had been cox of the Oxford crew that won the University Boat Race in 1901 and coxed the Great Britain Men's Eight to a gold medal in the 1908 Olympics.

He died on April 25th during the battle of St. Juliaan at the age of 36. His body was never found and he is commemorated on the Menin Gate. Brigadier-General Hull reported in January

1915 that Maclagan was 'a promising young officer who has a thorough grasp of his men who would follow him everywhere. Recommended for mention in despatches'. Bairnsfather wrote of his great friend 'Mac' that 'No one in this war could have hated it more than he did, and no one could have more conscientiously done his very best at it.' The same could have been said for most of his colleagues of all ranks who fought for the Warwicks in 1914 and 1915.

January 6th: 'We all met at the station Estaminet'- Le Café de la Gare at Steenwerck, on the right
Musée de la Vie Rurale de Steenwerck

Sunday January 3rd

We still continued to *peacefully look across* at each other. Determined these young subs shall build themselves a dug out and let me have a little privacy. Cave starts on an enormous one for himself. He says he is a married officer, and so is entitled to Field Officer's quarters. Wasey follows suit with one of his own designs, so rotten that the men only laugh at it and won't help him. A quiet night spent in my dug out, taking turn about for watch.

January 4th

Quite pleasant and quiet all day. The dug outs are progressing, thank goodness. *I sat on the parapet* and played the Austrian National Anthem. Four shots were fired at me, so I played Rule Britannia. I wonder why they didn't like the *Austrian air.*

January 5th

Cave's enormous dug out is finished and christened *Guy's Cliff.* We were *relieved by the Dubs* and marched back to La Crèche.

Photograph taken by Leutnant Zehmisch of N.C.O. Holland of the 134th Saxon Regiment with his booty captured from a British trench- coat, rifle, bayonet and a cap- possibly with a Warwicks' Antelope badge   In Flanders Fields Museum, Ypres

January 6th

Wasey and I, and the hunting horn, had a wet ride to work up an appetite for our smoking concert tonight. We all met *at the station Estaminet*, and had a most magnificent dinner, and many songs after. M. Guy Cave said he would see if he could round up some ladies for a hop, and produced four. The fun was fast and furious, and so was the dancing till the proprietor announced it was time we took the ladies home. *Young Bruce* was quite in his element.

peacefully look across: the Warwicks were lucky because elsewhere on the Western Front where Christmas Truces had been held, hostilities had generally restarted.

Leutnant Zehmisch's photograph of the ruined La Douve Farm which was behind the German trenches and was known to them as Wasserburg
In Flanders Fields Museum, Ypres

I sat on the parapet: although the ceasefire seemed to be still in progress, it was nonetheless a foolhardy thing to be doing.

121

Austrian air: Robert used his musical ability to provoke some inter-trench fun. Was it his playing or the Austrians' disappointing support for the Germans that provoked the shots fired at him? See his diary entry for May 30th 1915 on p.145 for his reaction to the Austrian anthem being played in an English Church.

Guy's Cliff: a bit of word play referring to Guy's Cliff, north of Warwick, an ancient site with caves.

relieved by the Dubs: before they arrived, during the night 'a German gave himself up to 'A' Coy in an intoxicated condition and was sent under escort to Div. H.Q.' It is strange that Robert should not have mentioned this unusual incident in his diary especially as it shows that discipline appeared to be slackening on the German side. This was Robert's last experience of Front Line conditions.

at the station Estaminet: the one at Steenwerck and well frequented by the Warwicks' officers.

Young Bruce: Bairnsfather has joined the fun from his billets at Neuve Église.

January 7th

Wasey and I had a nice ride. We called on the Plouvier girls who gave us tea, but would neither sing nor dance. We told them they should amuse the poor British officers who had such a dull time, and were so far from their homes. This quite fetched them, so they said they would just *sit on our knees*, which they proceeded to do. In came La Mère who remarked *"Eh, mais c'est la guerre"* and retired. Guy and I called in later on the station Estaminet where we found quite half the company. They insisted on standing us a cup of coffee and cognac. We stayed while they sang a song or two.

January 9th: 'the great Harwood'- within three days Robert had taken his leave of the Western Front. This photograph taken on June 1st 1916 shows 'the only two remaining Warwicks' officers of those who fought from August 22nd onwards'. Harwood is seated on the left and Major J.A.M. Bannerman in the centre
Royal Fusiliers Museum (Royal Warwickshire)

January 8th

Rode into Staenweck to attend a court of enquiry. A jovial young Major was the president, and we made short work of the business. We had a pleasant drink at my tavern, and then took lunch with the A.S.C. where I met *young I.K.Hamilton*, who has brought out a draft for the regiment. A nice lad who wants to be posted to 'A' company. We marched up to our farm.

January 9th

Rode down to post letters to Renie, and called in on the transport to see if *the great Harwood* had gone on leave, as I go when he returns. Found him quite unable to make up his mind whether he would go now or later, oblivious to the fact that unless he let the brigade office know one way or the other, he would throw the roster out, and our leave would be once more postponed. I therefore jumped on to Beauty, and rode straight to divisional headquarters, telling Harwood, that if he didn't want to get home, I did. There I found that Harwood was expected at Nieppe at 5.30 p.m. and that two other officers might go too. So I said "Right, that's me." I got my pass, and was told to wait at the transport farm for further orders. So returned to farm, and pushed off old Harwood, and took charge of stores and horses. The staff captain was there, and said he would do his best to get me off tomorrow. Too excited to sleep much.

Sunday January 10th

Got up early and went for a ride. A fine sunny morning. The padre held a service in one of the barns. The vet came to look at the sick horses, so I assumed a knowledge I had not, and all *passed off fine. Irvine and I rode in the afternoon round Neuve Église, and got back for tea before it started to rain, as if it had not rained for years.*

---

sit on our knees: meanwhile… back on the Home Front, Renie was dealing with the children, the farm and the animals… and the vicar and his wife…

"Eh, mais c'est la guerre": see his entry for October 8th on p.63.

young I.K. Hamilton: no relation, he died at Ypres in June 1915- see diary entry for February 10th 1915 on p.142.

the great Harwood: Captain T.H. Harwood is registered on the officers' list for 1916 and with Lieutenant-Colonel J.A.M. Bannerman, was one of only a few Warwicks' officers still serving in France in 1916. Harwood was mentioned favourably in Brigadier-General Hull's report as 'a hard worker who looks well after the comfort of the Battalion and is always up to time.'

Irvine: **Captain Gerard Faster Irvine** aged 23 died on October 24th 1916. His name is on the Thiepval Memorial in the Somme.

Neuve Église: north of Nieppe, across the border into Belgium where the Transport Farm was and where Bairnsfather was billeted with his machine-gun section.

January 11th
Rode up to headquarters to attend a *D.C.M. on poor Hadley* for desertion in the face of the enemy. Fear the worst. I said all I could for him. After the D.C.M. I was told there were no orders for my leave. Then I was told there were, so I got on the telephone, and rang up divisional headquarters, who told me that my leave was sanctioned, and that the bus started at 9 p.m. from Nieppe. The bus was lit by electric light, and very comfortable. Seven or eight other officers all very silent and happy. We reached *Hazebruck* at 10.15 p.m. to find there was no train till 3.30 a.m. Webb and I found a private house and sat down to dinner with Madame and her two pretty daughters. When we got back to the platform, we found all the other officers asleep, anywhere, so we woke the lot up, and made them play *the game* the children play on pavements with squares marked in chalk and a bung. We ended the night with the word making game.

D.C.M. on poor Hadley: Robert should have recorded it as an F.G.C.M. (Field General Court Martial): despite his pessimism, Robert's defence of Lance-Corporal Hadley succeeded as Hadley was found not guilty of desertion but guilty of absence without leave and was sentenced to one year's imprisonment and stripped of his rank. At the same Court Martial, Robert may also have spoken up for Private S. Greaves who was found guilty of sleeping at his post when acting as a sentry. His sentence was the death penalty, but this was commuted to three years' penal servitude. Five Warwicks' soldiers were not so lucky and were 'shot at dawn' later in the War:

Albert Henry Pitts (Lance-Corporal): 2/ Warwicks for desertion on February 8th 1915. He was the husband of Mrs A.L. Pitts of 44, King's Road, Bengeworth, Evesham. The location of his grave was lost, so his name was inscribed on the Ploegsteert Memorial.

Arthur Grove Earp (Private): A Kitchener volunteer for the 1/5 Warwicks, he was sentenced for quitting his post on May 1st 1916. At his trial on July 10th the Court Martial panel was told that he had been suffering signs of distress for some time and taking into account previous good service, a mercy sentence was recommended. However, this was countermanded by Army Commander General Hugh Gough who sentenced him to death, thus making an example of him at a time when the Battle of the Somme was raging. Earp had lived in Friston Street, Ladywood, Birmingham. He was buried in the Bouzincourt Communal Cemetery Extension.

Samuel Cunnington (Private): a regular who enlisted in January 1914 aged 19 in the 2/ Warwicks. He was the son of Mrs. Ann Cunnington of 25 Pope Street Birmingham, and was shot on May 19th 1917 for repeatedly deserting. He was buried at the London Cemetery, Neuville-Vitasse. According to the Commonwealth War Graves Commission website his brother 'also fell' but unlike his brother Samuel, at the hands of the enemy.

Frederick Broadrick (Private): 11/ Warwicks for desertion on August 1st 1917. A Kitchener volunteer, he was arrested in Calais and was already under a suspended death sentence for desertion. He was buried at Dranoutre Military Cemetery.

Charles Britton (Private): 1/5 Warwicks for desertion on September 12th 1917. He had absented himself from a company parade prior to going to the trenches. A conscript, he was the son of John and Ellen Britton of Allison Street, Birmingham and was buried at the Mendinghem Military Cemetery.

In total, 306 British troops were executed by the authorities on the Western Front, the majority of 264 were for desertion and cowardice, 7 quitting post, 5 disobedience, 19 murder, 4 striking a superior officer, 2 casting away arms, 3 mutiny, and 2 for sleeping while on sentry duty...

Hazebruck: spelled Hazebrouck, is the capital of French Flanders and a key railway junction with lines going to the Channel Ports and Poperinge. It became the major objective of Operation Georgette, one of the Germans' spring offensives in April 1918. The Allied line manned by Portuguese troops broke and Hazebrouck was threatened but saved by the intervention of the 1st Australian Division. On April 12th Field Marshal Douglas Haig issued his famous order- 'with our backs to the wall and believing in the justice of our cause, each one of us must fight to the end.'

the game: back at the trenches, the Warwicks were involved in a different 'game'- 'about 25 shells came over our trenches during the day without causing casualties. 2 wounded by snipers.' According to Sergeant Philpotts, after hostilities had restarted, a voice was heard from the German line asking "Are you the Warwicks? Any Brummagem lads there? I have a wife and 5 kids in Brummagem." The German chef from Birmingham elicited a sharp reply from the 'company wag'- "Yes mate and if you don't get your head down, there will be a widow and 5 orphans in Brummagem"!

TIPS BIRMINGHAM F.C. FOR PROMOTION.

Private Tapp, photographed in the trench he has so gallantly helped to defend. He is a keen Birmingham F. C. supporter, and has tipped them for promotion. His forecast, however, has caused a lot of argument in the trenches.

Private William Tapp: featured twice in The Birmingham Post's *Picture World on March 10th 1915, a member of a 'happy group of the 1st Warwicks'. His diary came to an abrupt end mid-sentence*

January 12th

Arrived at Boulogne at 7.30. Got our papers, and on to the boat quick and lively. Choppy crossing. Folkestone at 11.45 a.m. Wired to M. and Susan. Victoria 2.45. Left Waterloo 3.30 p.m. after *telling off a drunken captain of Kitchener's army. Okehampton 8.30 p.m.* Eat four boiled eggs on the restaurant car. Home 9 p.m. Renie arrived having motored all the way from Exeter. *All's well that ends well.*

———

telling off a drunken captain of Kitchener's army: after all that Robert had experienced as a 'regular' soldier, this incident would be upsetting for him. It did not augur well for the future as Kitchener's Army was the New Army consisting of the volunteers who answered the call-to-arms. They were also referred to as 'Kitchener's mob' by the 'regulars'.

Back at St.Yves, there was no incident of interest. In his diary William Tapp recorded that there was 'little sniping' and 'we can fetch water now without being sniped at' but on the other hand, a fellow soldier who 'stepped out of a ruined house smoking a cigarette' had a 'dozen shots fired at him' and Tapp commented that 'he won't do that again'!

'A happy group of Birmingham men of the 1st Warwicks in the trenches. They have experienced heavy fighting, but have repulsed the Germans. Private Tapp (second from left) was a recipient of one of the "Picture World" Christmas Boxes.

Okehampton 8.30 p.m: meanwhile in the trenches, the Dubs were relieving the Warwicks who returned to Hill 63.

All's well that ends well: a phrase Renie used on August 10th when her horse Gyp galloped around on the tennis court at Collaven without causing damage. For Robert, returning home marked a happy ending to the most eventful period of his life. Considering himself fortunate to be away from the danger zone of Plug Street, he would respond with great sadness on learning about the news of many casualties for the 1/ Royal Warwicks during the 2nd Battle of Ypres in late April 1915.

11

'A Day Unique in the World's History'

The Christmas Truce between the soldiers of the 1st Battalion of the Royal Warwickshire Regiment and the 134th Saxon Regiment, entrenched north of Ploegsteert Wood 1914

Christmas Eve:

'This is the day God made.' Soldiers of the Saxon 134th Infantry Regiment raised the roof of what was left of the half-ruined sugar factory with their rendition of the traditional Christmas hymn. The regimental chaplain reminded his packed congregation of the religious significance of the evening. The strains of 'Silent Night, Holy Night' drifted into the clear starlit night above.

"Just as the candles burn in the hands of our German warriors here tonight and on the Christmas trees in their billets, so do they burn at home and wherever Germans are to be found. We are a great nation and we will rejoice in this." His sermon was followed by the carol 'O happy, O blessed', a stirring 'Deutschland, Deutschland über alles' and the blessing. Leutnant Kurt Zehmisch noticed that several of his comrades had been moved to tears. He blew out the candle he was holding.

At 6 o'clock, with heavy hearts, Zehmisch's company assembled prior to their stint in the trenches. He ordered that "no shot is to be fired tonight or on Christmas Day unless in retaliation." The prospect of a peaceful spell of duty cheered them greatly as they marched to relieve 1st Company.

By 6.30 p.m. 'C' Company of the 1/ Royal Warwicks had settled into their trenches. Private William Tapp was struck by the lack of enemy gunfire. Instead, he could distinctly hear the sound of singing from the German trenches opposite and had a hunch that his prediction made two days earlier that 'we shall be pals by Christmas' might well come to fruition. He had enjoyed the pre-Christmas banter between the two sides when the Saxons' version of the British National Anthem was greeted by the Warwicks with, alternately, 'hurrahs' and 'boos'. His officer, Lieutenant Tillyer, had ordered the men to sing a song in return, which they duly did with gusto. The quality of the exchanges declined though, when Tapp shouted across the divide "Waiter! Sausages!"- which was followed up with five rounds of rifle fire.

The silence that greeted 'A' Company as they crossed the danger zone to the trenches, also made an impression on their commanding officer Captain Robert Hamilton. Disappointed at having to spend the festive season in the trenches, Hamilton and his Company were effusively wished a Merry Christmas by the Royal Dublin Fusiliers on their way out of the trenches. Their wishes were returned with an unseasonal bluntness tinged with envy. An officer warned Hamilton that something strange was in the air- the Germans were keen to parley.

Lieutenant Bruce Bairnsfather finished his glass of red wine and dragged himself away from the fire and conviviality of his dug out and joined some of the men of 'C' Company who were in festive mood. "You can hear 'em quite plain sir, singin' and playin' in a band or summat." When a repeat of 'Deutschland, Deutschsland über alles' reached a rousing crescendo, several of the Company's mouth organ specialists retaliated with volleys of ragtime and versions of German tunes they had heard.

Leutnant Zehmisch was aware that both sides wished to make contact. He started to whistle, which soon became cacophonous when his men followed suit. They were pleased to receive a similarly discordant response from the 'enemy'.

Zehmisch and Private Möckel, who had spent several years in England, called out in their best

English to suggest a meeting between the trenches for an exchange of German cigars and English cigarettes. Privates Möckel and Huss then carefully threaded their way through the barbed wire entanglements that guarded their forward trenches.

Bairnsfather turned to machine-gunner Sergeant Rea- "Sergeant, we'll go along the ditch to the hedge there on the right- that's the nearest point to them, over there." The two men made their way along the frozen ditch. Shouting could be heard from the Saxon trenches- Möckel shouted out "Varvickshires! Come over here!" He was greeted with raucous laughter and another dissonant recital by the mouth organ players.

Bairnsfather and Sergeant Rea continued down the line of the hedge and requested that the Germans meet them halfway. "But there are two of you" was the suspicious response so Bairnsfather's colleague proposed that he press on alone. As he approached, he held up both his hands; in one, he held a cap full of English cigarettes and tobacco. He came up to Möckel and Huss and wished them a Merry Christmas; 'C' Company listened in breathless anticipation. A muffled conversation was audible in the darkness. Their Sergeant held out his free hand and hearty handshakes followed. The meeting was greeted with enthusiastic applause and cheering from both sets of trenches. They lit each other's swapped cigars and cigarettes- the Sergeant inhaled his German cigar deeply, stepped forward and called out to the Saxon trench "I wish you all a Merry Christmas and a Happy New Year." Leutnant Zehmisch enthusiastically shouted back his thanks and wished all those in the Warwickshire trenches the same. To a man, 'C' Company called out greetings and promises to halt hostilities on Christmas Day. The men were illuminated by a star shell sent up by Zehmisch's Company- they shook hands again and returned to their trenches. A few minutes later Rea appeared to a loud cheer as he held up his haul of German cigars.

"No body to deal with then?" Redundant stretcher bearers in 'C' Company's trench groaned at Private Tapp's pun and struck up another carol. Their efforts were cheered by the appreciative German audience. Tapp turned to two fellow officers' batmen and expressed his appreciation of Sergeant Rea's decision to meet two Saxons on his own and of his return with a negotiated ceasefire for Christmas Day.

Similar inter-trench requests were made by 'A' Company and their opponents for a cigar and cigarette exchange. Captain Hamilton's former batman, Private Gregory, asked if he could go out halfway. Hamilton assented but warned him such a meeting would be "at your own risk". Gregory stepped over the parapet and met two Germans who were covered by another, fully armed behind them. There was much merriment when Gregory returned and, ostentatiously smoking his recently acquired cigar, told of the yarns he had spun about the Company's strength. He told Captain Hamilton that the German officer wished to parley with him on the morrow. After much shouting across No Man's Land, it was agreed that they would meet at dawn, unarmed.

Leutnant Zehmisch checked the English cigarettes and tobacco brought back by Möckel and Huss and then ordered that candles be lit and placed on top of the mile long trench. A full repertoire of Christmas songs and songs of the homeland were sung by his men. Sergeant Philpotts was impressed with the quality of the German singing and enjoyed their midnight version of 'Mid pleasures and palaces we may roam'. Charlie Pratt and those around him were transfixed by a cornet player whose rendition of 'Home Sweet Home' was a poignant reminder of those left behind at home- they applauded his effort enthusiastically.

Christmas trees adorned with burning candles were placed at regular intervals along the German trenches and each new tree received a rapturous reception. For the Warwicks, the display of Christmas trees and sparkling lights was a magical and spell-binding spectacle. Sergeant Rea had successfully read his officer's thoughts- "You should write one of your plays about all this when the war's over sir."

Men in both sets of trenches were trying to come to terms with the meaning of what had occurred and what the new day would bring. Many, like Leutnant Zehmisch, were too excited to sleep; for him it had been 'a wonderful night' and Tapp 'would not have missed this night for a lot.' Sergeant Philpotts, however, was one of many of the Warwicks who were still 'sore' about the way the Germans had treated the body of their commanding officer, Major Christie at Méteren Church on October 13th. Grudgingly he would join in the fraternisation.

Christmas Day

'No guns. No bullets. No voices.' At dawn, during stand to, men of all four companies of the Warwicks were overwhelmed by the pervasive silence. Private Harry Morgan chuckled when the spell was broken by a Saxon's attempt at a cock crow- he and others in 'C' Company expressed a few suggestions as to what they would like to do to the fowl impersonator if they ever laid hands on him.

It was a cold, beautiful morning; a low lying mist was slowly lifting. The previous night's Christmas trees were coated in glistening frost.

Leutnant Zehmisch and his men stood up in front of the parapets- when Morgan and Bairnsfather saw them walking about freely, it was a clear sign that the negotiated ceasefires had started.

As agreed, Captain Hamilton calmly marched into No Man's Land and met his Saxon counterpart whom he noticed was armed. They shook hands, and undeterred by the lack of a common language, concluded a 48 hour truce. Similar fraternisation broke out as far as the eye could see.

In most cases, the initial advances on Christmas Day were made by officers. Zehmisch met three officers with whom he was delighted to hold a conversation in English, French and German.

For all the soldiers in the area, meeting their enemies took priority over any expected duties. Meeting men who were suffering the same privations as themselves and a brief opportunity to ameliorate their wretched situation was to be grasped and savoured. Private Tapp pulled a button off his coat and exchanged it with a Saxon who did likewise. Like an excited schoolboy, Tapp was thrilled with his haul of cigars, two buttons and a cap badge and two cigarettes. He was surprised by how many of the Saxons whom he met could speak English and agreed with them that it was a 'pity to fire while we are up to our knees in mud'.

Lieutenant Bairnsfather mingled amongst the German soldiers, unashamedly making mental notes for future cartoons.

"Offizier?" Bairnsfather's uniform singled him out as an officer; he nodded and being 'a bit of a collector' pointed to his buttons and using a pair of wire clippers, removed them and received two in return.

Private Morgan was justifiably pleased with the bargain he negotiated- a cigarette case in return for a tin of bully beef!

Officers were taking advantage of the lull to order work on their trenches and barbed wire entanglements. It was also an opportunity to bury the dead. Zehmisch's men buried English and German bodies that had, for over up to a month, decomposed and been ravaged by rats. The smell was gut wrenching. At 7.30 a.m. Sergeant Philpotts saw three Germans approaching with a Red Cross. "As it is Holy Christmas we will allow you to bury your dead." Sworn enemies dug a mass grave on the edge of Plugstreet Wood and buried troops from both sides. As many as 50 of the Somerset Light Infantry, killed trying to 'straighten our line', were buried there. It was fitting, he believed, that a 'proper' military funeral followed.

Bairnsfather and Morgan joined a growing crowd of Warwicks and Saxons who were enjoying the bizarre sight of machine-gunner Jack Reagan, a barber by trade back home, cutting the lengthy locks of a Saxon who was patiently kneeling on the ground while the barber's clippers tidied up the nape of his neck.

Captain Hamilton was astonished to meet the Chef of the Trocadero and announced he would gladly swap his rations of bully beef for the Dinner he had enjoyed two years earlier.

"It was a quite capital Dinner Herr Chef."

"I could open a tin of Maconochie's for you now, Sir!"

The Chef reflected that a return to London was an unlikely scenario and was surprised that his former customer was no longer with the Norfolks.

"Have you seen any of your old comrades, Sir?"

"I think they are in the Wulverghem sector and have been billeted in Bailleul.'

Their conversation was interrupted by Lieutenant Black who was concerned that members of the Company were outnumbered by four or five to one by the Germans. He expressed his anxiety to Captain Hamilton who, despite being older than most of the Battalion's officers, was, he felt, less circumspect at times than he should have been. Eventually 'A' Company returned to their trenches after, to Black's amusement, much bowing.

Private Harry Morgan pinched himself again- he had now been in France for nearly two months and after the hell of life in the trenches he had found the whole experience unbelievable. Before dusk, one of his officers came through the trenches Father Christmas-like, presenting every soldier with a gift from H.R.H. the Princess Mary: an embossed box, which contained a pipe, six cigarettes, an ounce of tobacco, a tinder lighter, a Christmas card and a photo of the Princess and the King. "Bless her heart" he murmured in appreciation.

In Leutnant Zehmisch's section of No Man's Land, one of his subalterns, N.C.O. Holland took three photographs of mixed groups of English and German troops. Not long afterwards, a couple from 'C' Company brought out a football and using caps as goalposts started an impromptu and rigorous 'international' match. Handshakes followed and an honourable draw agreed until they returned to their trenches when, of course, victory was claimed.

In the late afternoon, efforts were made to arrange a grand Boxing Day match between the best players from the English and German Companies. Zehmisch regretted that a fixture might not be possible as he and his Company were scheduled to be relieved and a new officer would be in command.

Sergeant Philpotts engaged in a conversation with a German soldier who had been a chef in Birmingham and had left his wife and five children there when he travelled to the Front.

After dusk, soldiers on both sides mulled over what had happened. Tapp and three other officers' servants were of one mind that it had been an extraordinary day. He was amazed at how different it had been to recent Christmas Days he had spent, especially the one in 1910 when he had stood under the mistletoe with the girl he later married. The fraternisation in No Man's Land had been 'strange and unbelievable'. He had been struck by the superb Christmas lunch they had concocted and said to his colleagues- 'I hope everyone back home in England has as good food for their Christmas Day.'

Zehmisch and his fellow officers considered that it had all been 'so marvellous and strange'. How wonderful he mused, that after all, the Christmas Festival of Love, should have caused enemies to be friends for a short time. He nor anyone else present would ever forget their special Christmas and N.C.O. Holland doffed his Royal Warwicks cap to Zehmisch and wished him a Happy Christmas and, he hoped, a peaceful New Year. Lieutenant Bairnsfather was convinced that there had not been 'an atom of hate' shown by either side: suspicion maybe- Captain Hamilton doubled the sentries after midnight, just in case and to calm the nerves of young Lieutenant Black.

At 10 p.m. officers of all four of the Warwickshires' Companies met in 'D' Company's support trench for a concert. A couple of mouth organs foot-tappingly set the tone.

Robert Hamilton performed a number on the concertina he had found in a German trench weeks earlier and concluded proceedings with a resounding 'Tally ho' on his hunting horn. Bruce Bairnsfather performed a one man sketch that highlighted the differences between the light-hearted and humorous Warwickshires and the sombre, faded and unlovable 'Huns'. The heaving dug out rocked with laughter at his spontaneous Music Hall turn.

After midnight, they stumbled down to Captain Hamilton's dug out where they were confronted with an exhibition of the latest pin-up girls from *The Tatler*. The stove had been lit and warming cups of tea were much enjoyed. The 'A' Company officers concluded the proceedings with their party piece. Hamilton introduced it with sincere apologies to the nursery rhyme:

Ten little Pickelhauben advancing in a line
Bum crack Bum crack
Then there were nine

Nine little Pickelhauben marching to their fate
Shelled again Bum crack
Then there were eight

Eight little Pickelhauben case of Hell or Heaven
Crackfire, Gun Pop Popped
Then there were seven

Seven little Pickelhauben in a fix
The sentry drew a head on one
Then there were six

Six frightened Pickelhauben into cover dive
One round rapid
Then there were five

Five shaky Pickelhauben knowing what's in store
Just a sudden plip plop
Then there were four

Four tired Pickelhauben quite a sight to see
One more round of rapid
Then there were three

Three nervy Pickelhauben wondering what to do
An accidental enfilade
Then there were two

Two funky Pickelhauben about to run
A German shell Bum cracked
Then there was one

The last little Pickelhauben thinking of his wife
Raised his hands, dropped his gun
And thus saved his life

So…. Remember little Pickelhauben, altho' we be but few
In future be more wary
Of French's deadly crew

Well into the dead of night, the officers took their leave and returned to their dug outs, safe in the knowledge that hostilities were unlikely to resume in the morning. Lieutenant Black wandered back contented that it had been a very happy time and it had been such 'an extraordinary feeling strolling around about outside the trenches'. What a shame that his late 'poor servant' had been hit in the head just after making his lunch for him last time they were in the trenches, falling back into his dug out and practically into his arms. 'Such rotten luck when everything is so peaceful now,' he thought to himself.

As Lieutenant Bairnsfather bedded down in his dug out, he marvelled at his Christmas Day which had been for him, a perfect day for peace to be declared. After weeks of deadly sniping and shelling, it was as though the Truce had put a 'punctuation mark on all the combatants' lives of cold and humid hate'.

In the quiet of his dug out, Captain Hamilton sucked his pencil between his teeth, thought momentarily and entered in his diary- 'A DAY UNIQUE IN THE WORLD'S HISTORY'.

Boxing Day:

Soldiers awoke to a thin scattering of snow that covered the scarred ground between the trenches. Private Tapp was called into action at 7.40 a.m. as Lieutenant Tillyer was impatiently awaiting his breakfast. Saxons were walking on top of their trenches and there was more mingling between the two sides. Tillyer congratulated Tapp on the quality of his breakfast.

"You know Sir, I miss the sound of shots flying over- it's like a clock that's stopped ticking."

An hour later, Lieutenant Tillyer suggested to a group of Germans that they return to their trenches for their safety. Tapp sadly concluded there was little chance of a football match now.

Leutnant Zehmisch was disappointed that shellfire was exchanged by the artillery behind the lines and ordered his men to stay down low in their trench.

The desultory nature of the shelling convinced Tapp that it was safe to take a stroll to a nearby cottage where, usually, neither side dared venture. He had been ordered to look for coal and on his way, he met a German whose intention was to barter for a British Army knife. He made it plain that his knife was not up for grabs but the fruits of his negotiation were three coins, five rounds of ammunition and a cigar in exchange for his cigarettes.

Tapp and the German entered the cottage; the German helped him fill his bag with coal and it was only polite, he thought, to reciprocate. The German offered to shake his hand but not so courteously, Tapp refused. Shaking hands with a German, despite the peaceful Christmas, was something he could not countenance.

Late on Boxing Day night, Captain Hamilton cut the end off his German cigar with the knife his 'best man' John Atkinson had given him as a wedding present in 1907. Puffing on it, he wrote to his wife Renie about his most unusual festive season. Much as he had missed celebrating Christmas with her and their children, six year old Cynthia and three year old Richard, he had experienced an extraordinary day. This evening was a time for reflection and in his diary he recorded that 'I am told the General and his Staff are furious but powerless to stop it.' The words 'court martial' never passed the lips of the Warwicks officers but what they had actively agreed to and participated in was, they knew, little short of a treasonable offence. In the warmth of their 'convivial' dug outs, the officers were confident that if all the officers accountable for local armistices and fraternisation had been court martialled, the British Expeditionary Force would have no longer functioned as a fighting force.

Hamilton's perception of the mood at Head Quarters at St.Omer was correct; the fraternisation had definitely been a step too far and one of the Generals, Smith-Dorrien, had received intelligence about widespread local armistices. He issued the strictest of orders on Boxing Day that 'on no account is intercourse to be allowed between the opposing troops.' The well-being of their fighting spirit was vital for future military success.

The tone of memoranda issued by the General did not bode well for Hamilton and fellow officers in the Battalion. 'I am calling for particulars as to names of officers and units who took part in this Christmas gathering with a view to disciplinary action.' It will have dawned on him and all at St. Omer after receipt of the first 'particulars' that the gatherings had been so widely spread in not only the Ploegsteert area that the enforcement of disciplinary action would have been a pointless and impracticable exercise.

After Christmas:

Soldiers of all ranks in the trenches accepted the inevitability of an end to the ceasefire. Private Harry Morgan was disappointed that it was his side that broke the trust that had grown between the two sides. A German soldier was walking along his parapet carrying a bucket, when further up the line, a member of the Company shot him. The German response was not surprisingly a furious bombardment.

If Leutnant Zehmisch and other German officers had received edicts from their high command, some disregarded it. Private Tapp was astonished when on New Year's Day, a little dog trotted over No Man's Land and jumped into his trench. A message was tied round its neck. It was fussed over and the message gently removed and read out. 'How are you nicey Englishmen? We are all well, please send the dog back.' The dog was fed some bully beef and refused to return!

On New Year's Day, no one serving with the Warwicks was in any doubt that hostilities would recommence. General Sir John French's order was unequivocal- 'informal understandings with the enemy are to cease.' Any officers who allowed them would be brought before a court martial.

The officers of the Warwicks knew how to party and they welcomed in the New Year with much merriment at the *estaminet* in La Crèche where 'A' Company was billeted. They were joined by Lieutenant Bruce Bairnsfather who entertained them with his songs and cartoons which were passed around the dinner table and much admired.

Captain Robert Hamilton crawled back to his billet in the early morning fearing for his health. Head pounding, the thought of marching his Company to the trenches east of the village was not a happy one.

When Hamilton marched his men on New Year's Day to their trenches to reacquaint them with the enemy and the dreaded discomforts and dangers, torrential downpours dampened their spirits, drenched them to the bone and thoroughly extinguished their Yuletide *joie de vivre*. The spirit of Christmas was over.

Many of those involved in the fraternisation in the Ploegsteert area never returned to their families.

🔵 **Private William Tapp** fell at the 2nd Battle of Ypres on April 25th 1915. His diary provides a fascinating contrast to the written works of the privately educated officers Hamilton, Bairnsfather and Montgomery. Its poor grammar and sentence construction are transcended by the perceptive and colourful record of a batman's life in the trenches and behind the lines. Contemporary accounts of the warfare constantly mention the all-consuming threat of wounds and death. Mid sentence, Tapp's diary was cut short by an exploding shell. The diary survived but his body was never found- his name is recorded on the Menin Gate in Ypres. He died only five weeks after he received a mention in *The Birmingham Post's* 'Picture World' supplement on March 10th 1915.

● **Lieutenant Richard Bateson Blunt Tillyer**, aged only 22, was the son of Florence Anna Tillyer, of Marston Gate, Brockenhurst, Hants, and Richard Henry Tillyer. He also died at the 2nd Battle of Ypres in April 1915 and his name is listed on the Menin Gate, Ypres.

● **Lieutenant Frank Henry Black** fell in the same battle. On April 7th 1915 he wrote a letter in which he expressed a wish that 'this silly old war would hurry up and finish. I feel I have done quite enough soldiering. I have also got a touch of lumbago.' His father had been Hon. Sec. of the Royal Society of British Artists and Principal of the Camden School of Art. His commanding officer Colonel A.J. Poole wrote on Black's death, that 'he was the greatest favourite with us all. Personally I feel I have lost a great friend, and one that I shall never be able to replace as one of my officers. Unfortunately we have been unable to recover his body at present, but will make every endeavour to do so.' From his hospital bed, Private Roberts wrote that 'at 4 a.m. on April 25th, Captain Black led an attack on enemy lines and was shot through the head. It was impossible for any of us to do anything for him as death was instantaneous. Capt. Black was one of our most popular officers and his death deeply felt amongst the boys of the Coy.' He was buried at Pont-du-Hem Cemetery, La Gorgue.

The British and German soldiers who participated in the extraordinary events over the Christmas period north of Plugstreet Wood in 1914, did so in defiance of the wishes of their commanding officers. The Christmas Truce has never failed to fire the imagination: it was a moment, a 'punctuation mark' of pure theatre when the stage was the pock marked and desolate area between the trenches, bounded by barbed wire and rotting corpses. Soldiers provided music, singing, magical props, suspense and improvised dialogue in a three day long morality play, in which the Christian ideals of peace and friendship prevailed over the dark forces of hostility and hatred.

The final curtain fell with one rifle shot. The sequel was a reversion to the farce of senseless human loss and misery.

Andrew Hamilton

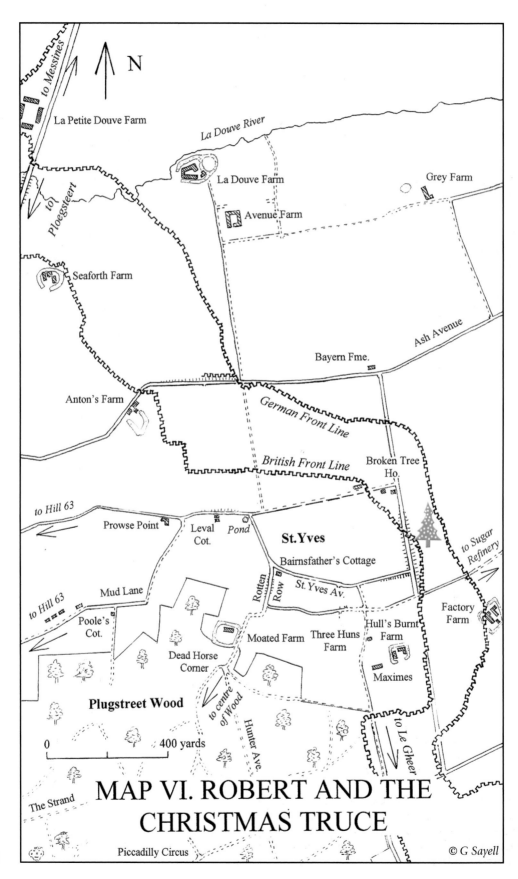

N

to Messines

La Petite Douve Farm

La Douve River

La Douve Farm

Grey Farm

to Ploegsteert

Avenue Farm

Seaforth Farm

Ash Avenue

Bayern Fme.

Anton's Farm

German Front Line

British Front Line

Broken Tree Ho.

to Hill 63

Prowse Point

Leval Cot.

Pond

St. Yves

to Sugar Refinery

Bainsfather's Cottage

Mud Lane

Rotten Row

St. Yves Av.

Factory Farm

to Hill 63

Poole's Cot.

Hull's Burnt Farm

Dead Horse Corner

Moated Farm

Three Huns Farm

Maximes

Plugstreet Wood

to centre of Wood

Hunter Ave.

to Le Gheer

0   400 yards

The Strand

MAP VI. ROBERT AND THE
CHRISTMAS TRUCE

Piccadilly Circus

© G Sayell

12

The Location of the Warwicks over Christmas 1914

The location of the Warwicks' Christmas fraternisation near Broken Tree House(s). Messines Church is in the background

The regular series of British Trench Maps 1:10,000 only started to appear in mid 1915. One dated July 17th shows the German Front Line. A useful one for reference is 'Ploegsteert 1.4.17' (see Map VIII) which indicates the location of the British and German lines which were to remain more or less unchanged until the German Spring Offensive of 1918.

A valuable starting point to study the entrenched lines at St. Yves is Leutnant Zehmisch's map (Map VII) which shows clearly the German position in early 1915. A larger scale map by Leutnant der Reserve Johannnes Niemann confirms the details of Zehmisch's map. It is interesting to note the different names given to the same positions by the opposing armies:

	British Name	German Name
The British side	Seaforth Farm	Englander Farm (Farm of the English)
	Anton's Farm	Heide Schlösschen (Little Castle of the Heath)
	Leval Cottage	Yves Schloss (Chateau Yves)
	Broken Tree House(s)	Söldner- Häuser (Mercenary's Houses)
The German side	La Douve Farm	Wasserburg (Moated Castle)
	Avenue Farm	Douve Farm
	Grey Farm	Abgebrannte Farm (Burnt Down Farm)
	Ash Avenue	Bayern-Strasse (Bavaria Street)

An invaluable source has been the plan drawn by Bruce Bairnsfather (see Sketch II overleaf) in which he shows, with a cross, where he met the Germans on Christmas Day and he also indicates where he positioned his machine-gun for the December 18th 'scheme' and where he had his 'sniping expedition at Anton's Farm' (see photo on p.120). He tells us in 'Bullets and Billets' that the Warwicks' position formed two sides of a triangle. In black, he filled in the square at the site of the cottage on St. Yves Avenue, where he drew his first 'Fragment'. On the pre-war plan of St. Yves the cottage was occupied by Edmond Verbeke a 'journalier' (a worker paid on a daily basis). On the opposite side of the road was the *estaminet* called 'Au Chant des Oiseaux' (birdsong) which was never rebuilt after the War.

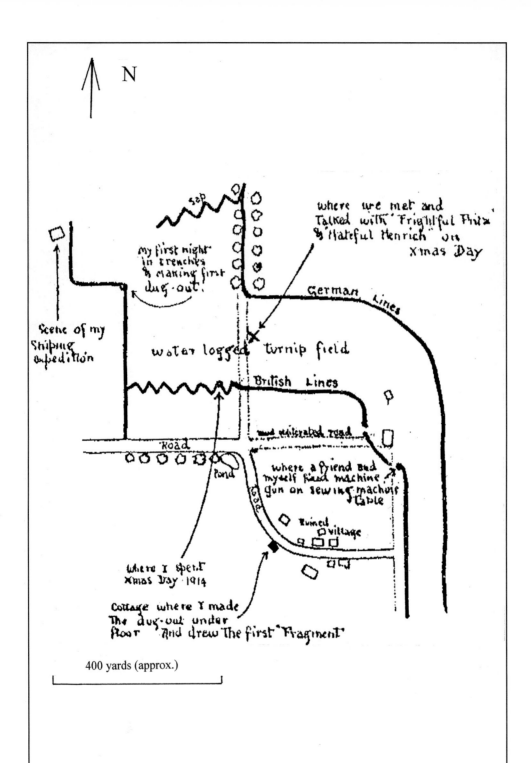

N

sap

where we met and
Talked with 'Frightful Fritz'
& 'Hateful Henrich' on
Xmas Day

my first night
in trenches
& making first
dug-out!

German Lines

Scene of my
Sniping
expedition

X

water logged turnip field

British Lines

mud obliterated road

Road

Pond

where a friend and
myself fixed machine
gun on sewing machine
table

Ruined
village

where I spent
Xmas Day 1914

Cottage where I made
The dug-out under
floor And drew The first 'Fragment'

400 yards (approx.)

SKETCH II. BRUCE BAIRNSFATHER'S
CHRISTMAS TRUCE

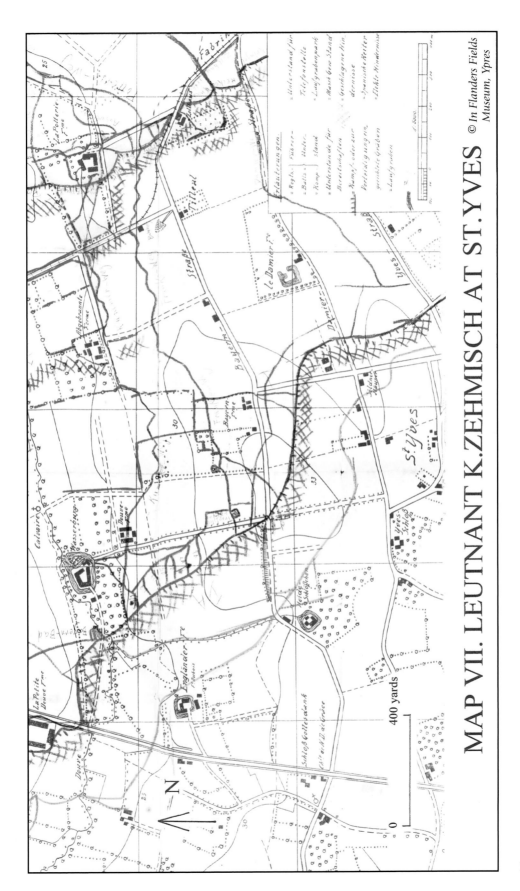

MAP VII. LEUTNANT K.ZEHMISCH AT ST.YVES

© *In Flanders Fields*
Museum, Ypres

400 yards

0

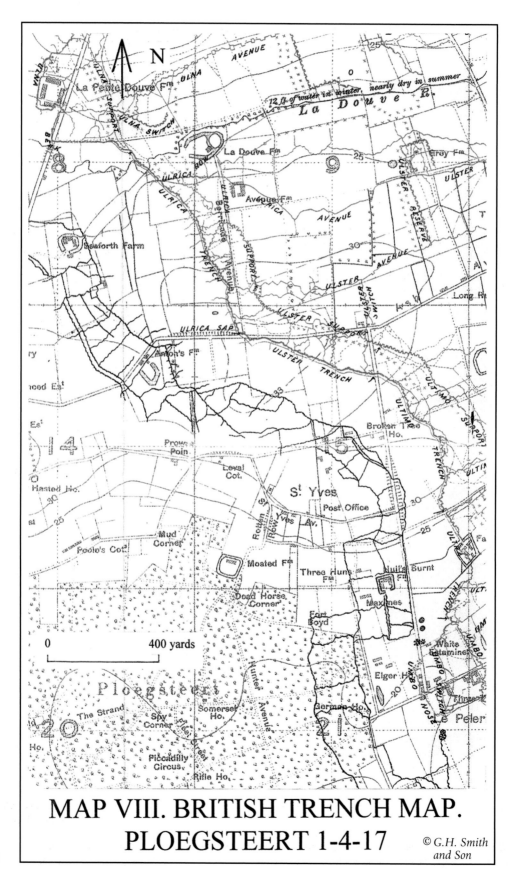

MAP VIII. BRITISH TRENCH MAP.
PLOEGSTEERT 1-4-17

© G.H. Smith and Son

Having studied the various accounts, it is possible to locate the front line positions of the four Battalions of the 10th Brigade in December 1914, as shown on Map VI. The Royal Warwicks and the Dublin Fusiliers were entrenched from Hull's Burnt Farm (named after their Brigade's Commanding Officer, Brigadier-General Hull) to Anton's Farm. The Seaforth Highlanders and the Royal Irish Fusiliers were in trenches from Anton's Farm towards La Petit Douve Farm.

The Warwicks approached the Front Line trenches from Hill 63 west of St. Yves; either they went along the road past Prowse Point or up Mud Lane on the northern edge of Plugstreet Wood and past Poole's Cottage(s) named after their Commanding Officer, Major Poole.

When going into the centre of the wood, they would have used Rotten Row behind Bairnsfather's Cottage. On the satellite image of the St. Yves area below, the opposing trench lines have been superimposed to show their location. A trench system is discernible in the Wasserburg area.

Robert refers to the 'sunken road' twice and to the Front Line being 'a few yards above us' not far from where 2nd Lieutenant Drummond of the Royal Field Artillery took the famous photograph of the Christmas Truce (overleaf).

La Douve Farm / Wasserburg

Anton's Farm   Prowse Point Cemetery   Bairnsfather's Cottage   'sunken road'   Area of Robert Hamilton's Christmas Truce

Satellite image of the Warwicks' Christmas Truce location- The British Front Line is blue and the red one is German. Robert was by the 'sunken road'. © 2008 Google © 2008 Cnes/Spot Image © 2008 Tele Atlas **139**

A reminder that the site of the Christmas Truce at St. Yves is still a dangerous area- Alan Reed and German friend in No Man's Land!

To the east of St. Yves part of the road going north/south below Broken Tree House(s) is distinctly sunken. The British Front Line lies just beyond, a mere 70 yards from the Germans according to Sergeant Philpotts and close enough for them to hear Robert play the Austrian National Anthem on January 4th. The low level of the road allowed Robert and his fellow officers to 'have our meals at a table placed in the sunken road' in relative safety on January 2nd. What a wonderful picture- British officers enjoying their lunch at a 'picnic' table within yards of the enemy! As he himself had commented about his ex-batman's meeting with the Germans on Christmas Eve- the officers' lunch was 'typically British'.

AR

Drummond's famous photograph of the gathering of the Warwicks and Saxons in No Man's Land near the 'sunken road'. Drummond's reminiscences were taped in 1976; not surprisingly sixty two years after the event there is, in our view, a degree of uncertainty in the transcript as to whether his photograph was taken on Christmas Day or Boxing Day. The general view amongst historians is that it was on Boxing Day. The British officer, second left, may well have been in Robert's 'A' Company and was not, as has been commonly believed, an officer in the Royal Dublin Fusiliers Imperial War Museum HU3580

13

'The whole world is waiting in hushed silence'

Extracts from Robert Hamilton's Diary 1915-1919
(commentary will be found within the text.)

January 14th 1915
The children and I played all sorts of games. I put them to bed and heard their little prayer.

January 15th
Played with Dickie and Toddles and put them to bed. They are the sweetest and best children I have ever seen.

January 19th
Did the dentist and ear specialist and then got an extension of leave till Saturday from the War Office with such ease that I was sorry I did not ask for more.

January 20th
Applied for a further extension of leave till 27th. And then had another morning with the snipe. They were very wild.

January 21st
Wire from W.O. saying if I wanted more leave, to send in another certificate; so wired to dentist to write another one till 27th.

Sunday January 24th
Renie wasn't very well which was a pity. We did not go to church in the morning as it was so beautifully fine and heard afterwards that the village had turned out to see me. We both went to the 3 o'clock service where there were a great many also.

- *On January 26th, William Tapp recorded that 'It is the Kaiser's birthday tomorrow so we shall look out for a surprise.'*

January 27th
Went to War Office and had my ears examined by two doctor Colonels.

Sunday January 31st
Motored in to Brighton and lunched at the Old Ship where I met some Norfolk recruit officers and Stracey. We had a walk on the front and the pier where we heard a bit of a concert. Tea at the Metropole where I met Col. Williams and Major Lancaster. Cinematograph show very good. We then motored back in the full moon after a good dinner at the Ship.

- **Major John Cecil Lancaster** *was killed just three months later on May 8th 1915- he is mentioned on the Menin Gate and has a grave at Oosttaverne Wood Cemetery- an oversight by the Commonwealth War Graves Commission that we are told will be rectified soon!*

February 1st
Left Waterloo at 10.30 p.m. and arrived Southampton 12.30 and went to Dolphin Hotel for the night.

February 2nd
Got onto the steamer for the Isle of Wight at 8.20 a.m. and proceeded through one continuous

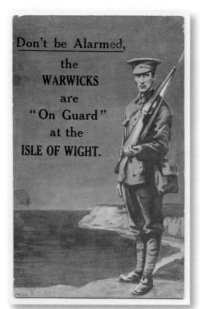

February 2nd 1915: Robert was responsible for training a draft of Warwicks to replace the increasing losses on the Western Front
Alan Reed Collection

line of ships of all sorts. Arrived at Cowes and trained on to Newport. Took a cab to the barracks arriving 10.30 a.m. All very pleased to see me. Guest night tonight with the full band.

February 3rd
The battalion went for a route march. I am to take over 300 men who are to form the next draft. There are 1700 recruits here and not a bad lot at all. 2,200 recruits and 57 officers have already gone from here.

February 4th
My company was distributed about the different barracks being taught musketry and bayonet fighting. Montgomery rolled up for lunch and seemed fairly fit. He has got a Brigade-Major job in the North of England somewhere.

• *Montgomery had recovered from wounds sustained at the Battle of Méteren on October 13th 1914. His star was by now in the ascendant but the letter below to Brigadier Tomes written 30 years after his departure from France, shows that he valued his grounding with the Royal Warwickshire Regiment.*

TAC Headquarters
21 Army Group
7/9/44

My Dear Tomes,

Thank you very much indeed for your telegram of congratulations from the Regiment. I value it very much. I never forget that I received my first education in the art of war in the Regiment and whatever success one has been able to achieve for the cause is due basically to those senior officers of the Regiment who taught one in the early days. To mention a few, Vaughan, Poole, Macdonald, yourself and many others.

Yours ever,

B.L. Montgomery

February 5th
Pte. Sperry turned up on the square and was very pleased to see me again. I have taken him on as my servant again. Took 'E' and 'F' Coy for a ten mile route march to the other end of the island. Guest night tonight with the band.

February 9th
Fine all day for a change. 'E' and 'F' Coys went for a route march and did a little tactical scheme half way. Had tea with Col.and Mrs. Clyne. Was President for the first time of a Court of Enquiry. Walked down to see what are now called the 'movies'.

February 10th
We were to have marched out to continue the Defence of the Island trenches but it was too wet a morning so I did a little squad scheme instead. Ian Hamilton turned up from the front where he has had rheumatism rather badly.

• **Lieutenant Ian Knox Hamilton** *of the 1/ Royal Warwicks died at the age of only 20 on June 1st 1915 and was buried at the New Irish Farm Cemetery. His father was the Rev. Edward Hamilton of Weston Road, Bath.*

February 11th
A beautiful day but very cold. Swinhoe and I walked down to get books to read. One Smithyson

of my company cut his throat and is not expected to live. I wired to his wife and she wanted to know whether 'she could see him.' I went to ask him in hospital and all I could get out of him on the subject of seeing his better half (apparently) was 'God forbid.' One lamb born at home. Lecture to the company on the position of the German Empire to the rest of the countries against her.

February 12th
Musketry on the range this morning- another lovely day. Another lecture on the causes of the war which the men seemed to appreciate. Walking back after the boxing show at 10.30 p.m. on the high road, I heard a cat mewing- I said to Swinhoe 'there's my black cat again' and sure enough up came a black cat and rubbed himself against my legs- I put him on my shoulder and carried him for a long way and then put him down. Funny the way these black cats find me.

February 18th
Toogood was sick so I took 'E' and 'F' Coys- 526 men. Impossible to make every man hear in the wind but they worked very well. Parade in the afternoon for the General tomorrow. Mrs. Sperry sent me two huge photos of her two children.

February 19th
We were inspected by General Campbell and marched past. Swinhoe and I had our photos taken in town. The Officers of the Battalion were photographed opposite the men- the regimental cat seemed to think that the photo would not be complete without her, so I took charge of her. Swinhoe and I played a game of billiards in the Warburton Hotel. Paid out the company.

February 20th
Route march, musketry and saluting parade. The C.O. and I went to Sandown to play golf- a lovely day but of course we both played abominably. Played auction after mess for 6d a hundred and won 7/6. Report that a liner was sunk in the Channel by a G. torpedo. Sperry had pinned up the photos of his two children above my mantelpiece.

- *On the day before, the Norwegian S.S. Belridge was torpedoed but did not sink.*

Hackett's latest drawing room yarns:
A parson took up farming and bought 200 ewes. Meeting a farmer one day he was told he would want some rams. The parson went to market and bought 200 rams...*and*

> There was a young lady of Ryde,
>
> Her ticket had failed to provide.
>
> A nice young conductor
>
> Came in and...kissed her
>
> And gave her a shilling beside.

Sunday February 21st
Church at 10 a.m. The usual service of four hymns and three prayers. Swinhoe and I hired a car and had a most delightful drive practically round the island. We were back for church in the town at 6.30.

February 24th
Route march and then company drill on the square- Toogood tells me that 'F' Coy is the best company in the Battalion.

February 25th
Company drill for the benefit of the young subs- Major Toogood and numerous other officers looked on. Toogood said he had never seen better results after only one month's training- his

own company had been here since November and he frankly owned they were not a patch on 'F' Coy. I hear a rumour I am to instruct the Battalion in bayonet fighting.

February 26th
Had a small scheme with the company. The inhabitants were much alarmed at my shells and thought there was an invasion on.

Sunday March 14th
Renie went to Church and I did not. Pte. Sperry with a party of lady friends arrived late causing quite a sensation- afterwards I told Sperry to bring Mrs. Sperry round and to my surprise it was not Mrs. Sperry.

March 20th
Field Day with my Company, 335 strong- Renie came out and was very amused at the battle. Sperry was in charge of the shell. We went to Whitwell where we had a most disgusting lunch.

March 27th
The Col. and I were going to Sandown to play golf but did not go- am not feeling at all fit these days.

April 7th
Solid drill all morning- men very slack. Seem to have forgotten all they knew. Had to get hold of a drummer to beat the time on parade as they could not even keep step.

April 9th
Went to the range and got caught in a blighter of a blizzard of snow and hail. Paid out all but the 9th Squad who are trying to make me believe that they cannot sight their rifles. They paraded at 2 p.m. and were to receive no pay until they could. It did not take long to discover how to do it. Appointment at Hereford as Commandant arrived from the War Office for me. The C.O. has to sanction it.

- *Commandant of the Military Detention Barracks*

April 16th
Left for Aldershot.

April 24th
Had an interview with Colonel Roy at the War Office. We had some lunch at one of Renie's restaurants where I thought some of the ladies were expecting something. We then got 2/- seats at the Palace and saw a wonderful show. We got on a bus and went to Putney Common which was Renie's treat to me and for which I paid. I shall soon have to buy her another hat to get square with her.

April 27th
I took the 1.30 from King's Cross to York. Met the Governor at Wakefield.

- *Prior to taking over at Hereford, Robert was gaining experience of a Detention Barracks at Wakefield.*

April 29th
My staff have all arrived and I have given them all a lecture which struck me later was pretty cool as they have all been at this sort of job most of their service. Many telegrams arrived asking for accommodation for criminals.

April 30th

18 men arrived- they will be washed and inspected and ready to be seen by me tomorrow.

May 4th

Met my spy man who is engaged by the Government as an interpreter for the West Riding District. He speaks with a strongly pronounced German accent.

May 14th

Major Leigh Lye inspected the whole of my Detention Barracks and made a report on them.

May 15th

Caught the 8.23 for home after signing numerous documents. Back home at 5.30. Renie and children very well. Rather too many weeds about and the fields have not been rolled.

May 27th

The work in the office seems to increase daily. It takes hours to read all the letters and correspondence and then the interviewing bad characters privately may be good work but it also takes time.

May 29th

Having cautioned once and let off once a certain worthless Private Dwyer, I had to inflict two days No.1 punishment diet on him for insubordination. This is the first man and I hope it may do him good.

- *No. 1 Punishment Diet: one lb. of bread per day and water only…*

Sunday May 30th

Church in the evening at St.John's Church where they had the affrontery to play the Austrian National Anthem to a quite unknown hymn.

- *See diary entry for January 4th on p.121 which shows that others did not like the Austrian anthem either!*

June 2nd

Now I have a fellow called Hamilton in. He is a thorough bad lot I am sure and I am going to have trouble with him. Have quite taken to Stoker Mordaunt- of course he knows no drill or anything and slouches about with a merry twinkle in his eye as much as to say "This is far better than stoking a battleship."

Wrote to Mrs. Black in condolence.

- *These may not have been their correct names, Hamilton and Mordaunt, as it is a slight coincidence that they bear the surnames of himself and Renie!*

- *Captain Frank Black had died in action at Ypres on April 25th.*

June 5th

Went to Oke great market to buy some young stock but there was nothing suitable- I walked up on the moor with the dogs and enjoyed the fresh air and sunshine to the full- spotted a nice little gorse bush which must come to Collaven in the fall.

- *Oke: Okehampton, nearest town to the Hamiltons' home.*

June 7th

The Sourton Sale at which we bought two yearling heifers and two nine months old steers. They must help to keep the two paddocks down as we do not intend to winter much stock this year and shall not require any more hay than last year.

June 12th

The tide of war has at last turned in favour of the Russians who are once more advancing and forcing back the Huns.

- *Huns- Robert uses the word more liberally than he did when in Flanders.*

- *Amongst Robert's papers was a letter Renie received from the Plouvier sisters of Steenwerck dated June 15th 1915 (see their earlier letter in diary entry for December 19th 1914 on p.107).*

'Madam,

We received your lovely letter from last month and we are all delighted to learn that your dear husband is in good health. His departure to England and his silence had worried us, this war is so terrible and murderous that it will have caused widespread grief. We send our sincere wishes and pray to God that he will remain in Yorkshire for the duration of the war.' They then apologise for their family having been unable to send a parcel of his clothes back to England. They tell Renie that their brother had been trying to find Robert near La Crèche where he had last been billeted. *'On returning from La Crèche he stopped at the café Joseph Charles near our station. Your dear husband must remember all the little places of our country. At the estaminet, he found two officers who knew Mr. Hamilton. One of them said "I will take the opportunity to give this to Mr. Hamilton and will take the parcel tomorrow," so a soldier came to collect it next day and our brother didn't think to ask the name of the officer being certain he would return it to you.*

Since your letter, we have been to the café to ask for information. According to what he says, it must have been Lieutenant Black, one of the officers who came from time to time to eat in the estaminet. Believe me Madam, that we are annoyed by this mistake. We would have preferred to have returned it directly to you. Please remember us to your husband. We send your children Richard and Cynthia our most tender kisses…

Bien cordialement,

Mlles Plouvier

- *The parcel probably never arrived because of the death of Captain Frank Black at the 2nd Battle of Ypres.*

'La Brasserie Plouvier'- the brewery owned by the Plouvier family
Musée de la Vie Rurale de Steenwerck

German Prisoners of War held at the Plouviers' Brewery
Musée de la Vie Rurale de Steenwerck

July 1st

Met my parish vicar as I was leaving on the subject of my walking out of his church when they played the Austrian anthem.

July 9th
Received 25 telegrams today asking for accommodation for prisoners. 15 of these telegrams could have easily been post cards instead- reported this to H.Q. Northern Command.

July 14th
The Padre and I called on Colonel Gordon Cumming and saw the German prisoners' camp at Lofthouse. They have more than every luxury that money can buy- they have plenty of money and have built themselves theatres, tennis courts and gardens and even have their own bands.

Sunday July 18th
Cathedral at 10.30. Had a sleep in the afternoon as my ear makes me feel all dizzy- when I woke up the SUN was shining brightly and it had stopped raining and as usual when the weather changes, my ears get better at once.

July 23rd
The children and I went up onto Sourton Tors. The hay is all cut.

July 28th
Went to York to see Major Hassall about special releases and petitions made by men to be reprieved and to go out to the Front.

August 7th
Dined with the Tews. The old man complained that the coffee was not hot enough, so I told him a bit of trench life would soon cure him of that complaint.

August 10th
Marriot hung on civil side for murder of his wife. The prison was full of officials all morning.

August 11th
Wrote to Col. Lawrence at the War Office for the Hereford job which should be better for the future than this.

August 20th
Parade of all men with sentences of 12 months and over to see about Special Release.

August 24th
Dashed up to Town and back. Met a doctor man in the Cri who had been a prisoner of war in Germany. Also another officer who was in the next lot of trenches to us and who had his hand shattered by a shell.

- *Cri: he may be referring to the Criterion Restaurant in Piccadilly.*

August 25th
Some of my Special Release men have not gone out yet because their regiments won't send escorts for them.

August 27th
Went out to see young Bobby Tennant, back from the trenches. A very good looking clean young English gentleman. He says that all are confident and cheerful out there. All the young girls for miles round came to pay homage to the young soldier. A telephone message announced the arrival of a Major Earle to take over from me. Met him later in the Strafford and did not take kindly to him.

September 2nd
The Bishop addressed the men on parade in the afternoon. This I should imagine is the first time a bishop has ever spoken to men undergoing punishment in a Detention Barracks. And it was very nice of him to do so.

September 8th

Dicky's birthday. Col.Turton came to inspect my barracks and made out a most flattering report for the W.O.

September 24th

A telegram from Western Command in answer to mine saying 'Report at Hereford when convenient.'

Sunday September 26th

Had a look at the Hereford Detention Barracks before going to the Cathedral and was quite favourably impressed. The service did not impress me. The sermon was by a fellow from the East pitying the life of the poor heathen Indian. I felt awfully inclined to tell him to get out to the Front and help us a bit first.

September 29th

Market day. Huge mass of farmers young and old. All seemed to be merry and bright and prosperous. The hotel was full up for lunch. Wrote to the War Office about them taking over and furnishing the Commandant's house.

October 7th

Recommended three for Special Release.

October19th

My overseas base kit arrived today with some of poor Taylor's things too.

- *Private Taylor his ex-servant (see p.61).*

October 26th

Plenty of admissions to see, including 2 Warwicks' men.

- *Three Warwicks were court martialled on October 2nd. Private Perry received 6 months imprisonment for being 'absent without leave'. He may have been sent to Hereford.*

November 12th

Many men to see and several cases to review for Special Release. A lad of 22 who had been in the Dardanelles and France came in for two years for desertion. He sounds and looks a good sort and we will see what we can do for him.

- *An example of Robert doing his utmost for those he considered as deserving soldiers.*

November 28th

Sold the four steers we bought at the Sourton sale on June 7th for £52.10.0.

December 9th

The children think their new house will be grand for hide and seek.

- *New house: The Commandant's House at Hereford Military Detention Barracks.*

December 18th

Borrowed Mrs. Holloway's gramophone for Renie who, when it arrived, very much turned her nose at it and said she hated the thing but ended by loving every note of it.

Sunday December 19th

We went to the Cathedral and disagreed about the merits of the sermon. The children soon tired of the gramophone.

December 25th

The children enjoyed their day very much. I played the gramophone to the men in the Detention Barracks who greatly appreciated it.

December 31st
A good finish to a terrible year.

January 1st 1916
Finished off the Confidential Reports on the Staff and told Lieutenant Chudleigh that what I requisition for, I expect to get without a pile of red tape correspondence to answer on the subject first. Renie not at all well- feeling very sick.

- *An early indication of his frustration with the bureaucratic nature of his job.*

January 3rd
Looks like another big draft going out.

- *Hundreds more were travelling to France and Belgium to replace those killed at the Front.*

January 5th
Poor Renie had a very bad night. The prawns she ate at dinner were apt to be too much for anybody.

January 8th
Pte. Elwood who was sentenced to two years, was released after being here a fortnight.

January 12th
Renie had tea with an unknown widow who had lost all her friends and relations and her husband in the war.

January 22nd
To Mold to take over. Clearing hop yards and cutting wood.

- *Detainees in Military Detention Barracks were often used for agricultural work.*

January 24th
What I requisition for I expect to get without a pile of red tape.

January 25th
Looks like another draft is going out.

February 1st
Learning to drive. Men from the barracks bound for Egypt.

- *British interests elsewhere in the world still had to be safeguarded. Egypt had been effectively under military occupation since the 1880s and was important strategically because of the Suez Canal and the route to India. It was declared a British Protectorate in December 1914 and became an important British military base.*

February 22nd
Renie said she thought the baby was coming.

February 23rd
At ten minutes past four in the afternoon, Oliver Anson was born. It was snowing at the time. Poor dear Renie, she had a worse time than with either of the other two and bore it all heroically. I started for the Dr. at 3.35- his town office telephoned to his private house and when I was told he had got the message, I bicycled to his house to make quite sure. When I arrived he had not made any kind of start, but he damned soon did.

February 24th
Aunt Nellie says she doesn't like the name Oliver. I can't stick the name Nellie so we are quits. The Battle of Verdun starts.

February 25th

I saw Major McDonald about the young shopkeepers who seem to expect me to recommend them for commissions in any of the crack corps.

February 26th

I think I should make a note of the particularly poor time I am having these days and if the children don't return soon I shall have to take to drink. The weather is deplorable.

- *It was a difficult time for the young family swapping between homes in Devon and Herefordshire.*

February 29th

The French are still holding their own against the German onslaught at Verdun.

- *The Battle of Verdun fought between the French and German Armies was the longest of the War lasting from February to December 1916. It was the costliest in casualties- the French Army with about 550,000 soldiers and the Germans 450,000.*

March 4th

2nd Battle of Verdun- Titanic slaughter with knives and bayonets only, plus the big guns. Germans no further forward.

March 27th

Started the order for 20,000 nosebags, 2,000 head ropes and 10,000 sandbags. The A.S.C. Sgt. asked us to take on making up 8,000 old sacks into 2,000 larger ones which we also took on.

- *Inmates to be engaged in useful work for the War effort. Nosebags for feeding horses, head ropes for horses and sandbags for the trenches.*

March 28th

Blizzard last night. Hereford isolated. Rheumatics seem to have moved up my neck now.

- *Rheumatics brought on by time spent in the trenches.*

March 31st

A big air raid on the East coast. Rumour says that ½ Fleet Street is bombed down and a bit of the Houses of Parliament.

April 12th

Oliver's christening at the Cathedral- the font was beautifully decorated by the Dean who did the service very nicely when he found his breath and had well cleared his throat. Everything went off very well and Oliver was as good as gold.

April 17th

Wire from Col. Turton to get ready 35 men for Egypt at once.

April 18th

Busy with the Egypt draft and the wood cutting party for tomorrow.

April 19th

Cabinet crisis over compulsion.

- *Conscription: was first introduced in February by Asquith's coalition government; single men and childless widowers aged between 18 and 41 were called up for military service. Such was the need for reinforcements at the Front that by June, married men were also bound by law to join the Army.*

Pacifists who refused to fight but who were prepared to aid the War effort joined the Non

Combatant Corps or the 'No Courage Corps' as the doubters dubbed it. Some found alternative civilian work which helped the War effort. 'Absolutist' objectors who refused to engage in any form of service that might help the military effort were convicted and sent to prison. Of these, 34 were sent from prisons around the country to France and the Government were forced to act quickly before the men were found guilty of non-compliance and executed.

On June 29th Prime Minister Asquith announced that Conscientious Objectors sentenced by Court Martial would have their cases reviewed by a Central Tribunal. Those classified as genuine cases would be released from prison to work under the auspices of the Brace Committee but those who refused this classification would be sent to Detention Barracks like those governed by Captain Hamilton.

April 24th
Oliver looked very bad. I fetched Dr. Whitfield. Packed the household of jabbering women off to bed at 11.15 pm. Astonishing how they can talk- and talk- after they have said everything twice.

April 26th
Sent Tom his wages. Bombardment of Lowestoft by a German battle squadron. The Irish Rebels seize the greater part of Dublin. Sir Roger Casement sent to London for trial. Wire from W.O. re. taking over Detention Barracks in Cairo.

- *Tom was the farm worker holding the fort at Collaven.*

- *Casement was born in Ireland and moved to the U.S.A. where he worked for the Republican cause in Ireland. After the outbreak of War he managed to secure arms for the Irish from Germany. On his return, he led the Irish Nationalist uprising in Dublin over Easter 1916 but was captured and hanged for treason in London. Other Irish rebels were sent to military prisons in England, two of whom were under the charge of Robert at Hereford Military Detention Barracks.*

April 29th
A wire from Col. Turton asking me if I would like to take over the Detention Barracks at Cairo, and I shall sleep on it.

Sunday April 30th
Cathedral in the morning. The Dean preached for some father who had just lost his son in the War. The Dead March (Chopin's) was played after the service for this son and a Captain Luard. Refused the Cairo offer- it would have been v. nice for me but rather far away for employment after the War.

- *Robert was referring to* ● **Lieutenant-Colonel Edward Bourryan Luard** *aged 45 of the King's Shropshire Light Infantry who died during the 2nd Battle of Ypres on April 25th and was buried at Lijssenthoek Military Cemetery in Belgium.*

May 3rd
Compulsion practically settled. Three of the Dublin rebels shot.

May 9th
A regular Con. Objector who told me that he was a disciple of the Lord Jesus Christ, came in yesterday. He refused to carry his arms, so I gave him 3 days No.1 P.D. to start him with.

- *This is the first time Robert was faced with the problem of someone who refused to fight and started him off with a bread and water punishment diet. Robert took a typically military view of Conscientious Objectors which was nonetheless more acceptable than that of Lieutenant-Colonel Brooke, Commandant of Wandsworth Detention Barracks. He was censured for his treatment of a Conscientious Objector who was put in a strait jacket twice for over 24 hours. On return from*

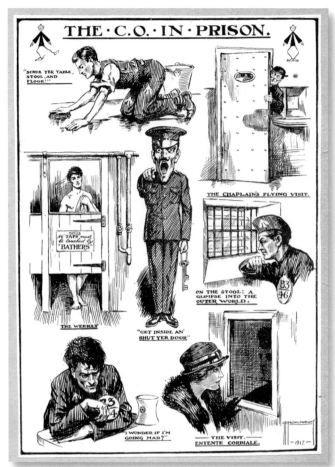

THE·C.O.·IN·PRISON.

"SCRUB YER TABLE, STOOL, AND FLOOR!"

THE CHAPLAIN'S FLYING VISIT.

NOTICE NO TAPS must be touched by "BATHERS"

THE WEEKLY

ON THE STOOL: A GLIMPSE INTO THE OUTER WORLD.

"GET INSIDE AN' SHUT YER DOOR"

"I WONDER IF I'M GOING MAD?"

THE VISIT, ENTENTE CORDIALE.

—1917—

June 3rd 1916: Postcard in support of Conscientious Objectors by G.P. Micklewright   Library of the Religious Society of Friends

a week in hospital, he was put on a bread and water diet for refusing to parade. When he went on hunger strike, he was forcibly fed. He was insulted by Brooke when in the strait jacket and spat at three times by him.

June 3rd
The Bishop's curate called about the Con. Objs and got little change out of me.

- *The Quaker movement was at the forefront of fighting for the rights of Conscientious Objectors like the Russian born Jew, Maurice Andrews, who was imprisoned at Hereford Military Detention Barracks where he was stripped of his civilian clothes and left for eight days in his vest and underpants. For four hours a day his hands were either strapped or handcuffed behind his back. A guard explained to a Quaker visitor that Army discipline could only be maintained by making detention so unbearable that a man would do anything rather than endure it.*

June 5th
The draft left for Aldershot. Capt. Burroughs was in charge and was very nervous about them but got them there alright.

June 6th
50 men started on the trench for the cable to the munitions factory. I went to Shrewsbury and lunched with Longdon. He spoke to Major Tyler on the phone about my hay leave- the rest of the business was forgotten owing to the drowning of KITCHENER and his staff on the Hampshire.

- *The Munitions Factory was located next to the Detention Barracks. Land around Rotherwas Manor was acquired by Hereford Council in 1912 and sold to the Ministry for Munitions in 1915. It was one of 12 Royal Ordinance Factories built during the War in England which tended to be located in open countryside, but near towns, with good railway communications and a large local labour force. By 1917, the factory was producing 70,000 shells a week.*

- *The Military Detention Barracks were housed in Rotherwas Manor and the military's job was to guard the Royal Ordinance Factory as well as the prisoners in the Barracks. A letter from the Home Office to the Herefordshire Gaol Visiting Committee on January 7th stated that it was 'not improbable' that the civilian prison would be required to accommodate soldiers sentenced to detention. There were no further civilian committals after March 1st 1915.*

- *Kitchener: Lord Kitchener of Khartoum, Secretary of State for War, was drowned on June 5th when on the way to meet Tsar Nicholas II. The cruiser H.M.S. Hampshire sank west of the Orkney islands after hitting a mine.*

June 7th

The Bishop's curate brought a Miss Sturge, a Quaker, to visit the Conscientious Objectors- as she held objectionable views I refused to allow her to visit them- a letter from the Bishop followed which I replied to, and expect more tomorrow.

- *The Miss Sturge to whom he is referring was Amy Sturge. She was the third of five sisters of a family of Quakers, a religious sect that believed in peaceful principles. Her obituary in the Quaker magazine* The Friend *described her as 'the ardent friend of the Conscientious Objector who found in Amy Sturge an understanding and sympathetic soul.' She was determinedly outspoken and in later years of her life was severely affected by arthritis. It is easy to imagine that she was, as far as the Governor was concerned, a difficult and forceful visitor to the Detention Barracks. She was related to Priscilla Sturge who married a 'chaplain' to Conscientious Objectors all over the country, William Albright, a Quaker and friend of Conscientious Objectors.*

June 8th

I got a most sarcastic answer from the Bishop.

- *In* The Hereford Times, *the debate over Conscientious Objectors raged during the summer months. On May 13th one correspondent argued that 'there is a good deal to be said for the opinion that if a man will not serve his country, he should not enjoy her laws or protection.' The Rev. G. Herbert Davies wrote on July 15th that 'it requires today far more moral courage to be true to their faith than to go along with the crowd.' The two views were as diametrically opposed as those of John Percival Bishop of Hereford and Captain Robert Hamilton, Governor of Hereford Detention Barracks, about the treatment of Conscientious Objectors.*

- *Bishop John Percival had been a member of a neutrality committee set up as War threatened in 1914. He, like another member of the committee, Gilbert Murray, Professor of Greek at Oxford University, changed his mind when Germany invaded Belgium. Percival, Headmaster of Rugby School before his appointment to the Bishopric of Hereford, wrote to* The Times *on August 12th 'in obedience to our Treaty obligations and in support of Belgium's just claim, our country had no choice but to take up the sword.' However, his attitude to Conscientious Objectors and Robert's treatment of them may have crystallised after the death of his youngest son on October 31st 1914.*

- **Lieutenant-Colonel Arthur Jex Blake Percival,** *aged 43 of the Northumberland Fusiliers and a member of General Staff, was one of the several Staff Officers killed when a shell hit Hooge Chateau where he was attending a conference on October 31st 1914. He was one of the first soldiers to be awarded a Cross of the Legion of Honour as well as a D.S.O and was buried at Ypres Town Cemetery. He married Cecil Henland in the same year as Robert's marriage to Renie in 1907; she was involved in founding the Princess Christian Hammersmith Nursery and the National Society of Day Nurseries.*

June 19th

A Quaker clergyman (so-called) arrived with permission from Col. Childs of the W.O. to visit the Conscientious Objectors.

- *The Quaker 'chaplain' was William Albright. An Anglican church warden, Robert was not a great supporter of Nonconformist, pacifist sects. Bishop Percival, on the other hand, was keen to attract Nonconformists to services in the Cathedral, an unpopular stance with many in the diocese.*

June 22nd

Went to Chester to see Colonel Dunne of the H.Q. Western Command on the Detention work. He is the head of this branch, but it is wonderful how little he knows about it. He seemed willing to advance one or two suggestions, so we will see if anything comes of it.

June 24th

This disgracefully treated boy Hill has been returned here again. He wrote to his mother saying good-bye as he was going to cut his throat and enclosed two farthings to be made into a brooch. I have brought him over here. Everyone needs a friend sometimes.

- *He was more supportive of a soldier in need than a Conscientious Objector.*

June 26th

Mrs. Hill came to see her son. She looks about 25 but is the mother of six.

June 28th

Sent a pretty stiff letter to Commanding Officers about men of theirs who should be at the Front.

- *Due to the huge losses at the Front, he was of the opinion that too many soldiers were being sent home for misdemeanours.*

June 29th

The C.O. of the 3/ Welch writes asking if I can recommend Shaw and Harries for immediate release. I replied 'With pleasure'.

July 3rd

The British and French offensive seems to have begun.

- *July 1st 1916 was the opening day of The Battle of the Somme, the so-called 'Big Push'. It is remembered for being the blackest day in the history of the British Army when there were 59,000 casualties including 19,000 deaths.*

July 4th

Had two special parades to pick out men for recommending to their C.O.s.

July 5th

Severe fighting on the Western Front.

July 6th

Inspected all the books- saw all the men including a boy of 15 and spoke to all the staff. Meant to have reported that I refused admission to Mr. Albright to see C.O.s.

- *William Albright was a tireless Quaker 'chaplain' to Conscientious Objectors, travelling to civil and military prisons throughout the country. In 1942, the year of his death, The Friend recalled 'his beaming smile and brilliant buttonhole' which he wore to overcome the official refusal to allow flowers to be taken in to prisoners. 'What stories can be told of his penetration into military detention camps in spite of orders! As a magistrate he was able to profit by this intimate knowledge of penal conditions.' A 'God-encompassed man' he had resigned chairmanship of a firm in Oldbury as he could not allow himself to share in any war profits.*

July 7th

Driving the Huns back gradually on the Western Front.

July 10th

Sent Q.M.S. and Sgt. Price to Cardiff to look for Hill. Captured at 11.15 p.m. by Sgt. Price after much excitement.

July 11th

Congratulated Tye and Price on their smart work in catching the young scoundrel. Two pimpled females from Smith's called to see me re. a Con. Obj. Let fly at both of them and kicked them out.

July 12th
Met Mrs. Holloway collecting in the pouring rain for the Prisoners of War so told her if she went in I would collect a sovereign for her.

July13th
Mr. Albright wired that he again had permission to visit the Con. Objs so I arranged for them all to be digging- he came and saw them and then had the cheek to ask if he might hold a service at 5.30 in their rooms. I said "no".

July 15th
Hill tried to hang himself. I went and had a good talk to him. Poor miserable kid. Had to write a long report to War Office on Spittle. A wire from Col. Childs saying that the Quaker man Albright was to be allowed to visit as a chaplain- such utter rot.

Sunday July 16th
Cathedral in morning. The Bishop (our friend) turned up just before the blessing for the 2nd Service. I was sitting in the choir stalls straight opposite his 'box' and I fancy he could not face it any more than his wife could Renie, when she called.

- *The Hamiltons and Percivals did not see eye to eye!*

July 19th
Col. T. inspected everything and everyone and found all correct.

July 20th
More about Con. Objs. entailing hours of extra work. The Rev. saw me about a letter Albright had sent him. I took a copy of it and sent it straight to the D.P.S.

August 9th
W.O. still on the worry about Con. Objs.

- *On September 19th military torture of Conscientious Objectors was brought to an end. The War Office ceased compliance by physical force. Courtesy was now expected from the Army.*

August 17th
Medical Board on two of my men- only 75 men in Detention now and it looks as if we shall soon close down altogether.

August 25th
My diary of the war is finished. Today's papers have long accounts of the doings to the Warwicks.

August 28th
Took my diary to the printers who want to charge me £5 to print it, so my Q.M.S. and Orderly Sgt. will do it between them.

August 31st
Met Mrs. Cuthbert- she says she can stand no more. Husband already killed, two sons in the firing line. Her daughter's boy of six is in her house with pleurisy. The daughter herself about to be a mother with her husband at the Front too.

September 1st
I fancy most of the so-called treasures will have to be sold to pay off the debt.

- *He is referring to the family home at Avon Cliffe, Tiddington near Stratford-on-Avon. His father had been facing serious financial problems.*

MISS CICELY MORDAUNT   MISS WINIFRED MORDAUNT

Miss Cicely Mordaunt and Miss Winifred Mordaunt are the two youngest daughters of Lady Mordaunt and the late Sir Charles Mordaunt, Bart., of Walton Hall, Warwick. Both have been at the front practically since the outbreak of war, and went out in October, 1914. Miss Cicely Mordaunt has received the Order of Elisabeth for excellent work during an epidemic of typhoid, and Miss Winifred Mordaunt has been decorated with the Croix de Guerre for gallant conduct during an air raid. In French Army Orders it was stated that Miss Winifred Mordaunt "showed an absolute disregard of danger"

The Birmingham Post July 11th 1918

Cicely Mordaunt's Great War Medals.

1   1914-15 'Star'
2   First Aid Nursing Yeomanry
3   Victory 1914-19
4   Order of Elisabeth (Belgian)
5   British War Medal 1914-18

For more detail on 1, 3 and 5 see p.171

September 23rd

Major Bairnsfather arrived at Walton for partridge shooting.

September 24th

Renie and I drove over to Avon Cliffe and talked things over with the parents. Got back to Walton to find Bruce Bairnsfather and a Mrs. Everett. Bruce did a sketch for Winnie. He has been given a pass anywhere on the French and Italian Front- he bought his father's place for him.

- *This would have been one of Bairnsfather's cartoons. He preferred to describe them as sketches rather than cartoons. He was now in a position financially to buy his father's house for him at Bishopton near Stratford-on-Avon.*

- *Winnie was on leave from France. Winifred and Cicely Mordaunt had performed in Bruce Bairnsfather's production of 'Ali Baba and the Forty Thieves' in January 1912. Winifred played Abdalla the Robber Captain and Cicely, Parizade, the Sultan of Baghdad's sister. The producer not only painted scenery that provoked much favourable comment but also took on the role of Ali Baba, according to a local report as a 'very effective one, in the company of a wonderful donkey' and his 'drollery was irresistible.' Miss Winifred Mordaunt apparently 'made a dashing Captain' and Cicely 'did quite well.'*

Winifred Mordaunt started the War with a month spent working in Leamington Hospital. She arrived in France in her own car on November 8th, drove for a doctor and was a Nurse until May 1915. She spent 10 months as a cook orderly and for the final months of the War was in the transport section of the First Aid Nursing Yeomanry Corps (F.A.N.Y.C.) as a driver and was mentioned in despatches on December 24th 1917 and on May 25th 1918. She received the French Croix de Guerre for gallantry during an air raid when she 'showed a complete disregard for danger'.

Cicely Mordaunt achieved the rank of Sergeant in the F.A.N.Y.C. and received the British War and Victory Medals for her work on active service in France, where she arrived on November 14th aged 25. She carried out a variety of roles; she was a driver from November 20th 1914 until May 1917, a cook in an auxiliary hospital in Tunbridge Wells from September 4th 1917 to March 11th 1918 and an assistant cook for transport convoys in Étaples from September 4th 1918 to July 7th 1919. Her British War and Victory medals would have cost her 6 shillings to purchase. She received the Belgian Order of Elisabeth. All work was unpaid.

Despite their sheltered upbringing, taught by Governesses and surrounded by servants at Walton Hall, Cicely and Winifred dedicated themselves to the War effort with great courage and determination.

September 30th
Quite busy in the office for a change.

November 8th
A little sunshine then heavy storms. I dread to think of the condition of the trenches on the Western Front.

- *Robert knew only too well from his experiences earlier in the War.*

November 20th
Finished Locke's 'TheWonderful Year' which is not as good as some of his others.

- *Locke had been the Librarian at Glenalmond College in Perthshire which Robert had attended*

November 22nd
Awful excitement at H.Q. and the W.O. over my report on Thornton the Irish rebel. Apparently one has only to refuse point blank nowadays in the Army to be treated like a hero.

- *Robert was constantly challenged by how he should deal with the Irish rebels and Conscientious Objectors and complained regularly at the lack of a decisive policy towards them from the War Office.*

December 3rd
Asquith blamed for the Somme push not breaking through- I think perhaps it is not altogether his fault.

December 4th
Have recommended two men for Special Release and shall be annoyed if they are not accepted by G.O.C. Lloyd-George resigns. Asquith should be hung drawn and quartered.

- *Robert seems to have changed his mind about Prime Minister Asquith. The Somme campaign came to a halt in mid November and the number of casualties for the eight miles gained was 600,000 for the Allies and 500,000 for the Germans. Lloyd-George resigned as Minister of War on December 1st starting a game of political musical chairs. Robert's wish was granted on December 5th when Asquith resigned to be replaced by Lloyd-George as Prime Minister on December 7th.*

December 31st
Haig created a Field Marshal. The dignified reply of the Allied nations to the hun proposal of Peace is magnificent.

- *The Germans submitted a 'peace note' stating that they were not responsible for the War and that they would agree to a peace settlement provided that their territorial gains were confirmed. The Allies refused to discuss peace until the Germans agreed to pay reparations and give an undertaking not to violate the independence of small nations.*

January 10th 1917
Was asked to take 32 men from one regiment- and an officer who had been cashiered and sentenced to six months hard labour- refused both.

January 17th
We went to an enormous meeting of agricultural people in the Shire Hall to hear Mr. Prothero the President of the Board of Agriculture speak about the need for the farmers to produce all they could.

January 24th
Wrote numerous letters to W.O. and Western Command.

February 3rd
America has broken off diplomatic relations with the Huns and their respective ambassadors have gone home.

February 7th
Colder than ever today- 27 degrees of frost. We had another capital game of hockey on the ice in the Lugg meadows.

February 8th
Dr. Sinclair died early this morning in Birmingham- he was 53 years of age and had been organist of Hereford Cathedral for 27 years.

February 10th
We both went to the Cathedral. One of Sinclair's 'children' broke down in the anthem which did not surprise me. One of his pupils played the Dead March. The music, his organ and his sympathetic nature, and the feeling of loss of his lovely music has quite upset me.

February 13th
Q.M.Sgt. Tye is offered the same job at Wandsworth which he accepts- I am very sorry to lose him.

February 15th
50 men and 5 N.C.O.s cleared Parry-Jones's Hop yard for him.

February 20th
The thaw has started and now for burst pipes and floods and not a plumber available.

- *Nothing changes…*

February 24th
The Town and County surveyors called about work they wanted my men to do for them. The British advance on the Western Front 1½ miles without any opposition.

March 2nd
My scheme re. 'Releases' is now quoted in detail in Army Council Instructions and issued throughout the different commands- very gratifying. Oliver photographed.

March 11th
Reported the escape and asked Western Command to detail a Court of Enquiry. Awful bore.

March 16th
The Russian Revolution. THE 'PUSH' ON THE WESTERN FRONT BEGINS.

- *Robert has been duped by propaganda. The Germans were in fact withdrawing to their heavily defended Hindenburg Line.*

March 20th
Walked out beyond Breinton to see the motor plough at work. It ploughs three furrows at a time and goes at 2 ½ miles an hour.

March 23rd
Mrs Cuthbert's daughter bounced in to ORDER me to send men to dig her mother's potato patch- she bounced out quick. A farmer man wanted the same but started badly by addressing me as Sergeant-Major.

March 26th
Our long expected order for coal came in today (20 tons)

April 27th
Promoted Major.

- *He didn't comment much about his promotion to Captain either.*

April 28th
Renie is on the grumble again. She wants to go back to Collaven but unfortunately there is a trying war on, and thousands and millions can't do what they would love to do- she has not discovered that she is NOT one of these.

(An insertion at top of the page by Renie)- By which remark I suppose you infer that I am doing what I love doing and have no trials or anything to put up with- a wholly mistaken idea- that she IS one of these would be more like it.

- *A marital diary-based tiff which underlines the pressures the family faced.*

May 1st
Sent off the W.O. return of names of men who I considered should be out.

May 2nd
W.O. wants to know how many men I have sent out from here. The S.M. and I struggled through the books and found that 94 had actually gone to France not including 34 I had specially released at their own wish to go to the Front.

May 4th
Another terrific battle being fought on the Western Front. Two million men at death's grips.

- *He is referring to the Battle of Arras on May 3rd. By now the Nivelle Offensive in the Aisne area had resulted in 150,000 French casualties and caused mutinies in the French Army.*

May 7th
Suggested to Col. Turton in answer to his letter that he should try and get me the 1st Class Commandant of Wandsworth.

May 30th
I had my first game of cricket and just managed to save a pair of spectacles by making one run in each innings but bowled 19 overs and got five wickets.

June 6th
The Chaplain General to the forces Western Command and Mr. Ward attended my weekly service and then lunched with me after- the children were not very taken with either.

June 9th
I am now i/c Troops and am responsible for orders in case of an air raid and for the protection of fallen aircraft but since there is not such a thing as a gun in the neighbourhood, I fail to see why an airship should fall here.

July 24th (back in Devon)
So that makes the HARVEST HOME. I reckon we have 12 to 13 tons of hay.

July 31st
Took the first dose of Dr Lan's medicine for rheumatism and three pills to produce sleep as I scarcely had an hour last night. Another great battle begins on the Western Front.

- *The start of the 3rd Battle of Ypres, known as Passchendaele which lasted until mid November at a cost of 310,000 British casualties.*

August 10th
A large convoy of wounded and gassed soldiers arrived for the hospitals at 4 a.m. All the V.A.D. ladies were sent for. They rightly complain that the authorities might have warned them they were coming for their own sake and for those of the soldiers.

- *Voluntary Aid Detachment: set up in 1909 as part of the Territorial Army Scheme, to tend to wounded and sick soldiers and care for garrison troops in local neighbourhoods.*

August 23rd

Ears and teeth still bad. Had a long eight mile walk with Jock after tea. A most perfect rainbow- a complete arc with a complete reflection also. When I got back a man was reported in a fit. I went to see him and sent for the doctor. He is only 20 years of age and has been at the Front 11 months and been wounded. He came to alright and when I asked him how he felt now, he said "Oh I'm alright sir, thank you." Three years ago today I sailed from Southampton for the War.

September 3rd

Had a hot route march round Sutton and saw the three dismal hay ricks still burning. 80 tons of good hay worth anything from four to five hundred pounds.

September 5th

Q.M.S. Fleming says all the Staff are against him- I'm really not surprised but will do what I can to keep the peace.

September 18th

Letter from father saying that poor old Alec has paid the extreme penalty- I don't know what Ida will do.

- *Ida, Robert's sister, lost her husband* **Captain Alec Campbell** *of the Sussex Yeomanry, who was killed on September 13th 1917 and buried at the Duhallow A.D.S. Cemetery.*

October 14th

Poor Trehearne's only son is seriously wounded and has had his right arm amputated.

November 20th

Sgt. Andrews arrived in place of Everrit and Parsons goes tomorrow to Aldershot. Both removals will be a lesson to the other members of the staff if they are thinking of messing about with the wives of soldiers fighting for their country.

November 21st

The push towards Cambrai according to the Evening paper is the greatest battle of the War.

- *The first time tanks were used by the British in significant numbers (476) and to good effect. After early gains, progress was halted by lack of reserves and German counter attacks- there were 45,000 British casualties and 50,000 German.*

December 11th (at Avon Cliffe, Stratford-on-Avon)

Poor Ida dreadfully altered and fearfully upset at the sight of me in uniform. I read some very beautiful letters she had received.

December 12th

I remained at Avon Cliffe and had another talk with Ida and sorted some of Alec's kit which she could not look at.

December 13th

The whole household has either a sore throat, stiff neck or a cold, and all delighted to see the end of 1917.

January 3rd 1918

A paragraph in the Birmingham Post about Winnie getting the 1914 Star and being mentioned in despatches.

January 4th
Wrote to Winnie to congratulate her on being mentioned in despatches.

January 19th
Renie went to her V.A.D. work in the p.m.

January 31st
Cynthia is getting far too fond of criticising and contradicting her parents and must be broken of this habit.

February 6th
Renie is very busy making herself a fancy dress out of two Union Jack flags.

February 19th
Mr.Wynne-Wilson called at 9.30 p.m. about tomorrow's funeral of poor young Geoffrey Bulmer who did away with himself after getting the M.C. rather than risk as pilot another's life and because he could stand it no longer.

- *Lieutenant Geoffrey Bulmer died on February 15th and was buried at Hereford Cemetery. He was awarded the Military Cross for action with the Royal Flying Corps.*

March 20th
Met one soldier without any legs being wheeled in a bath chair by another- also two blind soldiers being led by two flappers.

March 23rd
Our Western line has been forced back a bit by the Huns, but considering they have four to one of our soldiers, it is a wonder they have not broken through.

- *The start of the German Spring Offensives was made possible by the release of 40 divisions from the Eastern Front where fighting had ceased following the Russian Revolution.*

Sunday March 24th
The Cathedral was crammed to the roof for the Bishop's first sermon, which was a great treat. He read prayers at the end of his sermon for our soldiers fighting against the Hun hordes on the Western Front and for Victory.

- *The new bishop was Herbert Hensley Henson who became Archbishop of York in 1920. Robert had not found many of Bishop Percival's sermons a 'treat'.*

March 27th
The War news is bad- 50,000 prisoners, 100 guns and 100 tanks.

April 10th
Armentières and Plugstreet seem to be in danger of being lost.

- *This would have been a worry to Robert after all his efforts there and he would have been disappointed that they were lost.*

April 11th
The Army Council have informed the W.O. and the G.O.C. Western Command that they intend to take no further action over the Conscientious Objectors of Hereford Detention Barracks.

April 13th
Haig's order of the day 'to stand or fall' and 'no retiring' shows the perilous position of the Western Front.

- *Haig's order issued on April 11th was that 'there is no other course open to us but to fight it out. Every position must be held to the last man. There must be no retirement. With our backs to the wall and believing in the justice of our cause, each one of us must fight on to the end. The safety of our homes and the freedom of mankind alike depend on the conduct of each of us at this critical moment.'*

April 16th
Left for Avon Cliffe. Found poor mother very feeble. It is pitiable to hear her ask you to tell her where she is going. A sad and weary time for all. The War news is terribly bad.

- *The Germans took and then lost Méteren.*

April 20th
I went to see Maid of the Mountain which was not bad but was astonished at the number of young fellows in the cast- so went round to the back of the stage and found none had been out and they didn't see why they should be in the Army.

April 21st
Renie wired that Mother had died this morning- she had been unconscious for the last two days.

April 25th
The funeral passed off very quietly as was the wish of all. Read some of 'The Gate of Samaria' by William Locke, which I liked very much.

May 19th
Archdeacon Ingram preached a very nice sermon on the 'Spirit of God' and said it was that that gave the British troops the spirit to fight and win.

May 25th
Private Daley came to see me- I had got him off six months of his sentence last year. He had been captured on the Western Front and had just escaped from the Huns. He recounted his experiences in getting through the German lines. He and his pal strangled two Hun sentries and very nearly a young British Officer before they discovered they were in our lines.

May 27th
Captain Milburn asked permission to leave an Australian Officer under 'close arrest' with me while he rung up the W.O. A very nice father of about 30 years of age, two wounded stripes. Been out 3 years. Had the M.C. Married with 3 children in Australia. The W.O. replied it was alright. Thought they might have taken steps to find this out before this ignominious ordeal.

May 29th
Things on the Western Front are not going as well as one would like them to, but what can they do against such masses?

May 30th
The British are back on the Aisne and the Huns still advancing

May 31st
The Huns are now on the Marne and are advancing in a U or horseshoe formation. I should imagine Foch could do something here and capture a few thousand of them.

- *Marshal Ferdinand Foch was the French Allied Supreme Commander for the Western Front from April 1918.*

June 1st
Renie had breakfast at 7.30 and started bicycling for Avon Cliffe. How she can in this heat is beyond me. Mr. Jones is going up to London to voluntarily be given trench feet so that the doctors can operate on him and find out something they at present don't understand about. I think it is very brave and magnificent of him.

June 4th
Rumour has it that eleven divisions of Huns have been encircled by Foch.

- *The German advance was finally halted. American forces were now involved in the Marne area, adding substantially to the effectiveness of the Allies' counter-offensive.*

June 5th
The Huns made a further onslaught on the French and expected to reach Paris but the French held them.

June 6th
Eighteen American ships sunk by Hun pirates.

- *German U Boats (submarines) were operating in US waters.*

June 9th
Heard that Captain Hamilton who went out to drive an ambulance dropped in in time for a bombardment on the second day and was shell shocked and couldn't speak till he got home again. The Huns are making another desperate dash for Paris.

- *The effects of shell shock were understood by someone who had experienced them at the Front.*

June 11th
Cynthia and I went out after tea to see the Hamiltons of Breinton. He was looking very bad and seems to have lost his memory a bit. He says Paris fairly stinks of Americans and that the French are supremely confident.

June 12th
There is apparently not an apple in this part of the country so there will be no cider next year and a drink strike for certain.

June 13th
Much better news from the Front today- the French have counter attacked capturing over 1000 Huns and many guns.

June 18th
The English summer has started today. It rained all day.

June 20th
Made arrangements for the presentation of the M.C. to a Mrs. Pritchard, wife of an ex-police officer who has been killed in action.

- *37,000 Military Crosses were awarded during the War.*

June 21st
Went to see Mrs. Pritchard about her husband's M.C. but might have known she would want to dress out before appearing as the wife of Captain Pritchard. She turned up at 5 p.m. obviously dressed to kill and to be asked to tea. I couldn't ask her to tea as we already had more coming than we knew what to do with and so asked her to come tomorrow.

- **Captain Ralph Broomfield Pritchard** *from Jesmond, Newcastle-on-Tyne, of the Northumberland Fusiliers died on April 26th and was buried at Mendinghem Cemetery. He was 25 and was awarded the D.S.O. and M.C.*

June 22nd
Mrs. Pritchard is quite looking forward to as big a show as possible.

July 11th
Announcement in the Morning Post about Cicily and Winnie getting the Order of Elizabeth and the Croix de Guerre.

July 17th
The French and Americans are well holding the fifth Hun onslaught.

July 18th
Great French counter attack. 20,000 prisoners and 2,400 guns.

July 22nd
Allies cross the Marne- Huns in retreat- 200 prisoners.

July 27th
Hun retreat spreading- we pursue with cavalry and tanks.

August 2nd
Complete collapse of the Crown Prince's Army round Soissons.

August 6th
Colonel Banon wants me to take on the Ross area. I cannot work up any enthusiasm about it and am to let him know tomorrow.

August 7th
I sent him back his speeches, reports, letters and maps and said I was sorry I could not take it on. Haig continues to advance capturing villages, Huns, guns, booty by the thousand.

August 11th
The news is still glorious. The French take Montdidier and on the whole front the advance is extended to 12 miles.

August 13th
45,000 prisoners and over 1,000 machine-guns- something like a haul.

- *The 2nd Battle of Amiens started on August 8th, Ludendorff's 'black day' for the German Army when 27,000 casualties were sustained. It was the beginning of the end for the Germans.*

August 15th
Talked to the A.A.G. about the unfairness of sending men here who refuse point blank to put on uniform or do anything they are told. I pointed out that it was the simplest thing in the world for C.O. to wash their hands of these brutes, but my position, with my hands tied on account of the incompetence of the W.O. to deal with these wasters and their habit of invariably refusing to back me up, made it a very difficult one.

August 16th
More rot about Eldridge the Con. Obj. And the two Russian aliens.

August 17th
Still jawing and writing to the A.A.G. about men being sent here in mufti and Con. Objs.

- *mufti- non-military clothing.*

August 22nd
Saw the Irish rebel O'Donovan who openly says he wants to fight against England and no other nation. Got the A.C. priest to interview him, but the priest has no sympathy whatever with him.

August 26th
The Con Obj. Eldridge was tried by D.C.M. again this p.m. and I fancy had been given another long term of imprisonment. The British are advancing again successfully on a 35 mile front.

August 29th
The news is magnificent and the Huns retreating as hard as they can go.

August 30th
Bapaume, Noyon and Peronne have fallen and the allies still sweeping on. Magnificent.

September 3rd
Besides an advance of 4 miles the British alone have captured 10,000 Huns.

September 5th
Arrived at Bath- saw the doctor who ordered me baths and water and medicine and a needle bath. Drank 48 ozs of tepid mineral water.

September 6th
Went down into the Town with the Harley Street specialist and met a gentleman who wanted to know whether I had met his young brother who was a sub in the Warwicks with me and who has since been killed- this fellow turned out to be Hamilton, brother of I.K. Hamilton.

September 7th
The needle bath reminds me of hot needles alright and I should say was very good.

September 8th
Church in the Abbey. The singing and organ were nothing much and the sermon was about the Blue Coat School which did not interest me.

September 22nd
3 p.m. service at Sourton- Renie distinguished herself by playing the organ with conspicuous success and I read the lessons in my usual silky tenor.

September 24th
These dirty railway people are out on strike. Hundreds of Tommies from the Fronts can't get home.

September 25th
Attended a Medical Board. Papers all wrong apparently. Doctor says I must stay in Bath another month.

October 1st
The news from every Front is magnificent.

October 5th
On my return to Hereford heard numerous complaints from the staff, chiefly due to red tape and unnecessary office work.

October 6th
Went to tea with the old Dean- I was surprised at the old fellow being really jealous of my free treatment for rheumatism when he naturally had to pay. A trait in his character I did not think worthy of him.

October 10th
The magnificent news from all Fronts continues.

October 12th
All sorts of rumours that Kaiser Bill has abdicated and that Germany has chucked up the sponge. She will have to surrender unconditionally and lay down arms before we believe a word of it.

- *The Kaiser did not abdicate until November 9th.*

October 23rd
My left ear has gone just when I thought Bath had cured it.

October 24th
The British, the French and the Italians are now attacking and advancing again and given fine weather much may be expected of them.

October 25th
Went up on the Downs and then to the Pump Room. On my way I met W.J. Locke- just the same as he was 24 years ago. Had tea with him and a chat about Glenalmond past and present- I always thought he and Jeremy Taylor were pals- but not so- said he was the biggest liar he had ever met.

- *Robert later noted Locke's death on May 17th 1930.*

October 30th
Spent the morning finishing off my remarks on Turton's Report. There was not an item I could not answer with ease and truth but I fancy it will make little difference to the ultimate decision- but if Col.T. is the only one who wishes to down me and not someone at the W.O. I should not be surprised if he gets the chuck for being a d....d liar.

November 1st
I hear that brilliant funk stick Stanhope has been fetched back from Timbuctoo or somewhere where he received so many white feathers sent him, has been fetched back and roped into the Army- a bit late alas.

November 2nd
One cannot fathom the vast table turning that is going on these days. Nothing humanely possible can alter the fact that the Hun is utterly degraded for all time and on the brink of being hopelessly beaten.

November 3rd
Went to Tupsley Church, and not being able to hear a word thought about the present state of our affairs. Perhaps the nation's would have been more to the point. *However, the result was that I came to the conclusion that I have neither the wish nor the ability to become a General, and not the ambition to be anything out of the way. I think it would be best not to get the chuck now, though I don't really care much, as I have had enough of this alone, but I do think that allowance should be made for the personal element in every officer whether it is sport or anything else, and that an officer might carry on with a job quite usefully, without being prepared to go as far as the stake for it- or the workhouse.*

- *A cathartic and rather sad moment for Robert. It appears he is being removed as Commandant of the Hereford Military Barracks.*

November 4th
Great things still going on all over the bewildered world- any minute may now see peace. I wrote to the Sec. of the Devon cattle breeders Society re. membership. Made arrangements for the fifth military funeral since I got back from Bath.

November 5th
I took the men for a route march. Another big advance on the Western Front.

November 6th
The Allied Conference in Paris has decided to leave the terms of the German armistice to Marshall Foch thank goodness.

November 9th
The end must come very soon now. The Hun navy was ordered out to fight but refused.

- *The German fleet mutinied at Kiel on November 3rd.*

November 10th

Mons recaptured. The Hun given 72 hours to decide whether it shall be Peace or War. The whole world is waiting in hushed silence. Cathedral at 11 a.m. Walked back with Humphrey who bored me stiff. Renie should be here to ride Rhon in her Union Jack costume.

- *The British ended the War where they first engaged the German Army.*

Monday November 11th

THE END. Germany surrendered at 5 a.m. The official news was sent me by phone direct from the W.O. I acquainted the Police, the Mayor and the Times Office. The Town went mad. Where all the flags suddenly came from I don't know. On my way to tell the old Dean, I was mobbed by soldiers, munitions girls and the Hereford School boys and so kept in for the rest of the morning. An enormous Thanksgiving service at the Cathedral at 7 p.m. The Close was a black mass of people who could not get in. Bells and sirens rang all day.

- The Hereford Times *reported that 'It was noticed that by some freak, the flag at the Town Hall and another over a Commercial Street shop refused at the outset to go higher than half mast. Four long years of disuse had evidently put the hoisting tackle out of gear. The effect was ludicrous, but of course was of only brief duration…to describe in detail the groups and types of laughing joyous humanity would be a task. Suffice it to say that the fun was fast and furious.'*

- *Work stopped in the Royal Ordinance Factory at noon on November 11th and 15 year old Annie Slade, a munitions worker, recalled how 'we were all in our munitions clothes going round Hereford with flags the day peace was signed.'*

November 12th

Terms of the Armistice announced. Read them to the men and also the King's messages to his Army, Navy, Air Force and Dominions. Got a flag and mounted it on the highest point of the Detention Barracks.

November 14th

It seems to be exceedingly doubtful if we can make the Huns carry out the Armistice terms. After Office and fixing up the military part of the procession for the Thanksgiving Service on Sunday, I went shooting with Cox and Gilbert- we got 14 rabbits.

November 15th

Attended the meeting at the Town Hall and insisted on the military leading the procession if they are present at all and also that some of the idiotic Girl Guides should give place to the soldiers in the Cathedral. We went to a meeting about Women and the Vote at which the Bishop spoke.

November 16th

Wrote to Capt. Kennedy at the W.O. about an amnesty for soldiers in Detention and about this job generally.

- The Hereford Times *reported in November 1918 that 'while the influenza outbreak is being kept within bounds in the City of Hereford, the precautionary measures taken having had a beneficial result, the scourge continues more or less unabated in the County.' It was ironic that after the end of a war that had claimed nearly 10 million lives, an influenza pandemic should then claim an even greater number.*

Sunday November 17th

We saw the Procession and then got into the Cathedral- Magnificent service. The Bishop preached. Mr. Hull, the new organist, played for the first time since his release from captivity in Germany. His rendering of the National Airs was perfect. After tea we went to hear the Bishop at All Saints- another very fine sermon, but the service was spoilt by Roman rites at the end with candles and maces etc. and the donning by the Bishop of Trehearne's ridiculous garments. As Renie remarked-"Rubbish".

- The Hereford Times *marvelled at the 'Great scene in the Cathedral…numerous military officers including Major Hamilton were in the front near the pulpit…an awe inspiring sermon was preached by the Bishop based on the text, "He maketh wars to cease."' Renie clearly was of the opinion that the second service was too 'High Church' and verging on Roman Catholicism.*

November 19th

The Dean and Bannister handed the Herefordshire Regiment Colours to Wing and I in the Cathedral. The organ played appropriate music and the Dean made an appropriate speech. The regiment want their colours in France apparently to march into Berlin with. Fourteen went out today. Nothing yet from the W.O.

November 20th

Just when I thought I was getting rid of the men in Detention nicely, four came in belonging to the Inland Water and Docks R.E. from Chepstow (IWDRE or I Was Drunk & Re-Enlisted).

November 21st

Major Paris inspected a squad in Anti-Gas- I don't quite know why. Captain Rossiter telephoned to ask me to come to a Peace Dance, so I went at 8.30 and so enjoyed it that I did not get back till 2 a.m. Quite a select crowd. A little Irish girl from Presteign quite won my heart- she and two others danced like corks. We had the Highland Fling and the Gallop to end with.

November 24th

S. Sgt. Andrews was taken much worse. He expressed a wish to see me and I went at 3 p.m. He died at 4 p.m.

- **Frederick James Andrews**, *40, was in the Military Provost Staff Corps and was buried at Dorchester Cemetery. He and his wife Eva lived at 8, Shirley Terrace, Victoria Park, Dorchester.*

November 25th

Had rather a painful interview with Mrs. Andrews and her sister-in-law. Got together a subscription 35/- for a wreath. The body is to be sent to his home on a warrant. Several soldiers wanted extension of leave on account of sickness at home, and one or two to see me about employment. The fellow who swallowed a needle and who was sent to the general hospital to have it cut out, escaped from there. Not a word yet from the W.O. and I'm getting damned angry about it.

November 26th

Seabroke writes this a.m. to say that he is coming over here on the 8th to take over this show. The W.O says nothing. I got the necessary wood from Rowberry and made the coffin inside for Andrews.

November 28th

Another cool letter from Seabroke.

November 29th

The fellow who swallowed a needle said he had now swallowed another- because I did not believe him, he set to on his room and fairly did it in, besides setting fire to his bible. Put him in the padded room.

December 2nd

Wing and I inspected the two Hun guns which are to be drawn by Traction Engine through the town and country.

December 3rd

Took the men for a route march.

December 11th
Another body is arriving from Eastbourne to be buried with military honours at Mordiford on Saturday.

December 12th
I hear at last that I may proceed on leave pending instructions from W.O. Board of Officers. Reports on the two Irish shirkers my last official duty here.

December 13th
I stepped round and said good bye to the Fosters. We got off by the 12.50.

December 21st
A wire arrived ordering me to report at Tunbridge Wells on Monday- on the wander once more.

December 27th
Arrived at Tunbridge Wells at 5 p.m. Not at all impressed with future existence here and must see about some other job.

- *His next job was at Catterick in Yorkshire.*

December 31st
Heard from Seabroke who does not find things all joy at Hereford.

14

'Just like Brothers'

The London Gazette recorded on February 28th 1919 that 'Major R.C. Hamilton is placed on the retired list owing to ill health contracted on active service and is permitted to retain the rank of Major.'

Within six weeks, he left the Military Barracks at Catterick in Yorkshire, caught the 1 a.m. train from York to Paddington and never returned to active service in the Army. Robert mentioned tersely in his diary that he had received a letter from the Ministry of Pensions 'awarding me £30 as a gratuity for my 18 years of service'.

In the years after January 1915, disenchantment with his new role in the Army was a constant theme in his diary. Although relieved to survive the slaughter on the Western Front and return to his family, in his professional life he missed the comradeship forged in the face of adversity- he thrived on leading his Company and was delighted when the opportunity arose in October 1914 to lead 'A' Company into battle in the pursuit of victory against the 'Hun'. He had witnessed horrendous barbarity and had lost many fellow officers and soldiers under his command. They had all played hard in their billets behind the lines and at any stage, the drink in the *estaminet*, and the dance with the local girls could well have been their last. He missed the adrenalin rush of trench warfare and the rewards to be gained from working as a unit with fellow soldiers- his heart was never in his new role.

It was hardly surprising that his duties in Military Detention Barracks should have proved so unfulfilling. A professional soldier, only months earlier he had experienced military action of an unparalleled intensity and danger but now, he was faced with a daily grind of paperwork: the 'red tape rot' that he freely railed against. He had neither the training nor the skills to guide him through the problems posed by the Detention Barracks' intake of Conscientious Objectors and Irish 'rebels'.

His reaction to Conscientious Objectors and their Quaker and Anglican supporters was, to modern eyes, uncompromising and heavy handed. An officer who had fought in the trenches on the Western Front was unlikely, however, to have dealt sympathetically with the Conscientious Objectors under his control after the introduction of Conscription in May 1916.

As a trained officer, he considered it was his duty to support his fellow soldiers- he whistled to them to calm them down in the heat of battle and defended them at courts martial. He made no secret of his disappointment at the lack of similar support from his superiors at the War Office when his numerous requests for guidance and support over the Conscientious Objectors and Irish 'rebels' fell on deaf ears. The vacillating attitude that clouded the War Office's dealings with him, confirmed in Robert's mind that his days as a soldier were numbered.

His personal discontent was symptomatic of a wider national malaise in Britain after 1918. In August 1914, he and thousands of troops had set out from the English coastal ports to halt the German Armies' progress through neutral Belgium. Many more made the same journey to replace those who never returned and victory was ultimately achieved at a massive cost of human life in November 1918. The British Army, or what remained of it, having defeated the ambitions of Kaiser Wilhelm II, was engaged after the War in 'Strike Duties' in major cities which prompted Robert to write on March 20th that 'this looks like Peace doesn't it? We are to carry pistols and 50 rounds per man- 50,000 rounds in the carts.' More dispiriting for him was the mood of many soldiers. 'The men of 'A' Company marched *en masse* to the Officers' Mess to demand more lunch and a bonus paid to them similar to what some of the other men are getting. A most extraordinary proceeding but in these days of general discontent and strikes,

jor Robert Hamilton's Military Medals (miniature set):

Queen's South Africa Medal: three 'clasps' represent *vice in the Transvaal, Orange Free State and Cape Colony* *ing the Boer War*

King's South Africa Medal: with two clasps for the South *ican campaign in 1901 and 1902*

1914-15 'Star': awarded to those who served in Belgium *d France from August 1914 to December 1915; it was* *knamed 'Pip'- 2,350,000 were awarded*

British War Medal: for service from 1914 to 1918- *ueak'- over 6 million were awarded*

Victory or Allied War Medal: 1914 to 1919- 'Wilfred'- *out 6 million awarded*

p', 'Squeak' and 'Wilfred' were characters in a comic strip *ich first appeared in* The Daily Mirror *on May 12th 1919* *d became a popular craze in the 1920s. The script writer* *s Bertram J. Lamb and the artist Austin B. Payne. The* *ming of the characters is due to Payne's wartime batman* *o was known as 'Pip-Squeak'. Pip was a dog, Squeak a* *guin and Wilfred, who did not appear until later in the* *ies, was a rabbit.*

vas common for soldiers to be buried with their medals *ich may explain why Robert's original set of single medals* *10 longer in existence.*

I suppose poor Tommy is as fed up with the Government and all its doings as the strikers are.'

At the age of 42, suffering from acute deafness and rheumatism, Major Robert Hamilton returned home to Devon where he pursued a quiet existence as a gentleman farmer. He collected his medals from Budbrooke Barracks in Warwick on October 6th 1920. In the same week he was involved in the Church Service and unveiling of the Bridestowe War Memorial; he attended Western Front reunions and continued his Church Warden duties. Robert could concentrate now on his interests and loves-riding on Dartmoor, shooting, hunting, cricket and his family.

In 1919, on the death of his father Sir Frederic, he succeeded to the baronetcy as the 8th Baronet. Links with Stratford-on-Avon were cut with the sale of Avon Cliffe House which had become sadly dilapidated during the wartime years and the sale settled his father's debts.

Life in south Devon was relatively trouble free punctuated by the occasional problem that most parents are posed by their offspring. I could not resist including a letter sent to Sir Robert complaining of the behaviour of one of his sons:

Sat 5th
The Golf Club, Tavistock

Dear Sir,

It has been brought to the notice of our committee that Rule 38 of the Tavistock Golf Club was yesterday infringed by one of your sons, as he appears to have played a number of holes in excess of the amount allotted by the green-fee.

Heretofore, we have always relied upon the honesty of casual players and are naturally all the more pained at this flagrant breach of etiquette.

It was also noticed that quite apart from the unseemly language overheard and reported to us by Brigadier-General Leveson-Gower, D.S.O. of the D.C.L.I. your son constantly failed to replace an unnecessary large quantity of divots at a distance of about 100 yds. from most of the greens.

the complaining letter....

We have naturally been obliged to report this matter to the local magistrate, and pending further developements, we should be obliged if you would forward the extra shilling together with a fine of 5/-.

Yrs Faithfully,
Stewart Gordon Wetherby
(Hon. Sec. of Tavistock Golf Club)

Sir Robert would doubtless have been none too pleased about the alleged behaviour of his son but may well have grumbled at the letter's lack of a precise date and the spelling mistakes. He may have been aware that the complainant had served during the War with the Sherwood Foresters and not the Duke of Cornwall's Light Infantry.

His usual acerbic comment that 'a bit of trench life' was the best cure for such a complaint would not, in this instance, have been appropriate as Brigadier-General Philip Leveson-Gower C.M.G., D.S.O., had served with the Sherwood Foresters at the Front and was wounded twice in 1915. He received a Distinguished Service Order in 1917 after returning to action only a week after being gassed.

However, it would be interesting to know if, given Major Robert Hamilton's propensity for gentle criticism of the 'Top Brass', he was aware of Leveson-Gower's apparently inept leadership during the 2nd Battle of the Somme in 1918. On March 21st Leveson-Gower planned a disastrous counter-attack. Because of fierce German shelling, he countermanded the order to attack, but failed to inform one of the units involved, the 6/ Connaught Rangers who were wiped out and, as a result, had to be disbanded. At a time when battlefield communications were not too sophisticated, it may have been a case of 'Lions' being led by a 'Donkey'...

For the record, it is agreed by my mother and aunt that the perpetrator of the crimes of green-fee underpayment, profane language and divot replacement failure, was my uncle, Oliver Anson Hamilton. Despite his youthful indiscretions, he later survived the golf club's interviewing process to become a member of Tavistock Golf Club for many years!

Captain Robert Hamilton, as he was known for most of his time in the trenches in 1914 and 1915, failed to achieve a mention in despatches or a decoration. In what must have been a cathartic moment in his life, he wrote in his diary on November 3rd 1918 that, unable to hear a word of the service at Tupsley Church, he decided to contemplate his future and came to the rather sad conclusion that 'I have neither the wish nor the ability to become a General, and not the ambition to be anything out of the way.' His self-assessment may well have been correct but three letters amongst his papers give a clue to what the men he commanded felt about his leadership.

A letter was received from an address at Cothal near Aberdeen by his wife Renie when he was in the Plugstreet Wood area in December 1914; unfortunately the final page is missing so the identity of the writer is unknown; he obviously had connections with the Royal Warwickshire Regiment and visited the 1st Scottish Hospital at Rosemount School Aberdeen where several of the Regiment's wounded had been sent.

December 3 1914

Dear Mrs. Hamilton,

I have been keeping an eye on the men in the Hospitals up here to see if any Warwickshire men came in and I have had 7 or 8, and yesterday I found Sperry, your husband's servant, had just come in and so I thought I would write and tell you what he said about your husband. He simply adores him, and said "it was so bad getting wounded (his shoulder) for I had been with the Capt. all the time and he shared everything with me, I was able to make him a little comfortable and give him as good food as we could manage and how I can't bear to think I'm not there to look after him," poor fellow- there were tears in his eyes! He said your husband was so fit and well and always so cheery and kind- that he had some Warwickshire boys to dine with him every night while they were out at the farm and afterwards little Tillyer (our 'baby' of the last training) came to their little dug out and had dinner every night.

He could talk of nothing but your husband and how every night after dark he and Captain Hamilton went out for a walk "just like brothers"!

He says your husband had a concertina he found in the German trenches, and he used to amuse them all by playing it!

Before I left, Sperry said "now you will be sure to write to Mrs. Hamilton, for I would like her to hear about the Captain. I am going to write myself later but I want her to hear about him at once."

It really was touching his devotion to Captain Hamilton. He says the Dr. thinks he has a splinter of bone or shell in his shoulder and he is to have it x-rayed and may have to have it opened. He said "after I was wounded the Captain stayed with me all day and looked after me till I was taken away. It just happened at breakfast time, I had given him bacon and eggs and was just going to fetch his tea when I was struck"!!

Sperry looks well and I don't think will be very long in getting home.

I was very interested to hear about Captain Hamilton as I asked all the soldiers who have come up here but none of them could tell me…

Page 4

the Lord will reward him for being so good to others I think I have said all this time so I must wish your Husband the very best of Luck I can not wish him much better

Yours Sincerely

Mrs Sperry

Mrs. Sperry wrote to Renie in early December:

Page 1

Dear Madam,

Just a few lines thanking you for writing to my Dear Husband he sent the letter for me to read and asked me to write you a few lines I must say that each letter I have had from my Husband he has always mentioned

173

Mrs. Sperry's letter
continued...

...onths how good and kind your
...m I hope Husband as been to him
...see my and I hope and Trust in
Husband when he comes home the Lord that he will come
and then he will be able safly home to you very
to tell you all about your soon my husband told me
Dear Husband because I that he might be at home
know you will be anxious by christmas but he has
to hear about him and I suffered with his shoulder
shall also because he has I wish I could see him and I
been so good and kind to dare say you wish you could
my Dear Husband but see you Husband it seems

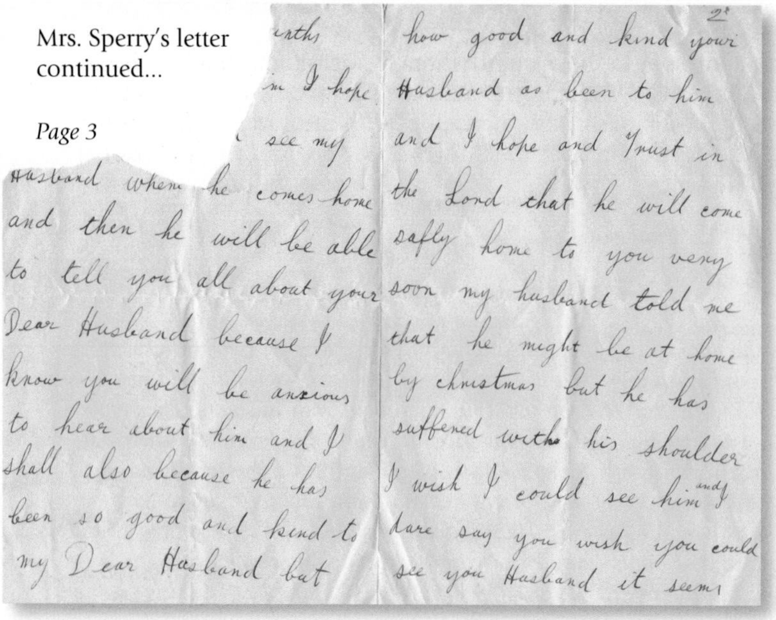

23/12/1914/ Mrs Sperry and i was pleased to
171 Cherrywood Rd find the Wife and
Bordesley Green children in the best
Birmingham of health and i hope
Dear Mrs Hamilton i and trust the lord
now take my pen with that the Captain
great pleasure to answer will get home for
your kind and welcome Christmas and i
letter that my Wife know you and
received and i am all his friends
very pleased to let will make it
you know that i
arrived from aberdeen
on satarday night

When Private Sperry
returned to Birmingham
he penned the following
to Renie which must
have boosted her spirits
over Christmas:

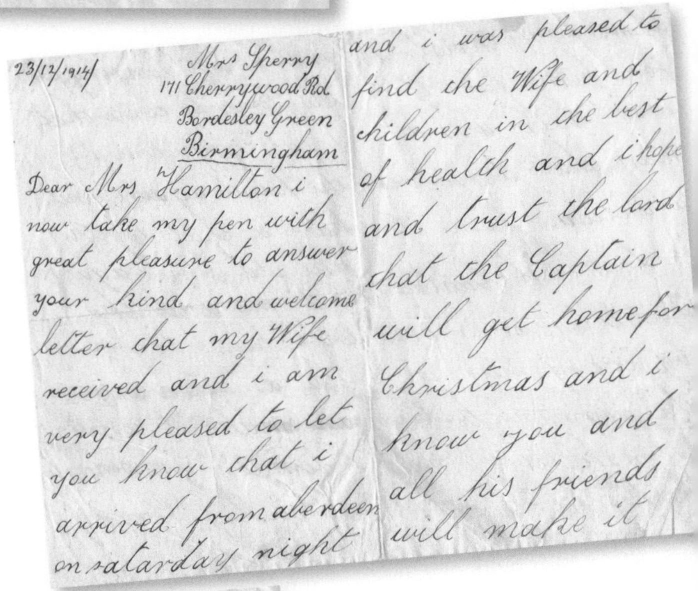

---

a merry christmas and i am longing for
for him for if the time to come that
ever their was a i can grip him by
man that derserved the hand again and
a welcome home it have a chat together
is dear old Captain like old times again
Hamilton he is loved and me and the
by every man in wife hopes to see
the regiment he tries you as soon as you
to make every man can make it convenient
happy like himself i remain yrs sincerly
Mr Mrs Sperry

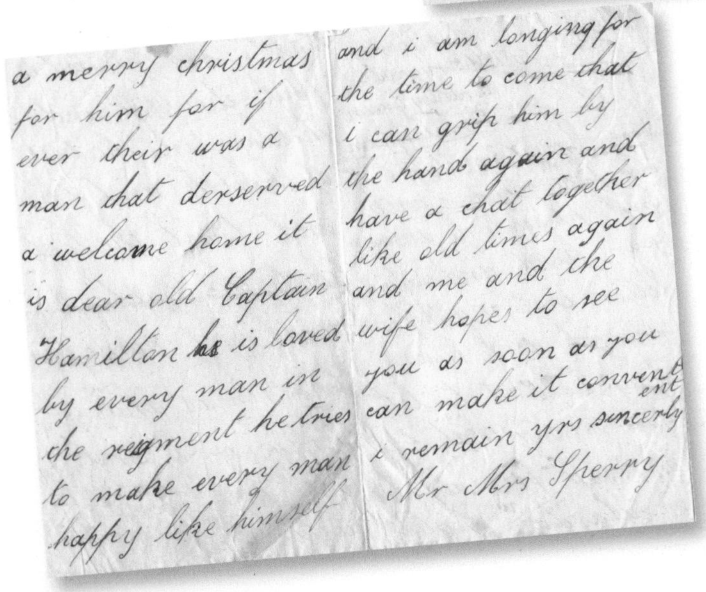

Despite an excellent reference from one of his batmen, (those he sacked may not have been so fulsome in their praise) Robert Hamilton concluded that he would not make a General. One of his friends in the Warwicks did achieve the highest rank- Bernard Montgomery who was ten years his junior. He survived his wounds suffered at the Battle of Méteren on October 13th 1914 and was awarded the Distinguished Service Order for 'conspicuous gallantry when he turned the enemy out of their trenches with the bayonet'. Although he avoided a return to active combat for the rest of the War, he continued in a worthwhile Lieutenant-Colonel post that had more career potential than the post of Commandant of a Military Detention Barracks.

In pre-war copies of the Warwicks' regimental magazine, *The Antelope*, Lieutenant B.L. Montgomery was successfully attending courses that would do his future career path no harm. He passed a Transport Course at Peshawar in June 1910 and in February 1913, he came first on a course held at the School of Musketry at Hythe in Kent. But he was also catching the eye of his superiors with his focused and single-minded determination. From his early days at St. Paul's School in London, he liked to be in control and disliked being under someone else's command. He, like Robert, was captain of his school's cricket XI and both took no prisoners on the Rugby pitch; Montgomery's style was ideally suited to a military career: he was 'vicious and of unflagging energy' according to the school magazine, and liable to commit such inconceivable atrocities as 'stamping on opponents' heads'. The sports' editor

ke Robert Hamilton, Bernard Law Montgomery was a fine cricketer, seated second from the ft in the St. Paul's School 1st XI photograph for 1906   Simon Sargent

may have been prone to youthful exaggeration but Monty's attitude was not quite the behaviour expected of the son of a former Bishop of Tasmania and the Secretary for the Propagation of the Gospel in Foreign Parts!

Montgomery was a fine all round games player and was appointed games officer for the Royal Warwickshire Regiment, based at the time in India. In 1911, the *Gneisenau*, a German ship docked at Bombay with the German Crown Prince on board. Montgomery was part of the guard of honour and was responsible for organising a football match with the Germans. Instructions came from on high that in deference to their guests, the Warwicks were to field a below strength side but to the watching British and German staffs, it was obvious that Lieutenant Montgomery had failed to carry out the request to the letter because the Warwicks beat the Germans by 40 goals to nil! When taken to task by his commanding officer, his defence was that "I was not taking any risks with Germans."

175

Montgomery went on to play his major role in World War Two. Only a few pages of his memoirs dwelt on the Great War, a period of his career when he may have been disappointed that his contribution had been affected by his wounds at the Battle of Méteren.

Captain Hamilton was a more cautious leader than some of his younger colleagues- he was in general ten years older than most and many of the young officers in their twenties were rash and fearless. One wonders why Robert did not feature in Brigadier-General Charles Hull's list of commendations in early 1915- maybe he had made known his feelings once too often or had been regarded as a prime mover in the unofficial Christmas Truce. One thing is certain- that the Captain was highly regarded by many of those he led- even his former batman Gregory was keen to impress him by offering to go out into No Man's Land on Christmas Eve.

Sympathy for those men under his command surfaces regularly from the pages of the diary. On September 5th, they were on their last legs- 'I am sorry for my men.' He wrote that 'little regard is paid to the comfort of the men' and when commenting on his men's billets he admitted that they 'were not very comfortable I'm afraid.' He appears not to have been aloof from them- on October 24th in a quiet moment he and three batmen enjoyed 'an excellent rubber of whist'.

Fellow officers must also have warmed to his concern for their welfare- a touching moment when all hell was let loose from the German trenches, was when Hamilton began to whistle to calm the nerves of 'poor' Lieutenants Black and Thornhill when their farm behind the line was bombarded.

Captain Hamilton freely dispensed criticism of his seniors in the safety of his diary. He was unhappy that in the Warwicks 'one doesn't ask, one does' and complained of 'regimental red tape rot'. 'Gunning to no purpose whatever' and a 'not worth the candle route march' were complaints expressed in late September and early October 1914. He made plain his feelings notably when an order was sent out that an officer and two men were to search for dead Germans; the reply was pithily expressed- "not in these trousers"! It is possible he aired his views too readily and may have paid the price when it came to commendations from above.

Robert and Renie Hamilton's Golden Wedding Anniversary on July 24th 1957. Robert died two years later and Renie lived on until 1969

What is apparent, is that whatever the privations and dangers that soldiers were subjected to in 1914, humour was often used to ameliorate the situation. Robert's wry humour and appreciation of the absurd must have helped boost the morale of those around him- knee deep in mud and faced with the consequences of another day of heavy rain, the mirth from the Warwicks' trenches must have been heard by the Germans opposite when Private Carter observed that the rain would 'lay the dust, sir, wouldn't it?' In his cosy and snug dug out, he and his officers relieved the tension of their spell in the trenches and amused themselves with stories of fellow soldiers and compositions like their 'The Fate of the Pickelhauben Patrol'. Robert and Bruce Bairnsfather both shared a similar sense of humour- much of Bairnsfather's early work was inspired by the stories swapped in the *estaminets* in La Crèche and Steenwerck- that Bairnsfather should have received so little official recognition for his work is puzzling but the 50th anniversary of his death in 2009 may rectify the situation and provoke an upsurge in interest in his work.

I scarcely knew my grandfather before he died on February 15th 1959. Only five years old at the time, I have limited memories of a very old man who, frighteningly for a young boy, shouted rather than spoke because of his deafness. As is so often the case, I failed to speak to my own father about his father's past and how Robert's War experiences had affected him and his family. The Great War was a subject that he, like so many others who fought in it rarely touched on, finding it too painful to share his memories of the horrors he had endured.

My grandmother Renie and great aunt Cicely lived on at Collaven for several years after Robert's death. I remember them sitting stooped over the kitchen table feasting on boiled eggs, the silence puncuated by the tap of teaspoon on egg and the occasional comment on the seismic and incomprehensible changes that were taking place in the 1960s which were "shocking, quite shocking".

After enduring and surviving the most destructive of wars, within just twenty one years of announcing the end of the War to the delirious townsfolk of Hereford, Robert wrote wearily in his diary on August 24th 1939 that 'The War news is hopeless- I do not see what is to prevent another European War.'

The pages of this book are littered with the names of those from all layers of society who died for their King and Country in the Great War. Some like Robert Hamilton were lucky to survive the snipers and shelling to record their story: a story that underlines the courage and heroism of those he fought alongside but it begs the question for the modern reader- what was the justification for such barbarity and massive loss of life?

Robert Caradoc Hamilton born March 22nd 1877 died February 15th 1959

Irene Hamilton born December 27th 1880 died October 24th 1969

Graveyard at the Church of St.Thomas à Becket at Sourton, Devon

AH

Acknowledgements

We should like to thank the following for their generous contributions without which this publication would not have been possible. If we have missed anyone out please accept our sincerest apologies- your name will be included in the next edition.

- Allsop, Robert (Eastgate Bookshop, Warwick): sourcing Bairnsfather material
- Baker, Chris (Western Front Association): information on units attached to the 10th Brigade
- Baynham, David: sharing his detailed knowledge of the Royal Warwickshire Regiment
- Bennett, Stephanie: scans of museum photographs and grants of permission from the Royal Regiment of Fusiliers (Royal Warwickshire) Museum's collections
- Bird, Dicky: information from the Royal Norfolk Regimental Museum
- Brown, Malcolm: information on the Christmas Truce
- Cazier, Régis (Archives d'Armentières): use of photographs
- Dendooven, Dominiek (In Flanders Fields Museum): for his enthusiastic welcome and provision of vital source material about the Christmas Truce from the German perspective
- Descamps, Béatrice (Sénateur Maire): information on the Battle of Méteren
- Deswarte, Jean-Pierre and Fache, Daniel: invaluable information and illustrations of the Battle of Méteren
- Dodd, Conor: information on the Royal Dublin Fusiliers (with apologies for my grandfather's comments about his uncles in the Regiment)
- Fache, Nathalie (Musée de Nieppe): information on the *Brasserie L'Espérance* and the Jeanson Linen factory
- Freeman, Birgit and her mother Jaeger, Hilde: deciphering the Zehmisch photographs' captions
- Godfrey, Wendy: description of the 1914 bombings in Scarborough
- Griffith, Rhys (Senior Archivist at Herefordshire County Records Office): information on Hereford Military Detention Barracks
- Hamilton, Alice: translation of the Plouvier sisters' letters to Renie Hamilton
- Hamilton, Anthea: editing, sound advice and forbearance of my many hours on the P.C.
- Hamilton, Elizabeth: background information on the Hamilton family in India, the Mordaunt family in Walton and the 'Warwickshire Scandal'.
- Hamilton, Imo: patience and tolerance faced with her father's lack of I.T. skills
- Harrison, Dahlia and Terry: information on Great War Nurses and Medals
- Hayward, Linda: information on her grandfather William Tapp
- Holt, Tonie and Valmai: information about Bruce Bairnsfather
- Mackenzie, Simon and Nightingall, Robert: access to Charles Nightingall's memoirs of the Great War held in the Liddle Collection at the University of Leeds
- Maclean, Rusty: material from Rugby School Archives on Major Christie
- Morgan, Harry: allowing us to quote from his father's memoirs
- Morgan, Tom: a mine of information on the Great War- visit his popular website- www.hellfire-corner.demon.co.uk
- Mundhill, Elaine: providing a wealth of detail for the reconstruction of Robert Hamilton's time at Trinity College, Glenalmond
- Rayner, Dick: providing information about Robert Hamilton and the Norfolk Regiment

- Reed, Ginette: for all her patience, support and good humour in the face of mounting piles of books and papers
- Renaux, Jean-Pierre (Président du Musée de la Vie Rurale de Steenwerck): use of Steenwerck postcards
- Richards, Anthony (First World War specialist at the Imperial War Museum) and the Museum Reading Room Staff: for information, welcome and help
- Roelens, Patrick: leads for information on the Ploegsteert area
- Sayell, George: thorough and precise work on the maps and thoughtful advice
- Seeney, David: research on Robert Hamilton's military background
- Smith, Ruth (Damson Creative): many thanks for the design of 'Meet at Dawn, Unarmed'
- Spencer, William (The National Archives): information about Conscientious Objectors and Regimental and Brigade War Diaries
- Vaux, David: enthusiastic advice and useful sources for the Royal Warwickshire Regiment
- Verhaeghe, Claude: use of his collection of photographs and details of St. Yves village- visit his restaurant- www.auberge-ploegsteert.be
- Warby, Mark: invaluable help on all matters concerning Bruce Bairnsfather- website- www.brucebairnsfather.org.uk
- White, Bruce /family/colleague: translation of Kurt Zehmisch's diary and captions to Zehmisch's photographs
- Wilson-Gunn, Paul: for information from Rugby School

Archives, Libraries, Museums and Websites

The following have been of great help in our research:

- Archives d'Armentières
- Bodleian Library, Oxford
- British Newspaper Library, Colindale
- Commonwealth War Graves Commission- www.cwcg.org
- Glenalmond College
- Google and Google Earth
- Herefordshire Records Office
- Imperial War Museum- Reading Room and Photographic Archive
- In Flanders Fields Museum, Ypres
- Musée de la Vie Rurale de Steenwerck
- Musée de Nieppe
- National Archives
- Religious Society of Friends
- Royal Norfolk Regimental Museum
- Royal Regiment of Fusiliers (Royal Warwickshire) Museum
- Rugby School
- Tavistock Library
- University of Birmingham First World War Studies (www.bham.ac.uk): 'Lions led by Donkeys' Archive

Original Sources

- 1st Battalion Royal Warwickshire Regiment War Diary: The Royal Regiment of Fusiliers (Royal Warwickshire) Museum, Warwick
- Bairnsfather, Bruce: Interview with Canadian Television November 1958- Mark Warby Collection
- Black, Captain Frank Henry: Letters 1914-1915- Imperial War Museum 82/3/1
- Drummond, Brigadier C.A.F: Tape- Transcript of Memories of World War 1- Imperial War Museum
- Gaunt, Lieutenant K.M.: Diary- Imperial War Museum 75/78/1
- Hamilton, Irene: Diary 1914- Andrew Hamilton
- Hamilton, Captain Robert: Diary 1914 to 1939- Andrew Hamilton
- Hull, Brigadier-General Charles: Report of 10th Infantry Brigade January 1915- WO95/1477, National Archives
- Jackson, Lieutenant A.H.K: Sketch of 1/ Royal Warwicks' position October 1914- National Archives WO/95/1484
- Judd, Corporal Samuel: Diary- Imperial War Museum
- Montgomery, Lieutenant Bernard L: Diary from *The Antelope*, Journal of the Royal Warwickshire Regiment May 1938 and letter to Brigadier Tomes 1944 - The Royal Regiment of Fusiliers (Royal Warwickshire) Museum, Warwick
- Niemann, Oberstleutnant Johannes: Diary- In Flanders Fields Museum
- Philpotts, Sergeant J: BBC Great War Series Correspondence- Imperial War Museum
- Pratt, Charlie (Royal Warwickshire Regiment): letter written on December 27th 1914 and published in *The Evesham Journal* on January 16th 1915
- Tapp, Private William: Diary- Imperial War Museum 66/156/1
- Tomes, Colonel C.T: The Great War Battle Honours from *The Antelope*, Vol IX Nos 2 and 3, Volume X No 1 and 2- The Royal Regiment of Fusiliers (Royal Warwickshire) Museum, Warwick
- Trench map 'Ploegstreet 28 SW4 Edition 4B' by kind permission of G. H. Smith & Son- trench map collection available from www.ghsmith.com
- War Diaries:1/ Royal Warwicks WO95/1484, 1/ Royal Irish Fusiliers WO95/1481, 2/ Royal Dublin Fusiliers WO95/1482, 2/ Seaforth Highlanders WO95/1483, 10th and 11th Infantry Brigades WO95/1477, 32nd Brigade of Royal Field Artillery and 1/ Rifle Brigade- National Archives
- Zehmisch, Leutnant Kurt: Diary (translated by Bruce White), Map and Photographs by kind permission of Rudolf Zehmisch and the In Flanders Fields Museum, Ypres

Published Sources

- *Antelope, The*: The Royal Regiment of Fusiliers (Royal Warwickshire) Museum, Warwick
- Arthur, Max: *When This Bloody War Is Over: Soldiers' Songs of the First World War*- Piatkus 2001
- Ashby, John: *Seek Glory, Now Keep Glory*- Helion and Co. 2000
- Bairnsfather, Bruce: *Bullets and Billets*- Grant Richards 1916
- Bairnsfather, Bruce: *Fragments from France*- The Bystander 1916
- Bairnsfather, Bruce: *One Night in Flanders*- The American Magazine December 1929
- Banks, Arthur: *A Military Atlas of the First World War*- Leo Cooper 1998
- Boulton, David: *Objection Overruled*- Macgibbon and Kee 1967
- Brophy, John and Partridge, Eric: *The Daily Telegraph Dictionary of Tommies' Songs and Slang 1914-18*- Frontline Books 2008

- Brown, Malcolm: *The Christmas Truce 1914: The British Story- in 'Meetings in No Man's Land'-* Constable and Robinson 2007
- Brown, Malcolm and Seaton, Shirley: *The Christmas Truce-* Papermac 1994
- Chasseaud, Peter: *Topography of Armageddon-* Mapbooks 1991
- Coombs, Rose: *Before Endeavours Fade-* Battle of Britain Prints International 1976
- Dendooven, Dominiek: *Kurt Zehmisch and the Great War in Waasten-* In Flanders Fields Magazine July 2000
- De Ruvigny: *Roll of Honour-* Naval & Military Press 2001
- Ellsworth-Jones: *We Will Not Fight-* Aurum 2007
- Gindre de Mancy: *Dictionnaire des Communes-* Garnier 1886
- *Glenalmond Chronicle, The-* Glenalmond College
- Hamilton, Elizabeth: *The Warwickshire Scandal-* Michael Russell 1999
- Haythornthwaite, Philip: *The World War One Source Book-* Brookhampton Press 1992
- Her Majesty's Stationery Office: *Field Service Pocket Book 1914*
- Hewins, Angela: *The Dillen- Memories of a Stratford Man-* Oxford Paperbacks 1981
- Hogg, Ian: *Dictionary of World War 1-* Hutchinson 1997
- Holt, Tonie and Valmai: *Battlefield Guide to the Ypres Salient-* Leo Cooper 2000
- Holt, Tonie and Valmai: *In Search of the Better 'Ole-* Leo Cooper 2001
- Hook, Alex: *World War 1 Day by Day-* Grange Books 2004
- Kingsford, C.L.: *The Story of the Royal Warwickshire Regiment-* Newnes 1921
- Maurice, Brigadier-General Sir Frederick: *The History of the London Rifle Brigade-* Constable and Co 1921
- Moorehead, Alan: *Montgomery-* Hamish Hamilton 1946
- Morgan, Harry: *Harry's War-* Rydan 2002
- Newspapers: *The Birmingham Post, The Daily Sketch, The Evesham Journal, The Hereford Times, The Stratford-upon-Avon Herald, The Tavistock Gazette, The Times*
- Pope, Stephen and Wheal, Elizabeth-Anne: *Dictionary of the First World War-* Pen and Sword Military Classics 2003
- Putkowski, Julian and Sykes, Julian: *Shot at Dawn-* Pen and Sword Books 2006
- Rawson, Andrew: *British Army Handbook 1914-18-* The History Press 2006
- Scott, Peter T: *Christmas Day in Plugstreet-* Stand-To Magazine Winter 1984
- Simkins, Peter: *The First World War (2)-* Osprey 2002
- Sommerville, Donald: *Monty- A Biography of Field Marshal Montgomery-* W.H. Smith Books 1992
- Spagnoly, Tony and Smith, Ted: *A Walk Round Plugstreet-* Leo Cooper 2003
- Spencer, William: *Army Records-* The National Archives 2008
- Stevenson, Davis: *1914-18 The History of the First World War-* Penguin Books 2004
- Weintraub, Stanley: *Silent Night-* Pocket Books 2002
- Westlake, Ray: *British Battalions in France and Belgium 1914-* Leo Cooper 1997
- Woodcock, Gerald: *The Book of Tavistock-* Halgrove 2003
- Woollcott, Alexander: *By Word of Mouth-* The American Legion Magazine July 1931
- Worsley, Gerald: *Devon in the Great War-* Devon Books 2000
- Wray, Frank and Maurice: *Christmas 1914-* The Army Quarterly Vol. XCVII October 1968/ January 1969

Index

There are main headings for
- Battles
- Cemeteries and Memorials
- Hamilton, Lady Irene (Renie)
- Hamilton, Major Sir Robert
- Medals/ Orders
- Mordaunt Family
- Places in Belgium, France, India, U.K. and elsewhere
- Regiments/ Units, British
- Regiments/Units, German
- Soldiers, German
- Soldiers, non Royal Warwicks
- Soldiers, Royal Warwicks

189

Overleaf: Photograph of Prowse Point Cemetery where 26 Royal Warwicks and
              46 Royal Dublin Fusiliers are known to be buried.   *Alan Reed*

Meet at Dawn, Unarmed
is dedicated to the 74 soldiers mentioned in the text
who died in the Great War.

- Staff Sergeant Frederick J. Andrews- Military Provost Staff Corps
- Private Arthur Henry Ashford- Royal Warwicks
- Private John Albert Baker- Royal Warwicks
- Captain Arthur William Balders- Norfolk Regiment
- Private F. Batchelor- Royal Warwicks
- Captain Charles Arthur Campbell Bentley- Royal Warwicks
- Captain Frank Henry Black- Royal Warwicks
- Private Herbert Bonham- Royal Warwicks
- Captain Thomas Rupert Bowlby- Norfolk Regiment
- Lieutenant-Colonel Sir Evelyn Ridley Bradford- Seaforth Highlanders
- Private G. Bradley- Royal Warwicks
- Lieutenant-Colonel Robert Henry Watkin Brewis- Royal Warwicks
- Captain Ernest Felix Victor Briard- Norfolk Regiment
- Private Charles Britton- Royal Warwicks
- Private Frederick Broadrick- Royal Warwicks
- Sub Lieutenant Rupert Brooke- Royal Naval Volunteer Reserve
- Lieutenant Geoffrey P. Bulmer- Royal Flying Corps
- Captain Alec Campbell- Sussex Yeomanry
- Private Stanley Chappell- Royal Warwicks
- Major William Charles Christie- Royal Warwicks
- Captain F.J. Cresswell- Norfolk Regiment
- Private Tom Crump- Royal Warwicks
- Private W. Crumpton- Royal Warwicks
- Private Samuel Cunnington- Royal Warwicks
- Private Henry Thomas Davis- Royal Warwicks
- Private Arthur Grove Earp- Royal Warwicks
- Private Frank. England- Royal Warwicks
- Lieutenant Thomas Algernon Fitzgerald Foley- Norfolk Regiment
- 2nd Lieutenant Kenneth MacFarlane Gaunt- Royal Warwicks
- Captain Cecil Glendower Percival Gilliat- Royal Warwicks
- Private J. Goodhead- Royal Warwicks
- Private Arthur Greening- Royal Warwicks
- Private Ronald Christopher Gregory- Royal Warwicks
- Private Sidney Hale- Royal Warwicks
- Private Harry Hales- Royal Warwicks
- Lieutenant Ian Knox Hamilton- Royal Warwicks

- Lance-Corporal Wally Heath- King's Royal Rifle Corps
- Private Harry Hobday- Royal Warwicks
- Captain Gerard Faster Irvine- Royal Warwicks
- Private G.R. Jackson- Royal Warwicks
- Captain G. H. Ker- Bedfordshire Regiment
- Captain William Miles Kington- Royal Welch Fusiliers
- Lieutenant O.A. Knapton- Royal Warwicks
- Major John Cecil Lancaster- Royal Warwicks
- Lieutenant-Colonel Walter Latham Loring- Royal Warwicks
- Lieutenant-Colonel Arthur Loveband- Royal Dublin Fusiliers
- Lieutenant-Colonel Edward Bourryan Luard- King's Shropshire Light Infantry
- Lieutenant Gilchrist Stanley Maclagan- Royal Warwicks
- Captain William Cecil Kennedy Megaw- Norfolk Regiment
- Corporal Benjamin Mole- Royal Warwicks
- Lieutenant Ronald Claud Nicolai- Royal Warwicks
- Lieutenant Wilfred Owen- Artists' Rifles/Manchester Regiment
- Lieutenant-Colonel Arthur Jex Blake Percival- Northumberland Fusiliers
- Lance-Corporal Albert Henry Pitts- Royal Warwicks
- Captain Ralph Broomfield Pritchard- Northumberland Fusiliers
- Brigadier-General Charles Bertie Prowse- 11th Infantry Brigade
- Lance-Corporal Thomas Henry 'Pat' Rafferty- Royal Warwicks
- Corporal Edward Thomas Sayell- Machine Gun Corps
- Private Milford Sayell- Royal Fusiliers
- Private Samuel Sayell- Royal Fusiliers
- Private William Tapp- Royal Warwicks
- Private Arthur Taylor- Royal Warwicks
- Private C. Taylor- Royal Warwicks
- Private R. H. Taylor- Royal Warwicks
- Lieutenant Geoffrey Holland Thornhill- Royal Warwicks
- Colour Sergeant Philip Thornton- Royal Warwicks
- Lieutenant Richard Bateson Blunt Tillyer- Royal Warwicks
- Lance-Corporal Samuel Tovey- Royal Warwicks
- Private Albert Tyler- Royal Warwicks
- Captain Henry John Innes Walker- Royal Warwicks
- Captain Arthur Edward Martyr Ward- Norfolk Regiment
- Captain Cyril Walter Carleton Wasey- Royal Warwicks/R.F.C.
- Private Frederick F. Yates- Royal Warwicks
- Sergeant Thomas Yates- Royal Warwicks

The authors recreating the meeting of the Warwicks and Saxons in No Man's Land at St. Yves!
Imperial War Museum HU35801